Regimental History of the

THIRTY-FIFTH

ALABAMA INFANTRY

1862-1865

by

Leroy F. Banning

HERITAGE BOOKS
2008

HERITAGE BOOKS

AN IMPRINT OF HERITAGE BOOKS, INC.

Books, CDs, and more—Worldwide

For our listing of thousands of titles see our website
at
www.HeritageBooks.com

Published 2008 by
HERITAGE BOOKS, INC.
Publishing Division
100 Railroad Ave. #104
Westminster, Maryland 21157

Other Heritage Books by the author:
Banning Branches
Banning Branches: Revised Edition

International Standard Book Numbers
Paperbound: 978-0-7884-1133-5
Clothbound: 9780-7884-8050-2

"It may well be said that no
Regiment made a more gallant
record in the Civil War than this
one built upon the nucleus of
LaGrange Cadets."

John Allen Wyeth, 1907

TABLE OF CONTENTS

LIST OF MAPS

FOREWORD

Any history of the 35th Alabama must involve some of the history of the LaGrange Military Academy because this "West Point of the South" gave birth to the 35th. Most of the officers and many of the men were Cadets at LaGrange.

The village of LaGrange, Alabama is located about 10 miles southeast of Tuscumbia, Alabama. Near this village, on January 9, 1826, a school for girls opened and was named LaFayette Academy after the French general that fought the British with George Washington during the Revolutionary War. Very shortly after opening, boys were also accepted. Due to the success of this school, four years later, in 1830, LaGrange College, named after General LaFayette's estate in France, was established. This college was the first college chartered by the state of Alabama.

Over the next thirty years some of Alabama's most distinguished families sent their sons and daughters to these two flourishing institutions. They produced some of Alabama's leading men and women of the 19th century.

Some time between 1855 and 1858 an effort was made to move the college to Florence, Alabama. The move was resisted, new buildings were erected, the name changed to LaGrange College and Military Institute and in February 1858 the school re-opened with Major James W. Robertson as Superintendent and Professor of Engineering. The Trustees shortened the name to LaGrange Military Academy in 1860. With the new name and management, the institution reached its highest prosperity and popularity.

As the clouds of war were gathering, the State of Alabama provided for the education, at LaGrange, of two boys from each county. The young men were to be selected by a competitive examination. 1861 saw 170 cadets enrolled, of which 47 were State Cadets. The teaching was the best, the discipline strict and the cadets earnest.

With the opening of hostilities in 1861, many of the older members of the Cadet Corps left school to enter the service of the Confederate States of America. By July 1 of that year, of 170 Cadets in the Corps, 48 had already volunteered. Many of them joined Company E of the 2nd Alabama Infantry and were known as the "Franklin Blues", after the county in which LaGrange was located. This unit was so badly mauled that it was disbanded on April 1, 1862.

With the coming of war, the flames of patriotism were raging high at this mountain top institution. Major Robertson wrote to Governor A. B. Moore in 1861, tendering his services and that of the remaining Cadet Corps, to the State and the CSA.

Governor Moore responded:

> "The country has greater need for you and your Corps of Cadets where you are than anywhere else at this juncture. It is not merely good raw material that we need so much now as trained men, and men capable of training others. -----"

> "I am anxious above all things, to keep our military institutions organized, that they may furnish to our Armies as they are needed, trained military men. --"

The entire Cadet Corps was assembled and the text of Governors Moore's letter read. Despite every effort of Major Robertson and the faculty, the youthful desire for glory could not be restrained. The Cadets began to leave in increasing numbers to join the army and fight for their country.

As the February 1862 term opened, it became obvious that it was all but futile to attempt to keep LaGrange open. Major Robertson again asked for permission to form a regiment. On March 1, 1962, he received permission and the unit that was to become the 35th Alabama started recruiting. Upper classmen went to surrounding counties asking young men to sign up for a three year tour of duty.

LaGrange Military Academy ceased functioning as an educational institution and became a "boot camp" for the drilling and training of recruits. Orders arrived on April 13, 1862. "March to Corinth, Mississippi and join the CSA troops in the defense of that city."

After that bright spring day when the Cadet Corps marched off to war, the campus was used from time to time as a training facility for other units. The 7th Kansas Cavalry under Colonel F. N. Cornyne arrived at LaGrange on April 28, 1863, during the course of a raid thru Confederate territory. They styled themselves "The Destroying Angels", and lived up to this name by burning every building on the campus to the ground. Nothing was left but the shell of one stone building and ashes.

For the next 42 years the mountain top was quiet. The grass and trees grew, healing the scars, until few signs remained that gallant young men had dreamed of youthful glory on a day long ago among these scattered stones.

Thursday the 19th of May, 1904 was another bright spring day.

10

Twenty-eight elderly men returned to the site of the youthful joy and dreams. On this day the survivors of the LaGrange Cadet Corps returned for a final rollcall. It was a reunion, to see the men with whom they had shared learning and joy as well as fear and death.

By 1982 the site of LaGrange Military Academy was difficult to locate and hard to reach. The only mark, a small weather worn sign, hidden by brush and weeds. Nothing remains but a few dusty books in dark library corners.

Roy Banning
San Antonio, Tx.
October, 1998

Saturday, March 1, 1862.

The weekend has arrived, and with it, good news! Classes were to have started in February, but so many Cadets have joined the Army that it is a waste of time and effort to attempt to keep LaGrange Military Academy functioning as an educational institution. For this reason, Major Robertson had written once again to the Governor of Alabama, stating the situation and requesting permission to raise a regiment. Today approval arrived and the older Cadets are leaving and going to the near by counties to enlist recruits for OUR regiment. They have been authorized to offer a $50.00 bounty to each man.

The war news has been mixed of late. Ft. Donelson in Tennessee surrendered on February 16th. Word spread that Jefferson Davis has been inaugurated on the 22nd as the President of the Confederated States of America. A little bad a little good. Just wait until we can get organized!

Patriotism is a very real thing at LaGrange, and as the word spread that WE are going to form our OWN regiment and show those "Yankees" a thing or two, about 90% of the remaining Cadet Corps signed up. A large number signed up with Capt. Hunt and his Company B because he had gone to West Point before becoming the Military Instructor at LaGrange. Besides, the Cadets just like him. Many other Companies are filling up also.

Most of the volunteers that are arriving at LaGrange have no previous military training. To solve this problem and get the men ready for war, Major Robertson appointed ten Cadets as Drill Instructors. The Cadets selected were Thad Felton, Joe Horn, James Hennigan, J.N. Thompson, John Harris, Sam Stewart, W.A. Russell and Lowe Dement, all from Alabama. In addition Hanson from Georgia and Cross from Mississippi are Drill Instructors. Now the fields and woods around our mountain top campus ring to the sound of men marching, learning how to load and fire the Academy's muskets, and in general, learning how to be a soldiers. Many of them brought their own musket and are good shots.

We found out that Federal troops are just about 60 miles northwest of us at Pittsburg Landing in Tennessee, and that a new General, U.S. Grant, took over as their commander on March 17. General A.S. Johnson is gathering the Confederate forces at Corinth, Mississippi, about 60 miles west of us. With this information in the back of our mind, training efforts are being increased and, at the same time, more and more recruits are arriving. With a sense of urgency, we are parching corn and getting our clothes and tack together so that we are ready to march.

Early April saw some of our old friends arriving. They are the Cadets that left LaGrange a year earlier and joined the 2nd Alabama. They called themselves the "Franklin Blues" and have seen a lot of action, so much so that their ranks were so reduced that the unit has been disbanded. We are sad and angry to learn that a lot of our school mates are missing. When the "Blues" heard that a new unit was being formed at their alma mater, they decided to return to LaGrange and sign up. They brought with them some of their friends, but more importantly, battle experience.

April 6, 1862, CSA troops under General Johnson maul General Grant's Federal troops in a surprise attack at Shiloh, Tennessee, just south of Pittsburg Landing. General Johnson was killed and General Beauregard took command of Confederate troops. The next day General Buell reinforces Grant, they counter-attack and the battle turns in the Yankee's favor. Reports indicate that Beauregard then retreated to Corinth. The casualties are high, with the Federal's having 1,735 killed, 7,882 wounded and 3,956 captured. The CSA had 1,728 killed, 8,012 wounded and 959 captured. That is a battle! Grant is pursuing Beauregard, and we hear that Federal troops crossed the Tennessee River at Florence, Alabama on the 8th! Florence is only a few miles from LaGrange. The Cadets, faculty and recruits start to pack up and get everything in order. The town folks know the young men will be leaving soon and they are giving all kinds of parties and dances. They also give us muskets, shot, powder, food and other supplies. They know many of our recruits do not have a weapon.

Monday, April 14, 1862.

Yesterday our orders arrived! We are to be known as the 35th Alabama Infantry Regiment, and we are to march by way of Russellville, and join the CSA Army at Corinth, Mississippi. This morning we are packing our gear. A lot of our boys had a problem deciding what to leave behind, extra clothing or pillows and other gifts from their mothers, sisters and sweethearts. Most of us feel that an extra pair of socks or a shirt will do us a lot more good. Company B got the rest of the LaGrange muskets, some of the others found some big cane knives, the rest of us figure we will get weapons somewhere along the way, if we have to take them away from the Yankees! We are ready to march!

14

Mid afternoon we start for Corinth. We are singing songs and talking about how we will run the Federal Army clear back to Washington D.C. when we get there. With US, the CSA will win this war! WE will make the difference. If any other troops want to come along for the fun, they are welcome to tag along. We will all be heros! We will be famous! The whole south will be talking about us!

After a couple of hours of marching, we halt at Spring Creek, about 6 miles southwest of LaGrange, and make camp. Most of the recruits that joined us were farmers and use to walking all day behind a plow. Others have been on the drill field for a month, but most of us have blisters and are stiff. We give each other a hard time, but everyone just laughs. A few more days of this and we can march a thousand miles!

Later that evening we hear a shot! A bunch of us head for the sound, and find that one of the Cadets in Company B, Ruben Spivey, has been accidentally shot in the right arm with one of the old muskets. His arm is a mess. Ruben has the dubious honor of being the first casualty in the 35th. We found out later that they had to amputate his arm, but he was going to be alright.

The next morning we are up bright and early, we fix our breakfast and the march resumes. The march takes us through Russellville, where we pause just long enough to smile and wave at the folks cheering us, enlist a few more recruits and accept the gifts of food, candy, etc. We stop again a Cedar Creek, because we were told that Federal troops were following us. We form a defensive line and Scouts are sent out, but they came back and tell us there were no Federal troops in the area. The march then continued to Burleson, where we make camp for the second night.

Two days were spent resting up and letting our blisters heal and then again we break camp and march to Jacinto, Mississippi. We are about one days march south of Corinth. At that point we are told to think about who our officers should be, that we will elect them on the 20th and get formally organized. The election was held and Major Robertson was elected as our Colonel, Edwin Goodwin to Lieut. Colonel and W.H. Hunt as Major. We confirmed our Captains, and elected replacements for the Captains that we promoted, as well as those that were appointed to other posts. Col. Robertson appointed men to be Adjutant, Quartermaster, Surgeon, etc. Thus, the 35th was finally organized and a part of the Army of the CSA.

April 23rd saw us on the march to Corinth. The 35th is assigned to the reserves as part of General William Preston's Brigade of General Breckenridge's Corps. Best of all we are issued Belgian rifles! With these weapons, we feel truly a part of the CSA Army. The story goes around about how the 35th was almost consolidated with the 16th Alabama. When they found out we had almost 400 men in our regiment, I guess the generals realized we were almost full strength and had the right spirit and Officers or we could not have enlisted as many men as we did. No doubt they realized that we were a unit that could whip the Yankees. In any event we are still the 35th Alabama!

The Federals have changed generals! Grant is out, Halleck is in and the Federals have only advanced 9 miles in the 20 days since the battle at Shiloh. By May 3rd, however, the Union Army is just a few miles northeast of Corinth and they are digging trenches and piling up earth for fortifications. Looks like they are getting ready for a siege. Guess they heard the 35th was coming. Over the next few weeks there were many skirmishes, but the 35th just sits tight. It looks like the Federals outnumber us by quite a bit, even though we have received many reinforcements. Some of our troops have been driven from our forward batteries. Let us at them!

Thursday, May 29, 1862.

Our officers tell us Beauregard does not feel that this is the time or place for an all out fight, so he has ordered his Grand Army of the Tennessee to evacuate Corinth, and destroy any supplies we can not take with us. All day and well into the night we load stores into rail wagons as well as horse drawn wagons and send them on their way down the Mobile & Ohio Railroad to Tupelo, which is 50 miles south. The troops move out and just before dawn of the 30th, the torch was put to all equipment and stores that were not on the move. At least the 35th got all the supplies we needed. The morning sky became colored with explosions and flame and dark pillars of smoke pierced the horizon as we retreated. There is a running rearguard action with the biggest skirmish taking place around Booneville, Mississippi, where almost 2000 men are captured by the Federal Cavalry.

The 35th is in "Camp Preston" near Tupelo, Mississippi. Each regiment has it's own area, as does each company within the regiment. Within the company, the men are in small groups for the purpose of cooking, etc. By now we have settled into the routine of camp life. We tell tall tails, play cards, clean our weapons, go hunting or sleep. On occasion, we have picket duty. The main thing we do is try and stay healthy. For some reason that is hard. Some of the men are in bad shape because of diarrhea, but even so the lack of action has the men grumbling. The folks back home are criticizing our officers due to their inaction. The Federal troops have occupied Baton Rouge, the Confederate forces have to evacuate Fort Pillow, Tennessee on the Mississippi River, Memphis is occupied. Why don't we do Something?

On June 19th we are ordered to retreat again. This time towards Vicksburg because the Federal army is still a lot stronger than

Beauregard's Army and they don't want the Federals to flank us. We should get some reinforcements from Vicksburg. What's wrong! Let us at them! At least this time we get to ride the train.

Forty U.S. gunboats, under Farragut, have stormed up the Mississippi and into the Vicksburg area! The Yankees hang around for three days and punch holes in some houses, but nothing caught fire. They do very little damage but cause a lot of consternation. The town people think that the enemy may land, but they do not flinch. They are a hardy lot. I heard one townsman say, "The enemy is all sound and fury and to brave men, contemptible." That is my idea of a man! Our gunners cripple several vessels and the fleet withdraws on the 29th. That put an end to their trouble making. June 27th brought news that Beauregard has been replaced by General Braxton Bragg. Maybe now we will see some action.

Our camp ground is in a low lying area and we are having a lot of our men coming down with fever and diarrhea. The Doc says it is the "malarious atmosphere" doing it's work. When we arrived in the Vicksburg area, we had 375 hale and hardy men. We now have about 225 fit for duty. We have to get out of this "malarious atmosphere".

On July 27th, we receive orders to board a train on the New Orleans, Jackson & Great Northern Railroad, and go to Tangipohea, Louisiana and from there, march to Camp Moore, as the enemy is about to attack our men! We have to defend the camp and then divert the Federal army so that we can fortify Port Hudson and thereby keep the Mississippi River open from the Red River to Vicksburg. They tell us that a large quantity of food stuffs and other supplies from the Trans-Mississippi region, move along that route and without it Vicksburg and the CSA effort in the Department of Mississippi would be doomed. Looks like we are going to get to see some more country and get some fighting done.

When we arrive at the railroad, we find there are just a few rail wagons. There is no room for anything other than men and ammunition. We are going to have to leave the rest of our kit. Upon arriving at Tangipohea on the 28th, we get the 35th together and march to Camp Moore, which is just out of town. When we arrive, we find the rumor of an advance by Federals on the camp is unfounded.

On July 30 we march to Baton Rouge and battle! Col. Robertson tells us that this time we will be in the thick of things. Because this will be the first time the regiment as a whole will be under fire, and because so many men and officers are sick, we need to reorganize. We are down to 200 men ready for battle and some companies have no able bodied officers. For these reasons the Col. places everyone into one of four companies, A, B, C, or E. He assures us it is only temporary and we will be back in our old companies after all our sick men get well and rejoin us. We are finally going to get to fight and half our men are sick!

A lot of our men are half sick because of all the rain and mud we have had to put up with the last few weeks. We had to leave our tents and food behind when we got on the train. Since we got off the train we have had to walk in the rain, sleep in the rain and eat in the rain. Folks around here have given us food, so we have enough to eat, but it is sleep in the rain at night and march in the rain and heat during the day.

The afternoon of August 4th, 3,400 tired and sick men reach the Comite River about 10 miles northeast of Baton Rouge, and make camp. We try to sleep.

By 11:00 P.M. we are up and find we have been assigned to the First Brigade of the Second Division. We move out of camp, cross the Comite River bridge and march down the plank road leading from Baton Rouge to Clinton. The 2nd Division has about 1,200 ready for action.

TUESDAY, AUGUST 5, 1862.

About 4 A.M., we reached Wards Creek bridge, on the Greenwell Springs and Baton Rouge road, where we took up our position in the line of battle, which was on the East end of town. The line was set up to the left of the main road, with the First Brigade's position being from the road to a point about 200 yards from a dense forest. The Second Brigade took up a position that ran through the forest and into a large field on the other side. The 35th occupied the left center of our brigade.

A thick fog was present which made us uneasy, but a little after daylight we were ordered to advance. We quickly covered two or three hundred yards and then encountered brisk fire from the enemy's skirmishers. Most of the fire was coming from our right where there were some houses surrounded by trees and wood fences. We fell to the ground in a pea patch and at the same time an enemy battery opened fire! A few minutes later our battery returned the fire and we were ordered forward again. The entire line jumped to it's feet running forward, shooting and cheering! The effect was something to behold! The enemy skirmishers fled and their battery was forced to seek shelter under the guns of the Federal arsenal to keep from being captured! A Federal battery and ours continued to exchange fire.

The First Brigade continued to advance across open fields and corn fields, receiving occasional enemy fire. We advanced and the enemy gave way, until they reached the woods on the other side of the fields. Here the Federals tried to establish a second line in front of their encampment. We were again ordered to charge, and the boys of the

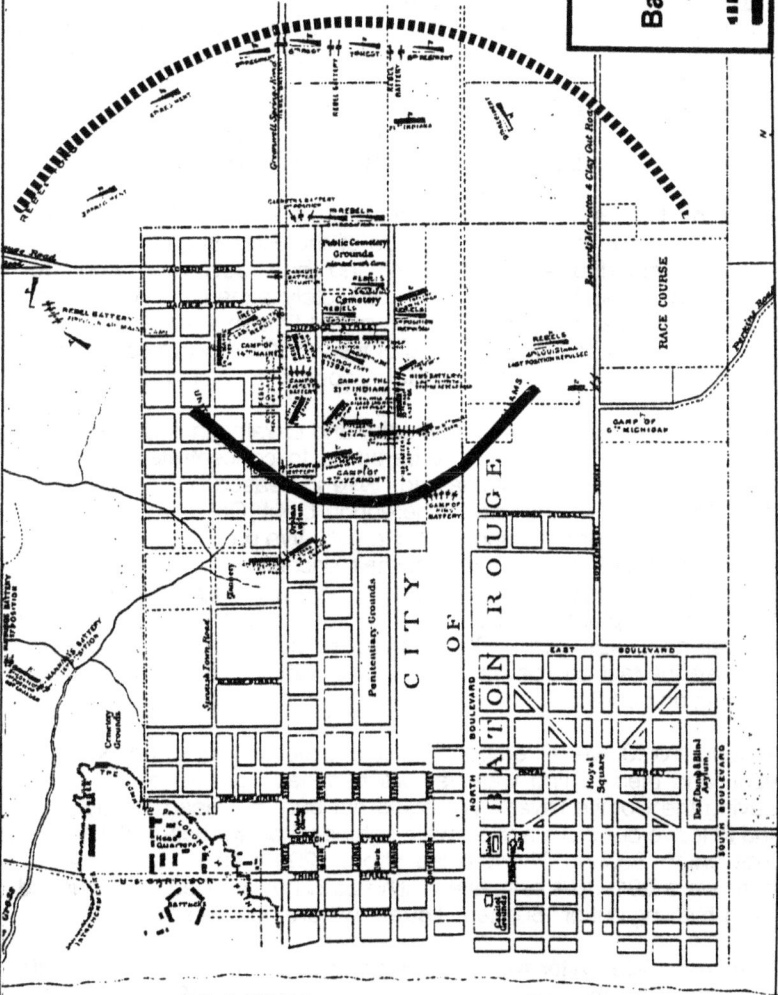

Battle Field
at
Baton Rouge, La.
August 5, 1862

CSA Lines
USA Lines

35th drove the enemy before them and completely overran their camp, which was between Main and Florida streets. Col. Robertson, noticing that the 7th Kentucky on our right was falling back thus leaving us exposed, ordered us to retire. The 6th Kentucky on our left did the same thing and took up a new position behind a fence in front of a cemetery on Dufroco street with us on their right. Both regiments moved forward a little and checked an enemy counter-attack by keeping up a heavy fire. The enemy had reformed behind their tents and began to rapidly advance. We opened a heavy fire and kept it up hot and heavy, as did the troops on our right and left. We halted the enemy advance. For more than an hour we held our position while under terrible fire from musket and cannon, all the while trading shot for shot with the Federals. The fighting was intense. For our baptism under fire, we had picked a hell of a battle! One of our boys said "the enemy gave as good as he got", which I must admit is true.

About this time, a messenger arrived and advised Col. Robertson that Col. Thompson, the officer in charge of the First Brigade, had been severely wounded and that command had devolved upon Col. Robertson. Col. Robertson was completely exhausted from recent illness and battle, and in no condition at that time to assume command. He therefor placed Col. Crossland of the 7th Kentucky in command of the right wing and our own Lieut. Col. Goodwin in command of the left.

We could see the enemy, both infantry and cavalry, in line of battle on our left. Lieut. Col. Goodwin ordered us to concentrate our fire on them, at which point they charged. We increased our fire and they started to falter and then fled, whereupon Lieut. Col. Goodwin placed his hat on his sword and shouted "charge"! We promptly replied to the order and drove the enemy from their encampment, back into town and under the cover of their gunboats. We did not have transport to remove the captured supplies, so the order to burn the enemy camp and fall back was given. The 35th was happy to be ordered back because the last charge had been made with less than one cartridge per man on hand!

At about 10:00, we retired from the field, collected our wounded as we went, and tried to find water as we had had nothing to drink since leaving the Comite River. We could not bury our dead because we had to leave our picks and shovels behind when we boarded the train. The entire Second Division had about 1200 men in the battle and there were 281 CSA casualties. The 35th had 4 killed, 21 wounded and 1 missing out of 180 men. I guess we are now veterans.

A few days later, after we have rested up at our camp on the Comite River, we hear that the enemy had 82 men killed, 316 wounded and that we had captured about 50 of the Yankees. The CSA troops gave them such a fight that they have abandoned Baton Rouge and have retired to New Orleans!

General Ruggles, who was our division commander, is assigned to fortify Port Hudson and make it ready for heavy batteries. So the 35th marches to Port Hudson, which is a few miles North of Baton Rouge, and we start moving dirt. They say Port H is now one of the strongest points on the Mississippi River, thanks to our work and the cannon that have been emplaced. More rain, more mud, more sickness.

August 23rd and the 35th gets to march again. O joy, o joy. We go back to Camp Moore where we will catch a train and return to Mississippi. Perhaps our sick will have time to get well.

We are at Jackson, which is good. The 35th will be able to regain it's strength because the climate is better and we have shelter. In addition, most of our men now have shoes and socks. Up to this point, about thirty percent of our men had been barefooted. Very few of us have uniforms. The officers all look splendid, but most of the men just have the cloths they signed up with. The government paid us for our clothes, but they are wearing out and all of us look ragged. We have been told that government issue clothing is on the way.

September 11th, and the 35th is ordered to Holly Springs in northern Mississippi. Upon arrival at Holly Springs, the division is reorganized, given additional equipment, and told to be ready to march and engage the enemy. We are assigned to the 1st Brigade of the 1st Division. Maj. General Mansfield Lovell commands the division and Brig. General Albert Rust commands the Brigade.

The entire camp is talking about the battle around Iuka, Mississippi. The Union General Rosecrans defeated our boys under General Sterling Price. There were a lot of casualties on both sides. Iuka is just a few miles east of Corinth, and the talk is that is where we are heading.

September 27th and we are on the march! Sure enough, we are on our way to Corinth where we will attack the Federal forces there and drive them out!

THURSDAY, OCTOBER 2, 1862.

Corinth is only a few miles away. We are to move to the North and come up behind the city. This morning we crossed the Tuscumbia bridge on the Hatchie River and headed for the Yankees. At Chewalla, 8 miles Northwest of Corinth, some of our cavalry and other troops run into Union skirmishers. After trading shots for an hour or so, the Federals retire toward Corinth. Our boys captured their camp, along with some quartermaster's and commissary supplies which we can use. About half mile past the enemy camp, the division is ordered

21

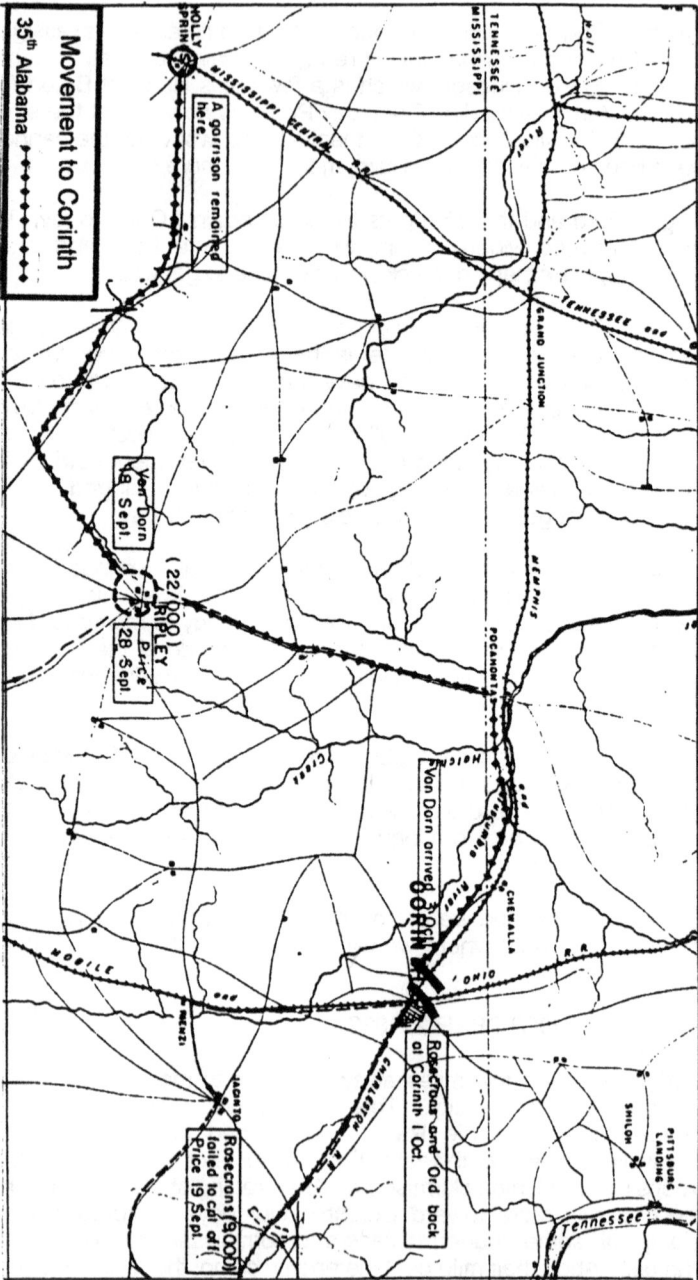

Movement to Corinth

35th Alabama ●●●●●●●●●

A garrison removed here.

Van Dorn 18 Sept

(22,000)
RIPLEY
Price
28 Sept

Van Dorn arrived 30 Sept
CORINTH

Rosecrans and Ord back
at Corinth 1 Oct.

Rosecrans (9,000)
failed to call off
Price 19 Sept

to bivouac in line of battle.

At 4:00 A.M. on the 3rd, the division starts moving Northeast, with skirmishers from General Villepigue's Second Brigade leading the way. When we are about three miles North of Corinth, CSA and Federal skirmishers come in contact on our end of the battle line and firing breaks out. The Federals are driven across Indian Creek, and our boys repair the bridge while the Yankees fire away. When the division has crossed the creek, each brigade takes their assigned place in the line. As our brigade holds the extreme right of the line, and this is where the action is, General Rust orders the 4th Alabama to relieve General Villepigue's men. The 7th Kentucky is to be held in reserve, with the rest of the brigade to close up and advance. As the fighting becomes general, we advance through a line of trees and approach the Yankees, who have taken up a position on the South side of the Memphis and Charleston Railroad, with his artillery on top of a hill. They have rifle-pits dug in a North-South direction and breastworks with a redoubt behind that. We got a problem, the Federals have a very strong position and we are going to get killed taking the fortifications.

The 35th is on the right side of the line, and when everyone is again in position, the entire division is ordered to charge. The troops in our area run forward, firing and yelling, and the enemy artillery opened up on us with terrific volleys of shell, grape and canister. Capt. Thad Felton of Co. B, who had been place in command of the 35th due to the illness of Col. Robertson, is killed. Capt. Mitchell as well as Lieutenants Hunter, Lawler and Collier are severely wounded while leading the 35th in this charge. Capt. Ashford of Co. C assumed command and ordered everyone to "fix bayonets and don't stop until we carry the breastworks!" The smoke, heat, noise and haze make everything a blur. Just as the 35th crested the enemy trenches and the Yankees are feeling our steel, the 7th Kentucky arrived to lend a hand!

General Rust had seen the storm of fire our end of the line was under and had released the reserves to come to our assistance. The 7th Kentucky had shared the joy and sorrow of camp life and battle with the 35th for over six months. In addition they were impatient to join the fray, and so they rushed impetuously forward to join the 35th and the 3rd Kentucky in driving our hated enemy from the field.

We paused awhile so that we could catch our breath and the rest of the division could even up the line. We replenished our ammunition and are then advised that General Rust's Brigade is to be held in reserve for the next stage of the battle. By this time it was late afternoon and the rest of the division had not advanced very far. Night put an end to the operations of an arduous and fatiguing but glorious day.

23

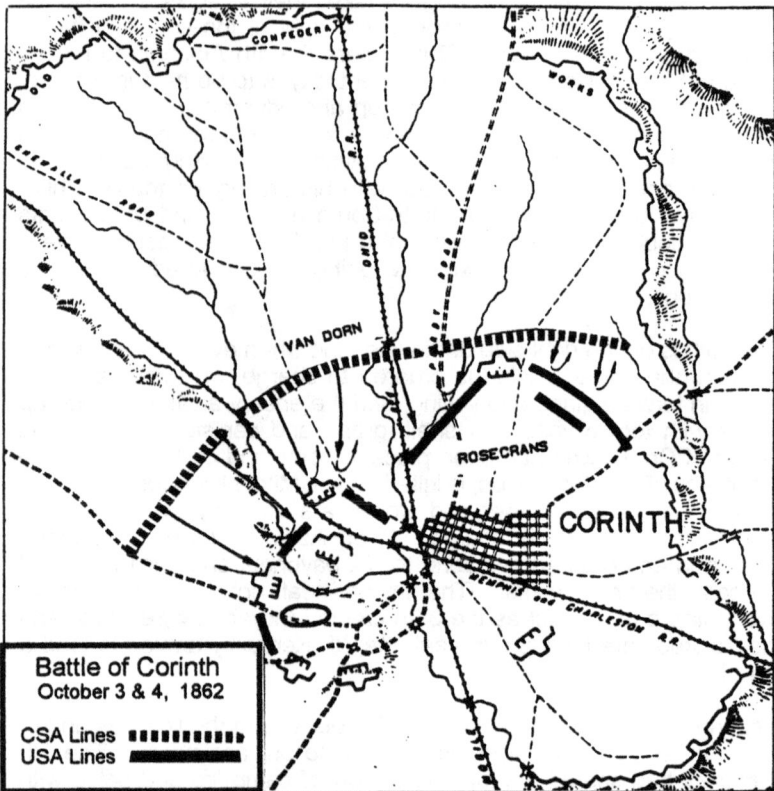

Battle of Corinth
October 3 & 4, 1862

CSA Lines ▰▰▰▰▰▰▰▰▰▰▰▰▶
USA Lines ▬▬▬▬▬▬▬

That night we spent bivouacked in the Union redoubt, among the abatis of timber that had cost us so many comrades in arms. The wounded were cared for and we buried our dead. The night was full of the ghosts of friends we will never see again and the thought of what tomorrow may bring. I don't think anyone slept very much that foggy night. Now we know what war is. Fear? Yes, but we had seen too much, been through too much, to let that take away our cause, our right to control our own destiny in the land we had opened with our own sweat and drive. Now you say your federal government should have all the power that your constitution gave to our state government! Most of us have never owned slaves, and most of those that do, didn't when they came to this part of the country to tear a farm out of the wilderness. If it had not been for us and our fathers, this land would still be nothing more than hunting grounds. We have created a way of life, an economy, a nation, if you will, where nothing existed before. We came here with nothing, Mr. Yankee, and did it by ourselves. Leave us alone.

The calm of dawn is shattered by the sound of a large battery of confederate artillery firing somewhere on our left. Today the division is assigned to the center of the line of attack, and they move forward with vigor, while Rust's brigade is held in reserve. We follow behind the 1st division as reserves, along a ridge, for about a mile and a half, moving toward the Union fortifications on College Hill.

The line of battle moves within 200 or 300 yards of several forts. The Federals have a long line of formidable breastworks with abatis in front. We can see hundreds of yankee troops within these fortifications. Enemy artillery opens a rapid, murderous fire, which the division withstood without backing up one inch. At this point, our brigade was ordered forward into the center position of the line.

About 9:30, the 35th was South of the railroad tracks. Somewhere to the left of our division the fighting was very heavy and the CSA line was giving away. The 2nd brigade was sent to their assistance, but the Federals had sent in fresh troops and the CSA line was still wavering. A short time later, we were ordered to fall back to the first position we had taken from the enemy this morning because our boys on the left had been compelled to abandon the field.

General Rust's brigade retreated in perfect order and set up a strong line of defense where we could repel the enemy should he advance along either of two roads or the railroad. Our artillery put an end to the pursuit of CSA troops by the Yankee cavalry. We held our position for exactly 40 minutes after the last regiment of our troops had withdrawn across Indian Creek and then followed, bringing up the rear, to Chewalla, where we rejoined the division.

During this early part of the retreat from the battle field, our brigade marched without any sign of disorder or excitement. The men of the 35th felt they had taken the worst the Yankees could throw at us and we had acquitted ourselves with courage and pride. We wanted to show that we may have yielded the field but we were not beaten! We were retiring with our pride intact, as should veterans who had seen the face of death and driven the enemy from strongly fortified positions. The 35th marched in better order and with more deliberation than at any time in the past.

On the morning of the 5th, we resumed our march with our division again acting as rear guard for the Army. It was not long before our brigade, along with Villepigue's was ordered to rush forward to the Hatchie River bridge, where the Army had been checked by re-enforcements of fresh Union troops. Villepigue arrived first and engaged the enemy with the object of holding them in check. Our brigade joined General Price and secured the crossing at Crum's Mill, where the CSA Army started to cross the river. Our division was assigned to hold the crossing and again act as rear guard. Rear, front, rear, they were sure keeping the 35th on the move.

For the entire 40 miles from the Hatchie River to Hickory Flats, our division continued as rear guard for the army. We would form into line of battle whenever the enemy was reported to be coming too near. A few shots would be exchanged, the enemy would halt, and we would resume the march. We would trudge along through the heat and dust undergoing long marches, loss of sleep, doing without food, but with our heads held high and our pride intact. It was a severe and trying ordeal, but the 35th and the division came through, bringing our wounded with us.

October 7th we passed thru Ripley and on the 8th, we returned to our camp near Holly Springs, Mississippi. During the retreat, we had some shortage of food and cooking utensils, everyone was foot sore, but that was behind us, and by the 13th we had settled down in our old camp. At the battle of Corinth and on the retreat, our brigade had 25 men killed, 117 wounded with 83 missing. Our division had 77 killed, 285 wounded and just over 200 missing. The 35th lost more than it's share of good officers and men. The story is that we killed over 300 Yankees and wounded 1800, while we captured 232. On the retreat we gave them another 500 casualties.

WEDNESDAY, OCTOBER 15, 1862.

General Van Dorn is in trouble for the way he handled the CSA Army at Corinth. Our total loss was 1423 killed, 5692 wounded and 2248 captured. They say he is going to be up before a court of inquiry. They have asked our own Col. Robertson to be a witness. The brass hats in the rear should stay off the back of officers that were on the field of battle. Until they have felt the heat of battle and heard the sound of a ball passing a inch from their head, they are not fit to judge the actions of a commander in the field.

The last six weeks of 1862 slowly passed as the men regain their strength and try to keep warm. In some ways there was not much action, and in others there was a lot going on. We left Holly Springs and retired to the mouth of the Tippah River due to the danger of Federal troops flanking us. General Van Dorn had lost a little "skin" at his trial, but had otherwise come out alright. Col. Robertson resigned from the 35th due to poor health and has taken an assignment in the Engineering Department of the army. Edwin Goodwin was promoted to Col. and has taken over command of our unit. Capt. Robert Pevy of Co. F resigned due to problems with his liver and kidneys. J.A. Flanagan took over as Capt. of Co. F. Mid November found us camped near Abbeville, but on the 30th our division was ordered to march to Grenada Mississippi and set up winter camp. On the way two men from Co. A, Pvt.'s Alexander and Bayless, were captured during a skirmish in Water Valley. That was in the first week of December.

The Yankees had accumulated a lot of supplies at Holly Springs after we left. General Van Dorn just could not stand that, so he took some of the men, and on December 20, he captured the Federal supplies along with 1000 Yankee troops. He took some of the supplies and burned the rest. The 35th did not take part in this action, but it put Van Dorn back in the good graces of the powers that be and Grant had to retreat to Grand Junction, Tennessee. We had our first Christmas in the field away from our family and most of us were downcast.

It had been quite a year for the 35th. We had gone from being students and farmers to battle proven veterans. We had marched hundreds of miles and fought two major engagements. We had made a lot of friends in the 3rd, 6th and 7th Kentucky regiments as we fought side by side with these men of proven valor. We had proven ourselves, to ourselves as well as our comrades and the general officers. We had adjusted to camp life and learned the truth about the "glory" of battle. In other words, we were soldiers.

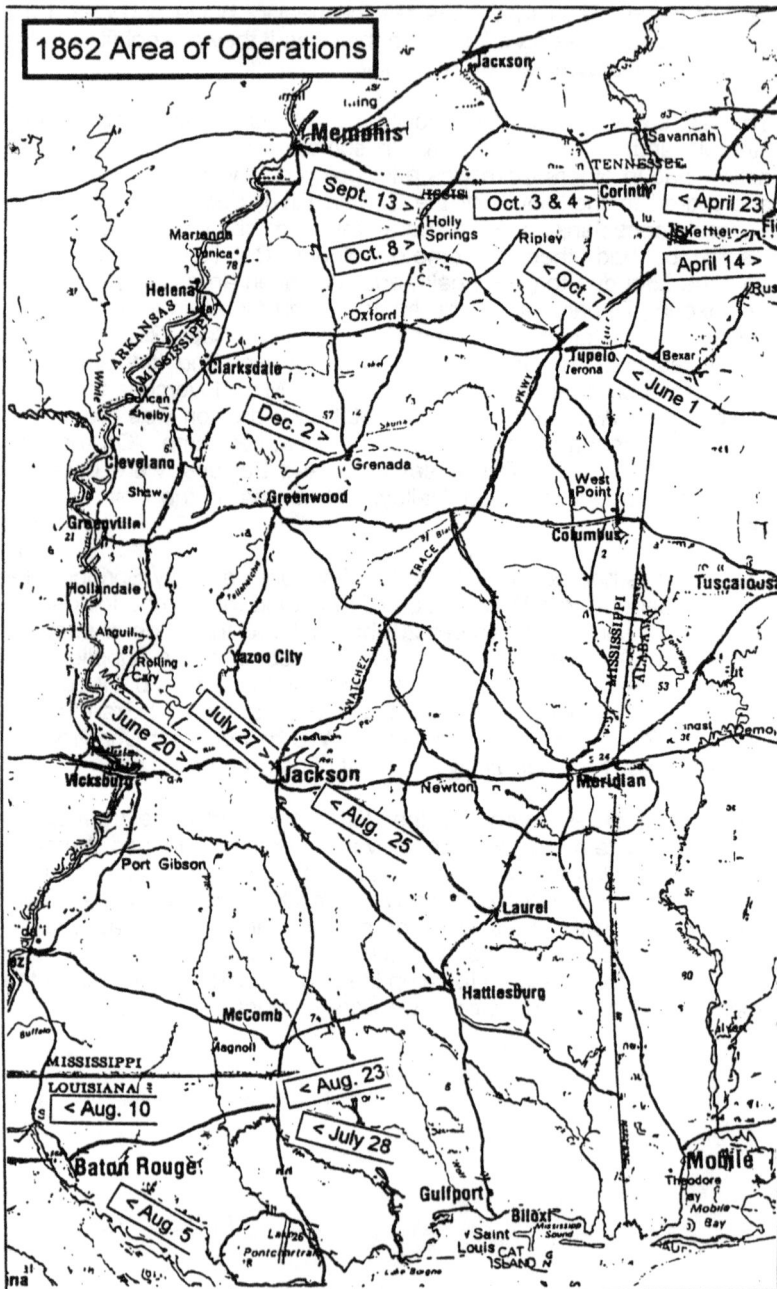

1862 Area of Operations

THURSDAY, JANUARY 29, 1863.

It is cold and damp. Our battle is with the weather. The camp at Grenada is little more than a field of mud with tents. Throughout January supplies come in and much of it is captured Union supplies. The men could care less. Union boots do a great job of keeping Confederate feet warm. Union tents can keep Confederate heads dry and Union rations taste pretty good.

General Grant's Yankee troops have poked their noses into just about every nook and cranny up and down the Mississippi River the past few weeks, trying to find a way to get at Vicksburg. They even have gunboats going up creeks and bayous, trying to get around Vicksburg. Grant has started work on his Vicksburg by-pass canal again! There have been a lot of skirmishes and small battles up and down the river as well as all over the state. There has been some minor fighting in our area, but we have stayed out of it.

On January 31st, General Loring's division is ordered to join in the defence of Vicksburg. General Albert Rust's Brigade, of which the 35th is a part, breaks camp and boards a train on the Mississippi Central Railroad. We pass thru Jackson and when the train stops, we find we are a Edwards Depot, which is about 15 miles east of Vicksburg. The 35th made camp about a mile from the railroad tracks and there we sat. The level of action was increasing on the river above and below Vicksburg and all around us.

MONDAY, FEBRUARY 23, 1863.

This morning we were ordered to break camp. After we had all our gear together, we boarded a train and moved to Osaka on the Mississippi-Louisiana state line. At that point, we began our march to Port Hudson. Most of us have mixed feelings about our return to this area. We remember mud, heat, bugs, sweat and a lot of hard dirty work. We will get to see some of our friends from our school days a LaGrange who are in the 27th Alabama, but the memories are hot, damp and unhappy. The 27th spent the winter at Port Hudson, and at least they should have some new tales to tell.

Upon our arrival at Port Hudson, We found that a lot of work had been done since we left. Our boys must have a hundred cannon in place, but we are put to work digging in and getting ready for an attack. The Federal's have a large gunboat fleet on the river between this point and Baton Rouge. We also hear that 12,000 Union troops have began to march out of Baton Rouge and headed our way! We will do our best to show them a hot time.

The Yankees made their move on the night of March 13th, when

Farragut's gunboat fleet tries to pass our batteries in the dark. It was one heck of a contest with the night being light as day from all the cannon fire. The gunboats poured shells into our positions and we rained shot on them. Many of the Union vessels were set on fire and otherwise knocked out of action. When dawn came, only two boats had made it past our guns! The rest had withdrawn. We had suffered a lot of damage, but we were more than ready for round two, whether it came from the river or the land. The second round never came. The gunboats returned to Baton Rouge, and the Yankee troops thought it best to march south to Brashear City instead of North where they would have to argue with us.

As March moved on, the 15,000 men now at Port Hudson continued to work on the defenses of the area. The Federals were going to have a hard time taking this place from us. The stories we hear about Vicksburg and Grant's attempts to get around it are the cause of a lot of laughter. He gave up trying to dig a canal around the city. It seems some of his gunboats got stuck in Deer Creek. Other gunboats are trapped and cut off in Steele's Bayou. Grant tried an expedition through Yazoo Pass and is blocked by our boys at Fort Pemberton. My o my, what a shame. You have to admit that Grant is trying, but he is not getting anywhere.

SUNDAY, APRIL 5, 1863.

Here we go again. We are to march out of here today, board a train and go to Tullahoma, Tennessee, wherever that is, via Jackson, Mississippi and Montgomery, Alabama. When we finally arrived at Chattanooga, we find out that General Rust has been transferred to General Sterling Price's Army, and that the 35th has been transferred to General Buford's Brigade. In addition, our orders have been countermanded, and we are to return to Mississippi. Well, we are getting quite a train ride out of it, but the 35th is scattered over 3 states. One way or the other we will all get back together.

On April 20th, we left Chattanooga on our way back to Jackson, Mississippi. I hope they know just where they want us. We are getting to see a lot of new country but all this riding around is not helping win the war.

The 35th arrived in Meridian, Mississippi April 24th and are immediately sent to Enterprise, which is 20 miles South of Meridian. About 1500 Union cavalry are approaching the town, and we are the nearest CSA troops. In addition, we are already onboard a train. So off we go like a bat out of hell! We come roaring into town with all guns firing, just as the Union cavalry enters the town. The enemy demanded we surrender the town to them. Our own Col. Goodwin told them to drop dead! The shooting started and the battle was on! A short time later, General Loring arrived with two regiments of

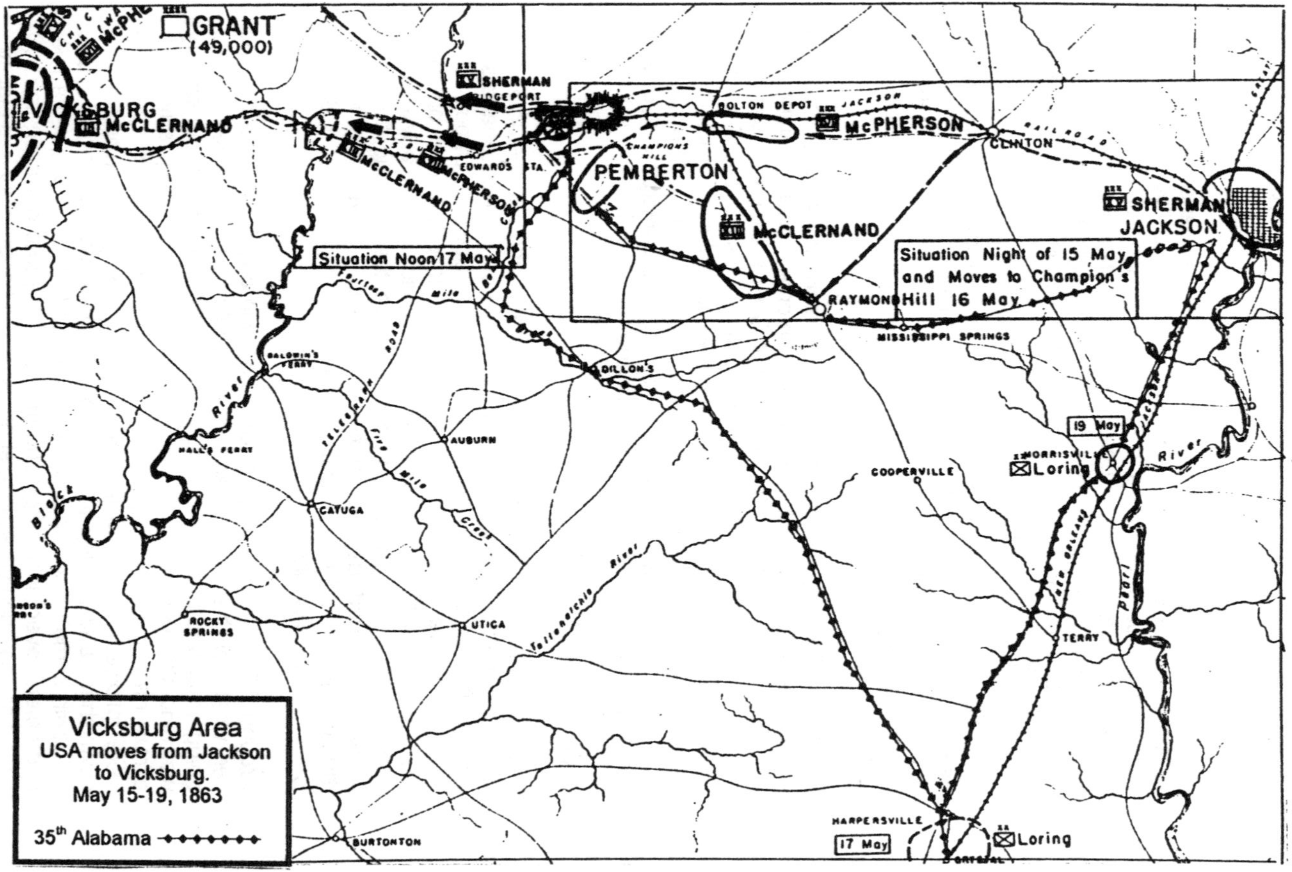

GRANT
(49,000)
SHERMAN
BRIDGEPORT
VICKSBURG
McCLERNAND
McCLERNAND
McPHERSON
EDWARDS STA.
BOLTON DEPOT
McPHERSON
CLINTON
CHAMPION'S HILL
PEMBERTON
McCLERNAND
SHERMAN
JACKSON
Situation Noon 17 May
Situation Night of 15 May and Moves to Champion's Hill 16 May
RAYMOND
MISSISSIPPI SPRINGS
BALDWIN'S FERRY
DILLON'S
River
AUBURN
HALL'S FERRY
19 May
MORRISVILLE
Loring
River
COOPERVILLE
CAYUGA
Creek
ROCKY SPRINGS
UTICA
TERRY
Pearl
HARPERSVILLE
17 May
Loring
BURTONTON
Vicksburg Area
USA moves from Jackson
to Vicksburg.
May 15-19, 1863
35th Alabama

reinforcements at which point the enemy retreated. This kind of thing will wake you up from a long train ride!

The Yankees were a part of Grierson's Raiders and was trying to capture supplies we had in Enterprise, as well as cut the rail line. They retreated about three miles out of town. General Loring took a regiment to pursue them, but he could not catch them on foot. They moved down the road toward Pauling so Loring sent some riders to burn bridges and telegrams for other CSA troops to cut them off. In any event they got away.

The 35th stayed in Enterprise a few days and on the 26th, the enemy was again about three miles out of town. On the 27th we could find no sign of them, so Loring mounted 150 men in Meridian and sent them to locate the Yankees. No luck. The last we heard, they showed up in Baton Rouge on May 2nd.

The 35th left Enterprise and arrived in Jackson on May 3rd where we were ordered on to Edwards Depot to reinforce General Pemberton. Pemberton was preparing to meet part of Grant's army that was trying to come up on Vicksburg from the East, after crossing the Mississippi River near Grand Gulf. On the 14th, Grant captures Jackson, after beating off our boys at Raymond, Mississippi. All this action is taking place within 25 or 30 miles of us. Pemberton's army, us included, is the only thing standing between Grant and Vicksburg!

FRIDAY, MAY 15, 1863.

Col. Goodwin is ordered to report to General Loring with the 35th. We march down the Raymond road until we find Loring's headquarters on the Ratliff farm about four miles south east of Edwards Depot. That evening, we are detailed for picket duty and move two miles on down the Raymond road to take position. We spread out a little with Co. F about 200 or 300 yards in front. Early in the evening the 22nd Mississippi joined us as the forward guard. From time to time throughout the night the quiet was broken by gunfire as CSA and Union cavalry exchange shots.

Around 7:00 A.M. on the 16th, Col. Goodwin decided to ride out and see what was happening because we could hear heavy skirmishing going on at a furious pace. The Col. found a few units of our cavalry watching the enemy. The Federal cavalry was slowly advancing across on open field. They were spaced about 40 yards apart and were followed by a long line of infantry. They were driving in our skirmishers and moving to their right as they moved forward. Col. Goodwin came back to our position, told us to form into a battle line, and defend every inch of ground from here back to our main line. At 8:00 A.M. the enemy began to shell us from a battery they had placed

Baker's Creek
Battle Field
May 16, 1863

Champion's Hill
Battle Field

May 16, 1863

Position of the U.S. Forces at 10.30 A.M.
" " " " 11 A.M.
" " " " 2 P.M.
" " " Rebel Forces.

Big Black River Bridge
Battle Field

May 17, 1863

somewhere to our right. The shells were bursting all around us and some men in the 22nd Mississippi were wounded, but all of us held our ground and were ready to meet the foe. Co. B was sent out to act as skirmishers and engage the Federal sharpshooters.

At 8:30 we received orders from General Loring to fall back and rejoin the main line. This we did until we regained contact with Col. Reid's 22nd Mississippi. Col. Goodwin, being the senior officer, ordered one company of the 22nd to join our Co. B at that point. The rest of their men were to fall back, but stay within 100 yards of us. The two companies on the point were engaging the Federals vigorously. Knowing they were trying to out flank us, Col. Goodwin kept vedettes on our flanks to keep us out of trouble. We continued to retreat slowly until additional orders arrived from General Loring, telling us to rejoin our brigade immediately.

We rejoined Buford's brigade which had taken up a position in the midst of heavy timber near the home of Mr. Ratliff. The brigade's right flank was on the Raymond road and the left joined with General Bowen's division. The press of battle forced Bowen to move left, which caused Buford to send his reserves into the line of battle to fill a 600 yard gap that had thus opened on our left. About 20 minutes later Buford had to shift left in order to maintain contact with Bowen's division, which had moved left again. We held this position till about 3:00 in the afternoon.

Due to the sound of heavy firing on our left, we knew the enemy must have massed their forces and charged that wing of our army. General Bowen had been pushed far to the left again, whereupon General Buford ordered his brigade to march a double time, by the left flank, until we rejoined Bowen's right flank. We had to cover two miles at this pace, through corn fields and broken ground, under a scorching sun. The heat got to some of the men. The enemy in this area was on a hill and they were taking pot shots at us. The further we went, the heavier the enemy fire became. When we made contact with Bowen's division, they were falling back in disorder before an enemy onslaught. Now our lines ran east to west, whereas this morning, we had a north-south line. As we were passing some slave quarters, General Bowen rode up and ordered Col. Goodwin and the 35th to follow him. At this point one third of our men had become separated from our regiment. Bowen found one of his aides and had him conduct us to the place where our boys were trying to establish a line of battle. We fixed bayonets and moved forward until we came upon General E.M. Green.

General Green ordered us to move to the right and protect the 1st Missouri Battery, which was under heavy attack by the enemy and in grave danger. The odds and ends of the 35th that were still with us ran in that direction until we found the "out of action" guns. We took up a position just to the rear of the battery, and let the hot lead fly. The battery men, thus reassured by our covering fire, rushed to their guns with enthusiasm and determination that undoubtly has seldom been seen. For over an hour the enemy poured volley after volley of shot, shell and canister on us. "Our" battery men worked like demons, knowing we were keeping sharpshooters away from them.

We had a good position from which to pick off the enemy and at the same time keep ourselves covered, but it was here that Lieut. George Hubbard was killed. He had been visiting old friends in the 35th when the action started, and Capt. Flanagan asked him to assume temporary duty as 1st Lieut. in Co. F.

The Federals had given up, we thought, just as "our" battery ran out of ammunition. The 1st Missouri packed up and drove off the field. Within two minutes the enemy opened up on our left, catching us in an enfilading fire. Col. Goodwing sent a courier to General Green requesting further orders, and we changed our front so as to meet the Union troops head on. At this time panic stricken CSA troops came running through our position. Col. Goodwin ran forward and ordered them to stop, but they would not obey his orders nor those of their commanders. Goodwin ran back to us and ordered a bayonet charge, but even the sight of men in gray charging forward did not halt the headlong flight. The colors of three regiments passed through the ranks of the 35th. All the officers and most of the men of the 35th collared passing CSA troops trying to get them to stop and take a stand. We begged, we threatened and cursed them, but it was no use. In the middle of this confusion, we received orders from General Green to follow the battery and provide cover. Accordingly, we followed the 12th Louisiana away from the Champion's Hill area and tried to locate the 1st Missouri Battery. A little later we were permitted to rejoin Buford's Brigade.

By the time we relocated our brigade, a general retreat was in progress towards Baker's Creek. The enemy was pressing, so we were assigned to act as part of the rear guard. We were then advised that the enemy had taken the ford across Baker's Creek, and were between us and Edward's Depot. Due to this, the part of the army we were with, mostly from Loring's division, was cut off from the general retreat towards Vicksburg. We started to move South in an effort to find another ford so that we could get back on the road to the bridge across the Big Black River. The roads were bad or Non-existent and some artillery had to be abandoned along the paths which necessity forced us to travel. The guns were spiked so they were of no use to the Yankees.

After marching about 12 miles, we found a guide and asked him to lead us to a ford. He stated that we could not get to CSA fortifications on the Big Black River, without passing through Union lines. The only way to save the division was to march passed the enemy flank and move toward Jackson. Vicksburg seemed doomed, as did some of the men of the 35th who had become separated from us, and must be with the rest of our army at the bridge over the Big Black River.

By neighborhood roads we moved during the night, passing the flank of the enemy, hourly expecting an attack. We could hear the Yankees conversing as we moved through the darkness, crossing ravines and creeks. About 3:00 Sunday morning, we reached Dillon's place on the road from Grand Gulf to Raymond, just a few miles from yesterdays battle field. The march continued to Crystal Springs on the Jackson and New Orleans Railroad where we camped Sunday night after marching 24 hours and covering 40 miles without provisions.

The next morning we got up hungry and continued toward Pearl River, then marched on to Jackson, which we reached on Wednesday, May 20th.

Upon arrival at Jackson it was found that the Federals had captured the town, destroyed all our Commissary and Quartermaster supplies and then departed. We were without food, blankets, shelter, extra clothing, guns and powder. The troops were in poor shape both physically and morale wise. In many ways, out condition was well nigh desperate. In other ways we were lucky, though. We had not been killed or captured, there was food to be had on farms around the area and the weather was warm, so sleeping on the ground without shelter or blankets of any kind was not as bad as it could have been. It did not rain on us, but each night brought a heavy dew, so the men got up each morning about as wet as if we had had a heavy rain. Under those conditions, the 35th and the remainder of Loring's division in the Jackson area waiting for reinforcements and supplies to arrive from Georgia and the Carolinas.

During this period we received news about what had happened to our comrades in arms. At Champion's Hill and Baker's Creek, we killed about 450 Yankees and wounded about 1900 more. We lost 2500 CSA troops killed or wounded, but about 1800 additional men were missing and I guess captured. Our boys that made it to the Big Black River bridge killed or wounded another 300 Union troops, but we lost 600 killed or wounded and had another 2500 captured. Those who made it across the bridge followed General Pemberton in retreat into the fortifications around Vicksburg. Before we had been back in Jackson 48 hours, Grant had launched two frontal assaults on Vicksburg, both of which were repulsed after heavy losses. Somewhere in all this action, the 35th had lost about a third of it's men. They are either dead, on their way to a Federal prison camp or in the trenches around Vicksburg.

A few days later, General Joseph E. Johnston arrived to assume command of the CSA troops in Mississippi that are not trapped in Vicksburg. Recruits and supplies began to arrive in an effort to bring our forces up to strength. It is understood that we are to attempt the relief of the besieged civilians and soldiers in the city of Vicksburg.

TUESDAY, JUNE 30, 1863.

The word has been passed today. We are to get our kit together and get ready to march to Vicksburg and raise the siege! The stories we hear about what is going on in the city are all bad. For more than a month Vicksburg has been under bombardment from gunboats on the river and batteries on the land. Every few days the Yankee troops try and storm CSA fortifications and are repulsed at great cost in dead and wounded. The civilians are living in cellars and caves in an attempt to get away from falling shells. They say our troops are eating mule meat and corn meal.

We know that there are a lot more Yankees around Vicksburg than there are CSA troops, but due to heavy action in Tennessee, Virginia and elsewhere, we are not going to receive any more reinforcements. We have to get the job done with the troops and supplies at hand. General Johnson had a letter read to us from Secretary of War, James Seddon. It said in part, "---the eyes and hopes of the whole Confederacy are upon you, with full confidence, ---- it is better to fail nobly daring, than, through prudence even, to be inactive." With these words in our ears, we pick up our guns and march out on the road to Vicksburg.

We arrive at the East bank of the Big Black River on July 1. Johnston sent out the cavalry on reconnaissance, trying to find a vulnerable place to attack Grant's outer defenses. For three days the cavalry probed the Union lines without finding a weak spot while we camped along the river cleaning our guns and thinking about the coming battle.

Our cavalry came tearing into camp on July 4th shouting that General Pemberton had surrendered! Vicksburg has fallen! 30,000 CSA troops captured including a lot of our friends! It is hard to believe. After all the many months of fighting, after all the dead and wounded, after all the hunger and hardship, Vicksburg and the Mississippi River is in the hands of the enemy! More of our friends and school mates in Yankee hands. Its sad. Its so hard to even think about.

Johnston's army starts the return march to Jackson the afternoon of the 4th. No sooner had we started back, than Federal troops attack our rear guard. With the fall of Vicksburg, thousands of union troops are available and are therefore ordered to attack us. We fall back to

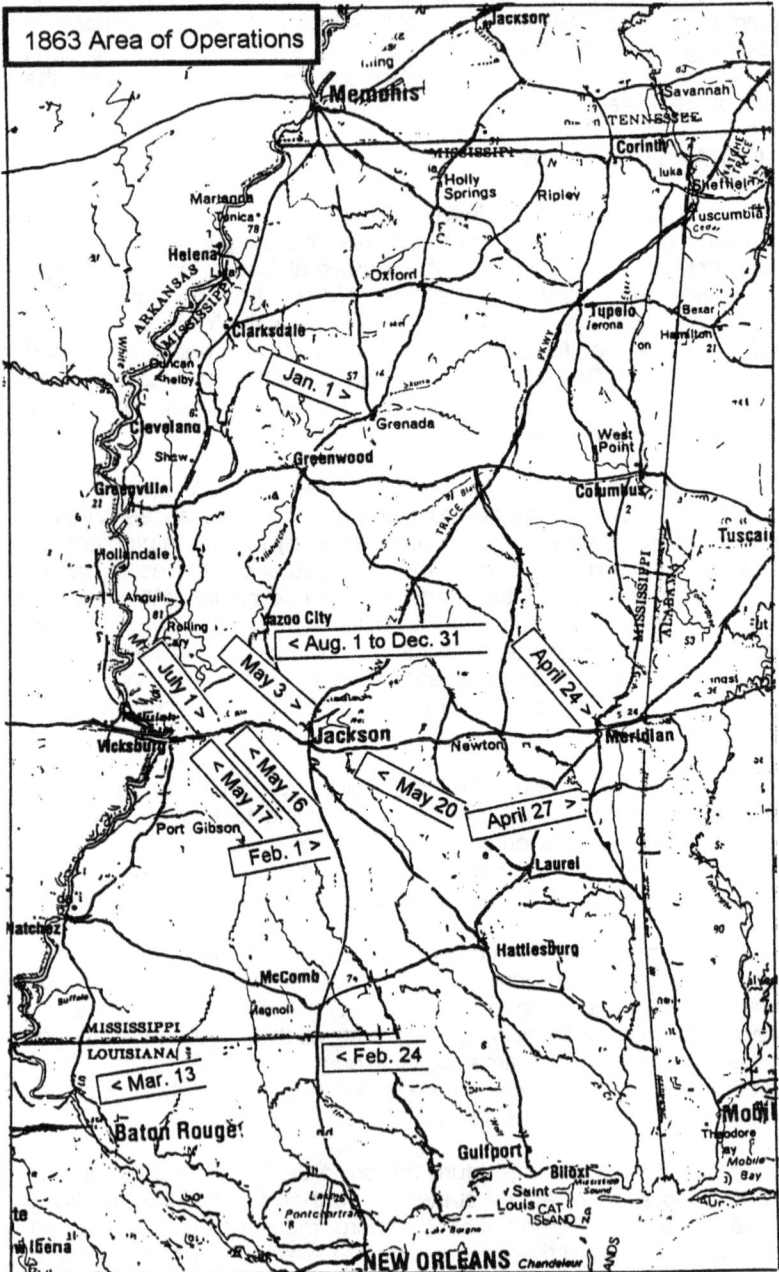

1863 Area of Operations

Jan. 1 >

< Aug. 1 to Dec. 31

July 1 >

May 3 >

April 24 >

< May 16

< May 17

< May 20

April 27 >

Feb. 1 >

< Mar. 13

< Feb. 24

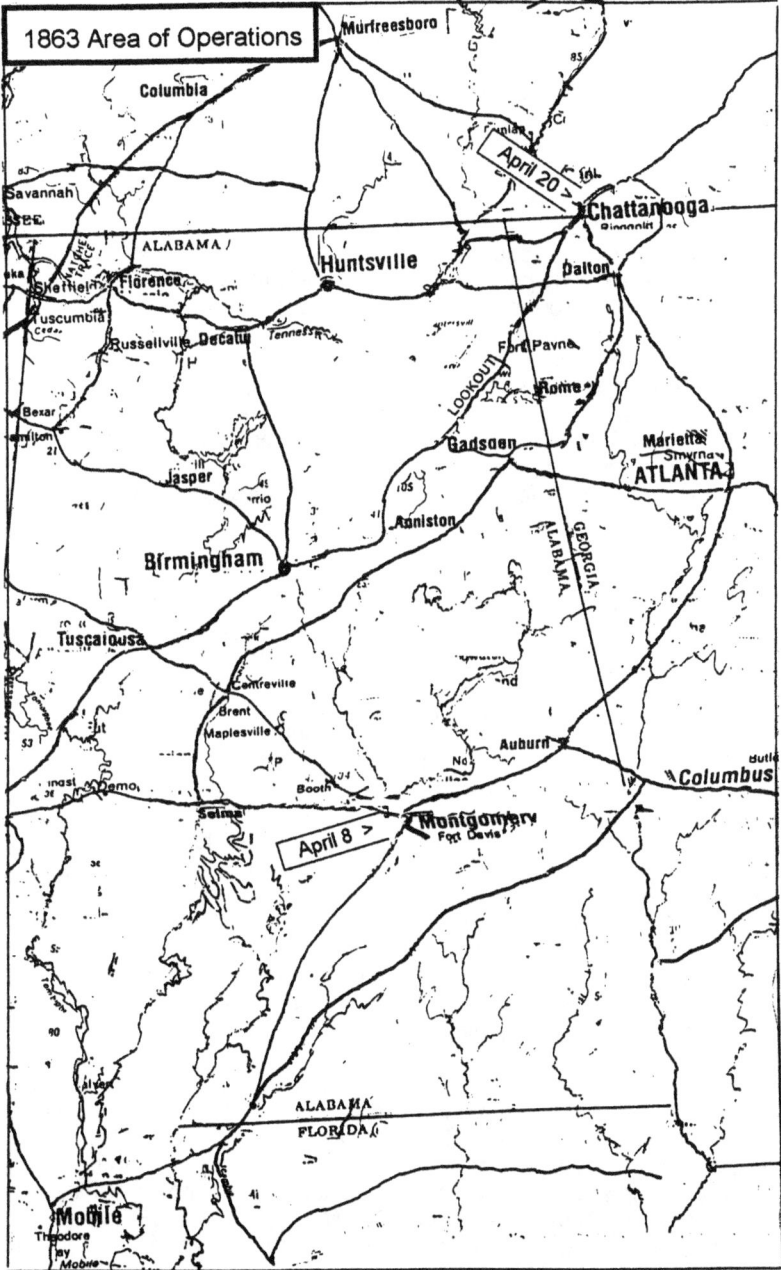

1863 Area of Operations

Murfreesboro

Columbia

April 20 >

Savannah

Chattanooga

ALABAMA

Huntsville

Dalton

Sheffield

Florence

Tuscumbia

Russellville

Decatur

Tennessee

Fort Payne

LOOKOUT

Rome

Bexar

Gadsden

Marietta
Smyrna

ATLANTA

Jasper

Anniston

GEORGIA

ALABAMA

Birmingham

Tuscaloosa

Centreville

Brent

Maplesville

Auburn

Columbus

Selma

April 8 >

Montgomery
Fort Davis

Booth

ALABAMA
FLORIDA

Mobile

Theodore

41

Jackson, and then retreat another 20 miles East to Morton, on the Southern Mississippi Railroad.

We moved on to Canton, Mississippi, and set up camp. The camp is very quiet and filled with gloom. Word Comes in that the Fort we worked so hard to build and defend at Port Hudson has surrendered. For a year and a half, the 35th has fought to keep Vicksburg and the lower Mississippi clear of Yankees, so that food and arms can move into the Confederacy. Now several states are cut off from us. We can Not use the ports in Texas and Louisiana. Federal troops are raiding all over the northern part of the state. We get reports of Skirmishes from all over. Around here there are a few minor firefights, but basically we just sit and brood while the officers talk about what to do. Our officers take care of us though. Our Captain came in one day with a load of tents and a few days later he came in with another load of tents. Well, we had more tents than we could use by this time, so he told the Lieutenant to trade them to another company in the 35th for boots, because he had a line on some shirts and trousers, but could not find any boots. We all became real "horse traders", but we tried to keep things within the 35th.

Summer passes, fall comes and goes, winters arrives and we just try and stay warm. It seems like Mississippi has become a backwater in the war. The cavalry are the only units really doing much fighting around here. I have seen enough action to last me a while though, I guess we should just try and take it easy, and be glad we are not being killed. A trickle of new men have been arriving, as have some of our boys captured at Vicksburg and earlier battles. When one of our old comrades come walking into camp after being lost at Big Black River or some other fight, it is cause for a real celebration!

The rumors are starting to fly again. The Yankees have been building up strength in south Central Tennessee and have started moving into the Chattanooga area. A few days later we hear about big battles at places called Lookout Mountain and Missionary Ridge. We are told that General Braggs has withdrawn from Chattanooga into Northern Georgia. The men of the 35th start cleaning up their guns and worrying about their clothes and boots. Some of our boys are making bets that our rest is about over.

While this is going on, our spirits soar, and then our hopes are dashed. Orders come down to have the 3rd, 7th and 8th Kentucky regiments mounted, and join General Forrest, who was then operating in the Northern part of Mississippi. They are to become a part of the cavalry! We had fought side by side with the gallant men almost from the day the 35th was formed and Col. Goodwin just knew we would get mounted and stay with our friends. Forms were filled out and signatures obtained, but to no avail. The 35th would stay on the ground and bid farewell to some of our best companions.

Mid December brings a new commander to the army in Mississippi. President Davis directs General Johnston to turn over his command to General Leonidas Polk. Everyone wonders what this change will mean for us. It does not take long to find out. Loring's division is ordered to join General Bragg at Dalton Georgia and aid him in the defence of Northern Georgia. The good news is that the 27th and 35th can leave right away, march through Northern Alabama, recruit some men, look for deserters and see the folks at home! Home! We have been away for almost two years. We do not have to be in Dalton until spring. It goes without saying that it did not take us long to break camp and head for Alabama!

WEDNESDAY, FEBRUARY 24, 1864.

We are back in Alabama! We got off the train at Demopolis and will stay here for a few days getting our gear in order for the march North to the valley of the Tennessee River. It will be a hard march, but we will be heading toward home!

Just before we left, Col. Goodwin died of an illness at Columbus, Mississippi. This put a damper on our joy at the prospect of seeing our families in northern Alabama. He was a good leader. Lt. Col. Ives became Col. Ives and took over command of the regiment. Everyone likes him, and he is doing well as our leader.

March 14th, we arrive at Mount Hope, Alabama, about 15 miles southeast of our old school at LaGrange. A Lot has happened since a group of happy young men marched out of LaGrange two years ago, with heads held so high. We had no idea what was before us that day. The young can be so foolish.

Our first order of business was to get the lay of the land, locate the enemy positions, pick up some recruits and arrest any deserters we came across. The 35th is down to 240 men and the 27th only has 280, so we need recruits.

We found the Yankees at Moulton just 12 miles East of us, and on the 21st, we joined with Col. William A. Johnson's cavalry and attacked the enemy. The fight started about 3 miles South of town, but the Federals took to their heels before we could fire a shot, so our cavalry chased them to Decatur. Seven of the Yankees were killed to the loss of one cavalryman. Col. Johnson was pleased with the way the 27th and 35th conducted themselves and said he would try and get us mounted and assigned to him. It sure would be nice to ride instead of walk, but we do not get our hopes up again.

March 24th sees us on the road again. We march to Russellville, about 15 miles West. Most of the men are given short furloughs to visit their homes. All of them are instructed to return with a recruit or two so that we can fill up the regiments. Col. Ives told us that he and the men not leaving camp would be somewhere between Russellville and Smithville, Mississippi, depending on what the Federals in the area were up to.

Loyal citizens in the area give Col. Ives enough horses to mount everyone left in camp. Most of us are sent out to a radius of 20 miles looking for deserters, but we do not have much luck. Col. Ives tells us on the 28th that he has received so many offers of mounts that he will request the Government to allow the entire 35th to become a cavalry unit.

As our men return to camp from their homes, we receive all kinds of information. The Yankees have thrown a bridge across the Tennessee River at Decatur and are fortifying that city. They have about 5000 troops at Eastport, just across the Alabama-Mississippi line. Huntsville is firmly in Federal hands. It looks like the spring campaign is starting to form. With most of our men back, we move 10 miles East to Newburg, Alabama. The men coming back from furlough have only brought in six recruits and eight deserters, 4 of which I am ashamed to say are from the 35th. On the night of April 12, part of the 27th and 35th, under command of our Col. Ives, cross the Tennessee River near Tuscumbia and surprised a camp of the 9th Ohio Cavalry. We kill 3, capture 3 officers and 39 privates and others. We also captured 65 horses and mules, arms and other equipment. All of this without sustaining a single loss. Half of the prisoners were turned over to the 27th. The other half were sent by Col. Ives to the Provost-Marshal at Tuscaloosa with one of our Captains and 14 men as guards. There was really very little risk in this raid, as we knew the country well and had spotted their camp earlier in the day.

By the 16th most of the men were on horse back, so we started to move around a bit more. On the 20th we were on the West side of the Flint River about six miles South of Decatur. We put on a show for the Yankees. They just knew we were going to attack, and they dug trenches and they moved guns sweating blood trying to get ready for the big battle they thought was coming there way. It was a sight to see,

because we knew that it was about time for us to move on to Georgia and that there was no army behind us coming here to attack them in the works they were desperately trying to put up. We would trade pot shots with the Yankees but I doubt we hit any of them. We just encouraged them to dig a little deeper.

The time had come for us to move on, so the 27th and the 35th headed South for Montgomery. At least this time we had horses and wagons so we could ride rather than walk. We arrived at Montgomery about May 23rd and were told to give up our horses and board a train for Resaca, Georgia. We were back on foot, but for the officers, of course. We got on the train and headed for Atlanta on the 24th. The train stopped for a while just across the state line in West Point, Georgia. When we started up again, our officers found their horses had been taken off the train to be watered, and had not gotten back on board in time, so they were on foot also. They laughed about it.

WEDNESDAY, MAY 25, 1864.

Our train stopped somewhere just North of Marietta, Georgia. I guess they did not want to risk having the rolling stock captured or destroyed. We were hustled off the train and rushed onto the road to the West. A big battle was going on at a place called New Hope Church, and our boys were out numbered two to one. We were needed fast! The 35th arrived in the area of the battle in the evening and were assigned to Scott's Brigade, Loring's Division of Polk's Corps. The fighting had died down for the day, and therefore our first order of business was to dig in - - - deep. All night long the thunder and lighting roared and rolled. The rain came down in buckets, but we keep working with spade and pick-axe. By dawn, we were wet and tired, but we were also strongly entrenched and in good position to do battle. Bring those Yankees on!

The next few days were a blur of charge and countercharge. Smoke and mud, never ending cannon and rifle fire, heat and blood. That is what I remember of the period. We had very little rest but neither did the enemy. Finally, General Sherman took his Union troops and moved off to the East, trying to flank our position. Our line moved to the right about two miles. Night and day there was heavy skirmishing and furious bombardment.

The Federals were still moving to the East, so on the 31st General Loring wanted to find out if the Yankees were still in front of us in strength. Our brigade and Featherston's started forward. After moving forward about 250 yards, firing broke out from Featherston's direction. We moved in that direction to provide them cover and found them in the process of dislodging a group of sharpshooters from a line of breastworks. We stayed on the flank, following the enemy line only a short distance, when we came upon another strong force behind a heavy line of fortifications. The enemy poured out a galling fire on our friends which we all returned, but we were then ordered to retire.

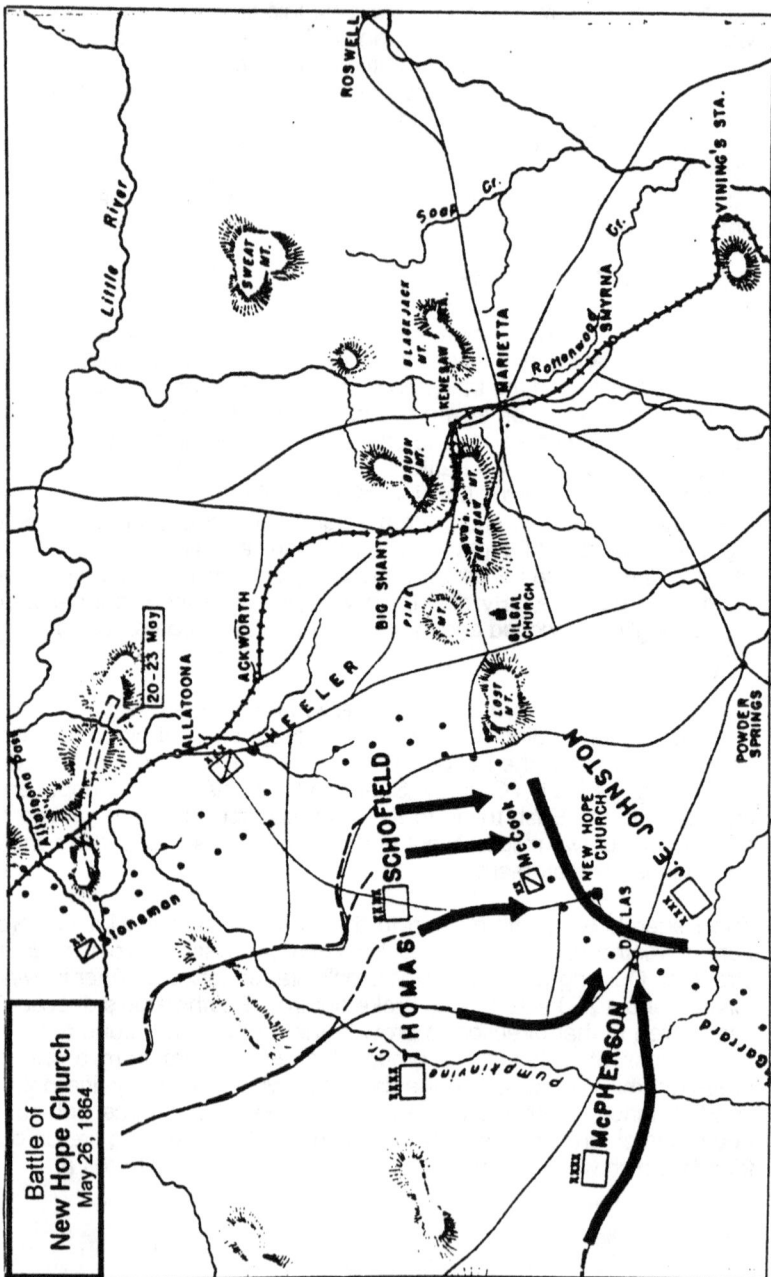

Battle of
New Hope Church
May 26, 1864

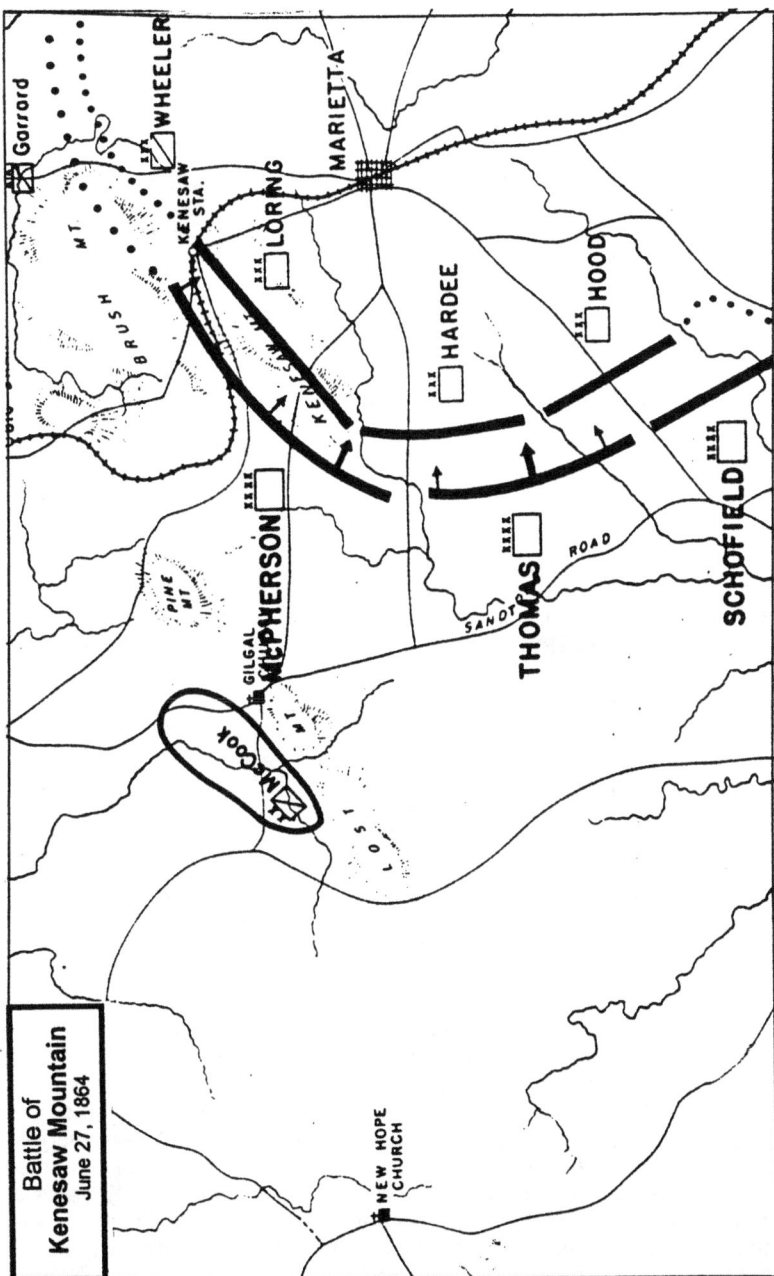

Battle of
Kenesaw Mountain
June 27, 1864

Garrard

WHEELER

KENESAW STA.

MARIETTA

BRUSH MT.

LORING

HARDEE

HOOD

SCHOFIELD

McPHERSON

PINE MT.

THOMAS

SAND TOWN ROAD

GILGAL

McCOOK

LOST MT.

NEW HOPE CHURCH

47

The 35th caught it's breath for a bit. It was at this point we found out that the 27th and 35th Alabama Regiments had been consolidated with the 49th Alabama back in April some time. We were told that the reason was our numbers had ben so reduced by illness, death and battle wounds to the point that we were just not big enough to be a regiment by ourselves. the only good thing about this was that our own Col. Ives would lead the 27th Consolidated Alabama, of which we were now a part. Col. Ives told us we could still call ourselves the 35th if we wanted, even though we were now just a few companies of the 27th Consolidated.

The word was that the CSA Army had lost about 900 men in the battle of the last few days, but that the Union Army had lost almost 3000. The Yankees had moved around our flank and were heading for the railroad to Atlanta. We had to cut them off, so there was no rest for the weary.

MONDAY, JUNE 27, 1864.

Over the last few weeks, we have fought and pulled back, fought and pulled back. Johnston set up a line running from Lost Mountain to Pine Mountain and then to Kenesaw Mountain. All the big CSA Generals were on Pine Mountain on June 14th, looking over the lay of the land and the Union positions, when the Federals fired just one round of cannon fire. The shell hit our general Polk in the chest and killed him. General Stewart took over his command. Shortly after that General Johnston pulled in all our troops to the Kenesaw Mountain area. Loring's division took up a position running from the base of Kenesaw, northeast to a point between the Bell's Ferry and Canton roads. Our brigade held the east end of our division's line.

Rain had fallen just about every day for over two weeks, but the mud and heat had not stopped the Yankees. Every day, somewhere along the CSA line, they charged. Our boys fight them off, shovel the mud and water out of the trenches and settle down for the next attack. Our end of the line does not see much action, which is just fine with us.

The morning of the 27th dawned bright and clear. General Scott had a full regiment, the 12th Louisiana, about 600 yards in front of our position on a skirmish line. About 10:00 A.M. the enemy came down Bell's Ferry road in full force. The men of the 35th could watch the approaching enemy, due to our position being about 50 feet higher. The 12th was well dug in and held their fire until the Union skirmish line, backed up by three lines of battle, were within 25 or 30 yards of them. At that point the 12th poured into the overwhelming enemy force, repeated volleys of minie-balls. the Federals went down rank on rank, in line abreast, eight and ten at a time, the soldiers behind, stepping over their dead and in turn joined the dying. The smoke of battle was so heavy it was getting hard to see. This thinned out the Yankees and caused them to falter, but did not stop their advance. Due to their heavy loss, the Yankees paused for a few moments to close up their lines. The 12th started to withdraw slowly toward our main battle line, knocking out some more enemy troops in the process.

When the advancing Union troops were within about 250 yards of our battle line the killing started again. Our artillery opened up a concentrated converging fire and our riflemen kept up the routine of load, aim, fire, load, aim, fire. Our batteries and muskets keep up their destructive and deadly fire for about an hour. The air was a sheet of flame. The fire was so galling and terrible and its results so severe, that the enemy retired, leaving their dead and wounded upon the field. As the sound of battle died down on our front, the wild and blood-curdling sound of a Rebel yell grew in volume as it moved down the line and was taken up by regiment after regiment. The fearful sound grew to a crescendo that drowned out all other sound. A few moments later we could once again hear Federal artillery on our right, firing upon General Wheeler's boys.

About 4:00 P.M., the Union artillery fire ceased and our skirmishers returned to their original position in front of our brigade. We could hear the cries and screams of the wounded for water and help, for escape from the pain. At this same time, the sound of battle picked up on our left, the direction of Featherston's brigade. As had happened all day long, the yell of Rebel pride would be heard, followed by the tremendous roar of hundreds of muskets and rifles being fired at one time, a pall of smoke would be seen, and then the normal sound of a pitched battle would prevail.

You have to admit the Union troops had courage, but this day was our day. The Federals had one hundred thousand men facing our forty thousand. We had the high ground, were well dug in and were fighting on our land, for our land. The Yankees had courage and this had to be recognized. At one point it was recognized. On one side of us the sound of battle stopped. We saw a Confederate officer and a Union officer talking on the breastworks. We could see that cannon fire had set fire to leaves, brush and grass, and that the fire was moving toward dead and wounded Union soldiers lying on the ground. These helpless men would be burned alive. A cease-fire was called long enough for CSA and Union troops to put out the fire. The Union removed their wounded, the two officers shook hands, walked away from each other and the fierce fighting resumed.

By mid afternoon it was over. We had shattered Sherman's army. We had not given up one foot of ground to him. Sherman had lost 9000 men this day, while General Johnston's losses were exactly 808 men.

Somehow in the aftermath of all the fighting we were just to tired to take much pride in having inflicted so much death and pain.

For the next few days there were sporadic skirmishes scattered up and down our line. July 2nd we saw the "Grand Union Army" on the move. They were moving down the valley toward the Chattahoochee River. Sherman had given up trying to take our positions. There was only one thing he could logically have in mind. He was going to march around our flank and into the city of Atlanta. We had to do something.

SATURDAY, JULY 9, 1864.

Earlier in the week, we had withdrawn from Kenesaw Mountain and moved into entrenchments that General Johnston had had built on the Chattahoochee River, in case Sherman flanked us. We were once again between the Yankees and Atlanta. Sherman was mad and thought he would be able to stride us a fatal blow, but good old General Johnston had him outsmarted, and we were once again in a good position to make the Yankees pay dearly for every inch of gain.

Word arrived that the Federals had moved into Roswell. Sherman then ordered every building and factory burned to the ground. Sherman then had every man and women that worked in the factories taken prisoner and shipped north. About 400 citizens were thus unjustly uprooted from their homes. Just a few hours after this story came in, another rider arrived with the news that Sherman had built a pontoon bridge across the Chattahoochee, northeast of us, and the enemy was pouring across. Flanked again!

Today we are throwing up new fortifications that run from the Chattahoochee to Peachtree Creek. Dig, dig, dig. Retreat, retreat, retreat. What can you do when you are outnumbered more that two to one. Every time the Union troops come at us head on, we give them a licking. I guess that is the reason the Federals are afraid to take on our General Johnston and instead they just move around our flank.

General Johnston is getting ready to move back to Atlanta within the imposing fieldworks that the Georgia Militia under General Brown had built. Johnston felt that his veterans behind those breastworks would inflict vast losses on the enemy. We would gather our strength for a time, and then start on the road to final victory. The fortifications were well dug in, had deep rifle pits and strong revetments for our cannon. They ran all the way around the city, and at every point, had several hundred yards of cleared ground that would provide us with a good field of fire. The area we now occupy has to much timber and brush. The Yankees can hide to easily.

President Jefferson Davis has just committed the biggest blunder of the war! He has just replaced our good General Johnston with General John B. Hood! The news was not to be believed. All the men trusted and liked Johnston. We would have followed him anywhere, executed any order. He is a good man. He talks to the troops and is a fine general. But he brooding untrustworthy Hood? What goes on in the minds of the people in our war department is hard to understand. If Hood had been in charge these last two or three months, we would all be dead and the Federal flag would be flying over Atlanta! Johnston's general staff are outraged and say they are going to resign from the army. Some of the officers and a lot of the men say they will not fight under Hood. All the Generals, Colonels and company officers went to a meeting called to forestall trouble. When it was over cooler heads had gotten everyone to reconsider. The troops still grumbled, but Hood took over on the 17th. An army that was filled with cheerful optimism and confidence became gloomy and pessimistic over night. Once again the brass hats show they have no idea what they are doing. The first thing Hood did was to scrap General Johnston's plan to move into fortress Atlanta, and told us to get ready to attack.

The sun rose clear the morning of July 20th, and as the day wore on the temperature went up. July in Georgia is hot. We were part of Stewart's Corps, which was to the left of Hardee's Corps. Loring's Division held the right flank of Stewart's Corps. The 35th was on the left of Loring's Division. Anyway, we were just to the left of the center of the CSA line.

A lot of officers were coming and going so we knew that something was up. At 1:00 P.M. orders came in from General Scott to the effect that the entire division was to move by the right flank one division length. We packed our kit and followed Fetherston's brigade along our line of entrenchments for about a mile and a half to a point one half mile east of Pace's Ferry road. Here we were ordered to deposit our knapsacks in the rear of the brigade and form up for action in front of our entrenchments by 4:00 P.M.

At 4 o'clock, col. Ives told us to move forward and to the right, and when we found the enemy we were to "allow no natural or artificial impediment to check our forward progress." The boys in our company decided that meant we were to find the Yankees and run them back to Ohio.

When we arrived at the CSA skirmish line, we were ordered to check our bayonet's, form into line of battle and load our muskets. This we did, and then moved forward, driving the Union skirmishers back into their main works. Our regiment and part of the 12th Louisiana was advancing through timber, while the rest of the brigade had 600 yards of open fields to cross. At this time, John Abernathy, from the old 27th, captured the colors of the 33rd New Jersey Regiment. We had moved within 100 yards of the Union trenches, when Col. McAlexander, who was in charge of the right wing of our regiment, was ordered by someone on General Scott's staff, to fall back. Whereupon, Col. Ives ordered us back.

We had moved slowly and reluctantly about 50 yards to the rear, when another member of General Scott's staff rode up and told Col. Ives that an order to fall back had been given. The rider indicated that the enemy works on our right flank had been taken. All of this was going on while we suffered under a most galling crossfire from the Yankees, and our color bearer, Marcus Green, was hit in the leg. One of the color guards seized the flag. We immediately did an about face, and in one long, yelling, smokey charge, we overran the Yankee works, captured several prisoners as well as three artillery pieces.

The Federal troops had offered feeble resistance to our last charge and in there precipitous flight, threw away their knapsacks, guns and other equipment. Our marksmen encouraged their haste by taking careful aim and shooting the Yankees that were slow to leave. A Few minutes later, Major Wright, in charge of our left wing and McAlexander on the right, advised Col. Ives that our regiment had no support on either side! Scott's staff officer did not know what was going on! The result was that we were in a crossfire from the right and the left.

The enemy on our flanks and in front of us had rallied and even though Fetherston's brigade had joined us on the right, our ranks were being gradually thinned. When Col. Ives decided we were not going to get support on either flank, he ordered us to fall back about 150 yards, to the cover of a ridge. Here the fight continued. General Scott knew that victory could still be won, if he could only get back the brigade (Adam's) that had been detached a few days earlier. Scott's presence in the midst of all the shot and shell the rest of us were in, had a cheering effect on everyone.

It was now getting dark and the fighting started to die down. We received orders to move back into our old works at 9:00 P.M. We removed our wounded from the ground in front and retired to our mid-day position. A Lot of sweat and blood was spent for nothing. The 35th, or 27th Consolidated, had 2 men killed and 31 wounded.

We found out later that our losses were lighter than any regiment in the brigade, and the general area in which we were fighting, had been almost quiet, when compared to what had been going on elsewhere up and down Peachtree Creek. The 57th Alabama, which was part of our brigade, had lost 157 men out of 330. The CSA had lost 4500 to 5000 men. We are not strong enough to take that kind of loss and have not one inch of ground to show for it.

Sherman now held the railroad to the north, which would enable him to bring in fresh troops and supplies. He held part of the railroad to the east, which cut us off from reinforcement and fresh supplies. We now felt sure that General Hood would take us into the 10 mile circle of fortifications around Atlanta. It had to be the most strongly protected city in the country. All it needed was battle hard veterans to man them. With the troops we had left, we could hold those breastworks forever.

The morning of July 21st started out hot and stifling. Just as we finished breakfast, white flags of truce started going up all over our lines as well at those of the Federals. We were told that a truce had been called to allow both the Federal and Confederate troops to bury the thousands of dead scattered across yesterdays battle field. Everything was quiet as this distasteful chore was attended to. The only sound was that of spade and pick-ax. The sight of the horrible wounds that our comrades had suffered gave us all pause to think and wonder about our own mortality. With a quite word or gesture the Yanks would show us where some of our boys had fallen, so that they could be buried by men that cared. We did the same for them.

When the days dreadful task was done, the white flags came down and everything along the bank of Peachtree Creek was still. As night fell, the order to break camp and march into Atlanta was given. It seemed like Hood was going to do what he should have done a few thousand dead earlier.

As we are on the move into Atlanta, we could see strong redoubts on the hills, all connected by high breastworks and good deep rifle pits. The entire fortification was revetted with heavy timber. The outside of the works were protected by tens of thousands of abatis, which were made of big tree limbs that had been sharpened and firmly planted in the ground at an angle pointing outward. There was also "chevaux de frise" which is criss-crossed sharpened poles, that have been tied together to form a barricade. There also was a deep trench in front of the works. Sherman would be plain crazy to try and storm this bastion, if we had enough men to man the works.

Just as we started thinking that things were going to be alright, word started filtering in that Hood had ordered General Hardee's Corps to march right on through Atlanta and by marching all night, attack a part of the Federal army that was near Decatur. Hood was then going to send Cheatham's Corps, which had not been in yesterday's battle, northwest up the railroad to attack another part of Sherman's army. Not only were we outnumbered two or three to one, but Hood was going to split us up and try some more attacks! What a fool.

Battle of Ezra Chapel
July 28, 1864

54

By nightfall we had been able to get a little rest, but then Hardee's Corps started arriving back in town. They had lost the fight and in the process been shot to pieces. Another 7000 of our men lost! As worn out as we are and as out numbered as we have been, we should have been defending not attacking!

SATURDAY, JULY 23, 1864.

Sherman and the Union army had pressed in close to Atlanta. They were erecting their own forts and had mounted siege guns within easy range of any point within the city. The bombardment began. They were pouring explosive shells as well as red-hot cannonballs into our positions. We just kept our heads down. The civilians suffered through the inferno of incessant shelling with us. A lot of citizens left on trains that used the two sets of tracks that were still in our hands.

On July 28th Loring's division, along with another from Stewart's Corps, was ordered to move out with General S.D. Lee's Corps, and prevent the Union troops from cutting our last rail connection to the outside. The Union army was on the west side of the city moving south, so we marched out of Atlanta following Lickskillet Road. Stewart's Corps stopped and took up a position near Ezra Methodist Chapel to wait for the oncoming Yankees. General Stewart's two divisions were to be held in reserve, so we took up a position to the rear and a little to the left of Lee. We were about a mile and a half outside the fortifications of Atlanta. Just after noon, the Union army started arriving and the shooting started. As both armies clashed, our boys charged the Union skirmishers and pushed them back to a small hill where resistance stiffened.

From our position we could see what was going on and something was wrong. What had started as a all-out assault had fizzled out. There seemed to be nothing but confusion. Some of our troops were pushing the enemy back, some stopped half way and others hardly moved from their original line. The order of battle had been misunderstood or something. The enemy started to move forward but was halted. Even though not actually engaged in the battle, our division was having a good many men killed and wounded by enemy fire. We were in an open field in the immediate rear of our battle line and could not return fire because our boys were between us and the Yankees. We were suffering from Union fire without being able to reply.

Our boys repulsed all enemy attacks but it was obvious that General Hood's idea for an assault had been ill-conceived. There was one final useless surge forward in the late afternoon and then the attack was called off by General Lee. Hood's recklessness and CSA courage had cost the defenders of Atlanta another 4000 to 5000 men, of which 27 were members of the 35th Alabama. Sherman had only been slowed

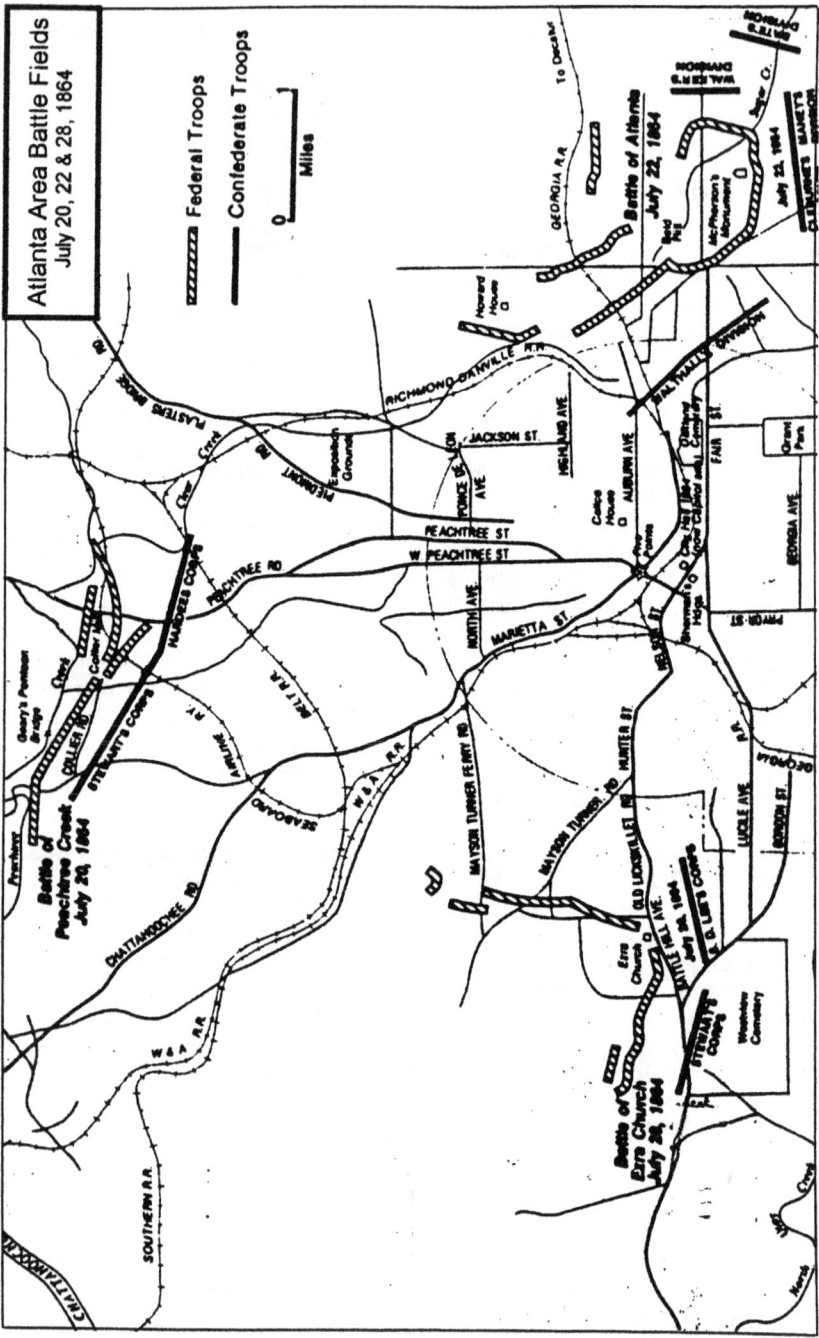

Atlanta Area Battle Fields
July 20, 22 & 28, 1864

Federal Troops
Confederate Troops

0 Miles

To Decatur

GEORGIA R.R.

WM. H.T. WALKER'S
DIVISION

WM. H.T. WALKER'S
DIVISION

Battle of Atlanta
July 22, 1864

July 22, 1864

CLEBURNE'S DIVISION

McPherson Monument

Bald Hill

Sugar Cr.

Howard House

RICHMOND-DANVILLE R.R.

FAIR ST.

JACKSON ST.

HIGHLAND AVE

AUBURN AVE

PONCE DE LEON AVE

Inman Park

Confederate Breastworks Ground

Calico House

Five Points

WHEELER'S DIVISION

FAIR ST.

GEORGIA AVE

PEACHTREE ST.

W. PEACHTREE ST.

PRYOR ST.

PLASTERS BRIDGE

Clear Creek

PEACHTREE RD

NORTH AVE

MARIETTA ST.

NELSON ST.

HUNTER ST.

W. & A. R.R.

HARDEE'S CORPS

STEWART'S CORPS

COLLIER RD

COLLIER RD

Peachtree Creek

Geary's Pontoon Bridge

Battle of Peachtree Creek
July 20, 1864

CHATTAHOOCHEE RD

BELT R.R.

AIRLINE R.Y.

SEABOARD RD

W. & A. R.R.

MAYSON TURNER FERRY RD

MAYSON TURNER RD

OLD LICKSKILLET RD

LUCILE AVE

BENSON ST

GEORGIA

Battle of Ezra Church
July 28, 1864

Ezra Church

BATTLE FALL AVE

S. D. LEE'S CORPS

STEWART'S CORPS

Westview Cemetery

SOUTHERN R.R.

CHATTAHOOCHEE RIVER

North Cr.

Utoy Cr.

56

for a short while. We started moving south toward the rail junction at East Point so that we could keep supplies moving into Atlanta.

A few days after the battle at Ezra Chapel, Loring and Walthall's divisions returned to Atlanta. For more than a month red hot shells fell on buildings and homes setting many fires every day. The volunteer fire fighters were never able to get much rest. Almost half of the citizens have left the city. A lot of the people still here have been living in "shebangs" or small caves that they have dug in an effort to get away from the shelling. Food is all but gone. Very little comes in on the one rail line still open, due to Yankee raiders tearing up the rail line and attacking trains when they can. Confederate Cavalry under General Joe Wheeler tries to defend the long stretches of track. The civilian population has been living on starvation rations. We have very little more.

On August 25th Sherman's guns had fallen silent. It was the first day in more than a month that Federal shells did not fall on Atlanta. Most of us thought that they knew that the town was nothing but a pile of rubble. As far as buildings were concerned, the town was dead. But even if that was the cause, we knew the Yankees were up to something and we would have to respond.

THURSDAY, SEPTEMBER 1, 1864.

A few days later we found out what Sherman was up to. The Union army had cut the West Point Railroad just below East Point, about 7 or 8 miles south of Atlanta. Half of the Yankees were holding that position and the other half were advancing on Jonesboro to cut the Macon and Western Railroad. Hood had to act and act fast.

Cleburne and Lee's Corps left Atlanta on August 30th to join Hardee's Corps at Jonesboro and on the 31st a big battle began. That afternoon Hood ordered Lee's Corps to move toward East Point and attack Federal troops preparing to attack Atlanta from the south. Cleburne was left to face six Federal corps. Cleburne's boys were chewed up badly. Cleburne gathered the men he had left and retreated south to Lovejoy Station. This left Hardee cut off at Jonesboro, lee caught between two strong Federal forces and Cleburne in disorder at Lovejoy. The only troops left in Atlanta was the Georgia Militia and Stewart's Corps, of which we were a part. Atlanta could no longer be held. The city was lost.

Today the CSA is moving out of Atlanta. We blew up the powder magazine and destroyed any supplies the Yankees could use. At 5:00 P.M. Hood and his staff left for Lovejoy. The Georgia Militia left next. Stewart's Corps, with the 35th, was the last to leave. As we marched out the folks remaining behind watched us with accusing and tearful

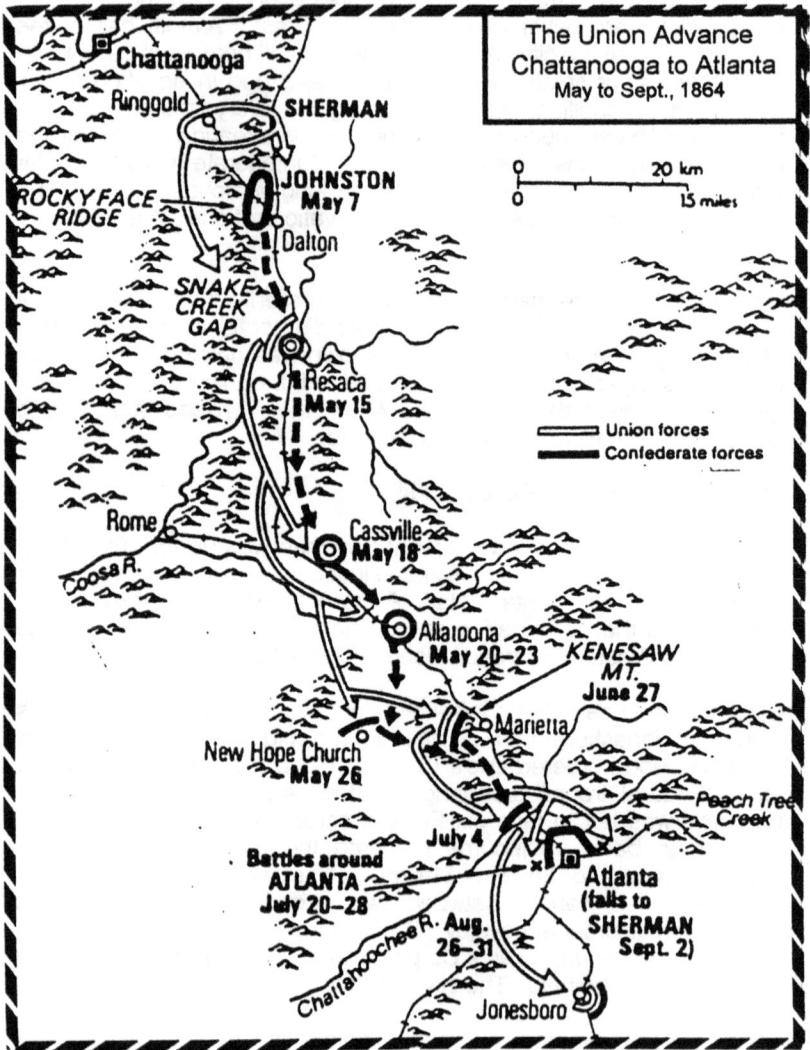

The Union Advance
Chattanooga to Atlanta
May to Sept., 1864

Chattanooga
Ringgold
SHERMAN
ROCKY FACE RIDGE
JOHNSTON
May 7
Dalton
SNAKE CREEK GAP
Resaca
May 15
Rome
Coosa R.
Cassville
May 18
Allatoona
May 20-23
KENESAW MT.
June 27
Marietta
New Hope Church
May 26
July 4
Peach Tree Creek
Battles around ATLANTA
July 20-28
Chattahoochee R. Aug. 26-31
Atlanta
(falls to SHERMAN Sept. 2)
Jonesboro

20 km
15 miles

▭ Union forces
▬ Confederate forces

eyes. By midnight the only troops left inside "the most strongly fortified city on earth" were some cavalrymen detailed to blow up 81 freight cars full of ammunition, some locomotives and the Confederate Rolling Mills. As we marched south we could hear the explosions. It was louder and more freighting than anything I can remember. The cavalrymen caught up with us and told us that every building within a quarter mile of the ammunition train explosion had been flattened. When we got to Lovejoy's Station, 20 miles south of Atlanta, some of Cleburne's boys told us they heard the explosion and saw the fire ball.

September 2nd saw Federal soldiers march unopposed into Atlanta. September 20th Sherman forced everyone who was not a Yankee sympathizer to leave. Thus more than 1600 men, women and children were taken from their homes, kicked out of town and left to starve. The city of Atlanta was left with less than 100 civilians. Nice guy, this Yankee General Sherman. Well, at least the CSA army was back together. We have lost half our men, but we are still an army.

For the next three weeks there was scattered skirmishing all around. While the 35th did not see any action, General Joe Wheeler's cavalry all but wiped out 5000 Yankee cavalrymen in two running battles between Macon and Newnan. Wheeler did this with about 500 confederates. I always did say one of us is worth ten of them.

President Davis came into camp on September 25th to see Hood and give us a pep talk. He wound up being embarrassed. Davis called for a review of Hood's army and what he saw was the hungry, tattered, dog tired remnants of General Joe Johnston's once unbeatable Confederate Army. We did not want to listen to Jeff Davis' speech. The troops took up a chorus. "We don't want a speech! We want old Joe back!"

President Davis finally finished his speech. The main thing he had to say was that he and Hood had a great plan. We were going to march around Atlanta and move over the same ground that we had been fighting over since spring, them move into Alabama and Tennessee. In other words, Hood was going to win the war by taking an army that this "Skill" had slashed to half it former strength, into the stronghold of the enemy! I wonder how long it will take Sherman to get a full report on the "grand strategy"?

Hood's army moved out of Lovejoy's Station on September 28th & 29th. We head northwest, cross the Chattahoochee River and then we head for the rail line near Kenesaw Mountain. Sherman's troops are nipping at our heels all the way. When we reach the railroad, we tore up track, bent the rails around trees, destroyed switches and did anything we could to make the road unusable for a long as possible. We wanted to make his life as miserable as we could.

We generally follow the railroad north doing as much damage as we can without allowing the Yankees to catch us. From time to time, we capture a few squads of Union troops. But our main job is to destroy Sherman's supply line and stay alive. Most of us are sick and hungry. Some of our troops have no shirts, trousers are in tatters. Many of our men are shoeless. We live on parched corn and have to put up with dysentery and scurvy. We are just skin and bones. Some of our men had known only the finer things in life and now are living on food that a few years ago, the poorest of us would have scorned. We fight on and trudge northward.

WEDNESDAY, OCTOBER 5, 1864.

Yesterday we passed Big Shanty again, took a few prisoners and tore up some of the railroad. Hood found out there was a Yankee supply depot at Altatoona Pass, guarded by a detachment of Union troops. This morning Hood sent in a demand for immediate surrender. Lord knows we could use those supplies. When the Yankees would not surrender, Hood ordered an attack. By this time Sherman was closing in on the rear of our army, so the attack was given up and we moved on to the north.

The army kept moving north through Cassville Station, Adairsville, Calhoun, Resaca and Tilton, tearing up track, destroying block houses and doing all the damage we could. Dalton was reached on the 13th. We attacked a fort there and captured something over 400 troops of the 44th U.S. Colored, and some much needed supplies. At this point Hood left the railroad and we headed west for Alabama, and Sherman returned to Atlanta.

I am not sure of the day, but I think it was October 18th or so when we crossed the state line into Alabama. We were heading southwest toward Gadsden so that we could avoid the Yankee troops in Huntsville and the northeast part of the state. At Gadsden we marched northwest again toward Decature and Tuscumbia.

As we neared Decature, General Loring's division was ordered to attack the Federals in that city in an effort to draw Union troops down from Tennessee.

The 26th saw the main army continue the march toward Tuscumbia, forty miles to the west. Loring's division made ready and launched the attack that day, with the 35th proudly in the lead. We attacked the Federal positions boldly but with a bit of care. Our goal was not to overrun the fort and take the town but to give them a good enough scare that they would call for reinforcements. We kept up a good fight for several hours. Our attack coupled with their knowledge that Hood's

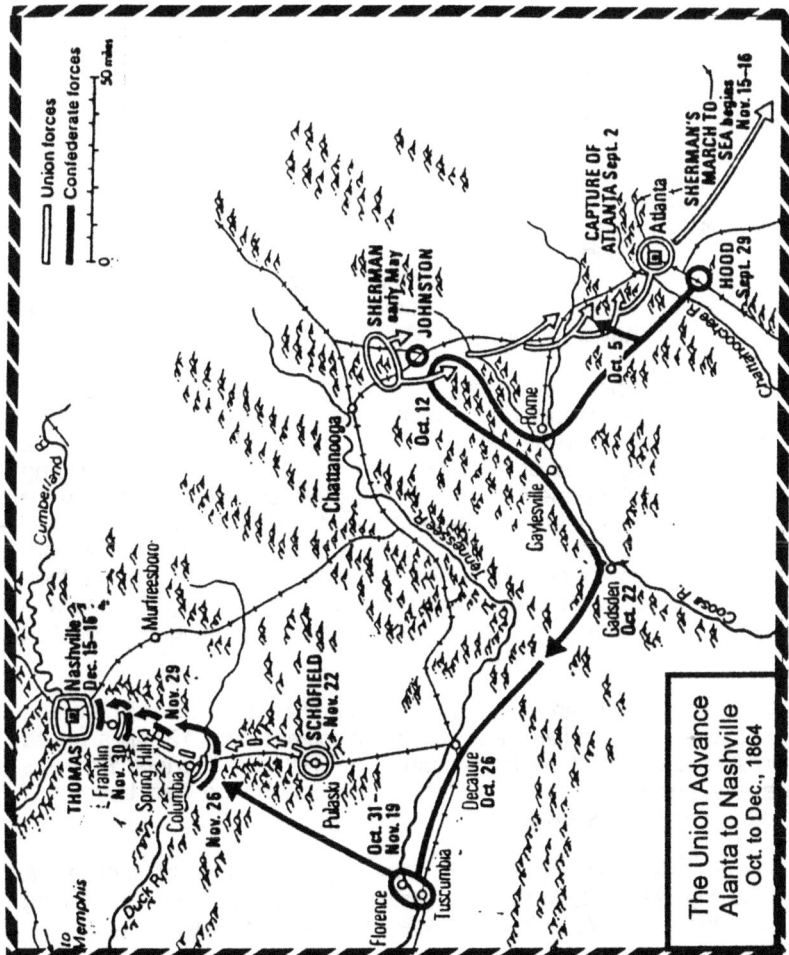

The Union Advance
Alanta to Nashville
Oct. to Dec., 1864

Union forces
Confederate forces

0   50 miles

Memphis

Cumberland

Nashville
Dec. 15–16

THOMAS
Franklin
Nov. 30
Spring Hill
Columbia
Nov. 26

Murfreesboro

SCHOFIELD
Nov. 22

Pulaski
Oct. 31–
Nov. 19

Decatur
Oct. 26

Florence

Tuscumbia

Duck River

Chattanooga

Oct. 12

Gadsden
Oct. 22

Gaylesville

Rome

Oct. 5

SHERMAN
early May

JOHNSTON

CAPTURE OF
ATLANTA Sept. 2

Atlanta

HOOD
Sept. 29

SHERMAN'S
MARCH TO
SEA begins
Nov. 15–16

Chattahoochee

Army was in the area, gave cause for concern I am sure, but it was not without cost. The 27th Consolidated, of which the 35th was a part, had 35 men killed or wounded.

After a few days of causing trouble for the Yankees, we followed the main army to Tuscumbia, and home for many of us. Home! Our old school was just a few miles away and even though it had been burned by Yankee raiders, it still held many pleasant memories. It is hard to believe all we have seen and done in the past two and a half years since a bunch of foolish boys marched off to war.

When we came into Leighton, we started to come across the camps of the army. The further we went, the thicker the camps. We finally found a good spot outside of Tuscumbia and set up our camp. The whole army spent the week foraging for supplies. Even though we were late comers, we were able to fill our needs quickly because we knew so many people in the area. We saw old friends, many of whom we had to tell the sad story of how their husband or son died. It was a sad-glad time. After three years of war, the citizens did not have much to share, but they all gladly gave what they could.

One evening about sunset, somewhere, in some camp, a few ragged, half starved, war weary troops started singing "Home Sweet Home". The sound gathered as camp after camp took up the melody. In a short time thousands of men for miles in all directions were singing softly. Many of the men in the 35th could not sing because they were crying. These were men that had been through the shot and shell, seen the blood and gore and knew the smell of death. They were home. So many of our friends will never come home, never see their mothers, wives or children, never again know the feeling of being with friends and listening to a song. After five or ten minutes, the song faded and the night was totally silent.

More supplies arrived at Barton which was the eastern terminus of the railroad. The supplies then had to be moved over 12 miles of the worst kind or roads, to Tuscumbia. The 19th saw General Forrest's cavalry join us and advised that a pontoon bridge had been built across the Tennessee River.

The next day, November 20th, with only three days of supplies in hand, the cavalry lead the way across the river, followed by the long gray line of CSA soldiers. We are on our way to Nashville, Tennessee.

SATURDAY, NOVEMBER 26, 1864.

For the last few days, we have been running into Yankee scouts and today we have found the main Union army, just north of the Duck River near Columbia, Tennessee. If we can beat the Federals to Spring Hill, near Columbia, Tennessee. If we can beat the Federals to Spring Hill, we will have them cut off from Nashville, then we can knock them out of action and have 20,000 to 30,000 less Yankees to fight at Nashville.

We follow General Forrest's cavalry across the Duck River to a point about six miles east of Columbia. Forrest drives the Federal cavalry before him and takes up a position at Spring Hill to wait for the foot soldiers to catch up with him. Chetham's Corps has literally been fighting a running battle in the race. Chetham arrives at Spring Hill in time to aid Forrest in cutting off the escape of the Yankees. The rest of Hoods army arrive in the afternoon and the job of "mopping up" the Yankees is underway.

Only about 5,000 Federals made it into Spring Hill. The remainder, about 25,000 troops are back in Columbia! We have done it! We have cut them off! We have about 25,000 CSA troops in front of Spring Hill and can polish off the Yankees here this afternoon, do an about face, march the 12 miles back to Columbia, where we will rejoin the rest of our army, and 50,000 strong, beat the Hell out of the rest of the Yankee army!

At this critical point, General Hood orders us to make camp! There is a few hours of daylight left, a job than can be done in that time, and Hood says make camp? An easy victory to be had, after months of taking a whipping, and Hood says "make Camp"!

Scott's brigade, of which the 35th is now a part, spent the night near the turnpike about three miles from Spring Hill. We used the time cleaning our weapons, learning our position in the line of battle for tomorrow, and trying to get a little sleep.

As the sun rose on the 30th, reports came in that the enemy was no longer in Columbia. At the same time our skirmishers reported that there were no Yankees in Spring Hill! Some of our scouts came in and reported that the last of the Federal army was moving into Franklin and throwing up breastworks. While General Hood had slept, the Union troops had marched around our flank, withdrawn from Spring Hill and moved on to Franklin. Their army was no longer split and they were once again between us and Nashville. Hood had avoided victory again!

Hurried pursuit was begun, with the 35th Alabama in advance of the entire CSA army. Contact with the Union forces was made about three miles south of Franklin early in the afternoon. The enemy occupied a strong position on hills that flanked each side of the turnpike. The 35th attacked the enemy on their left flank with a rebel yell and a lot of pent up frustration. We drove them out of their positions and back into the fortification around the southern part of town.

63

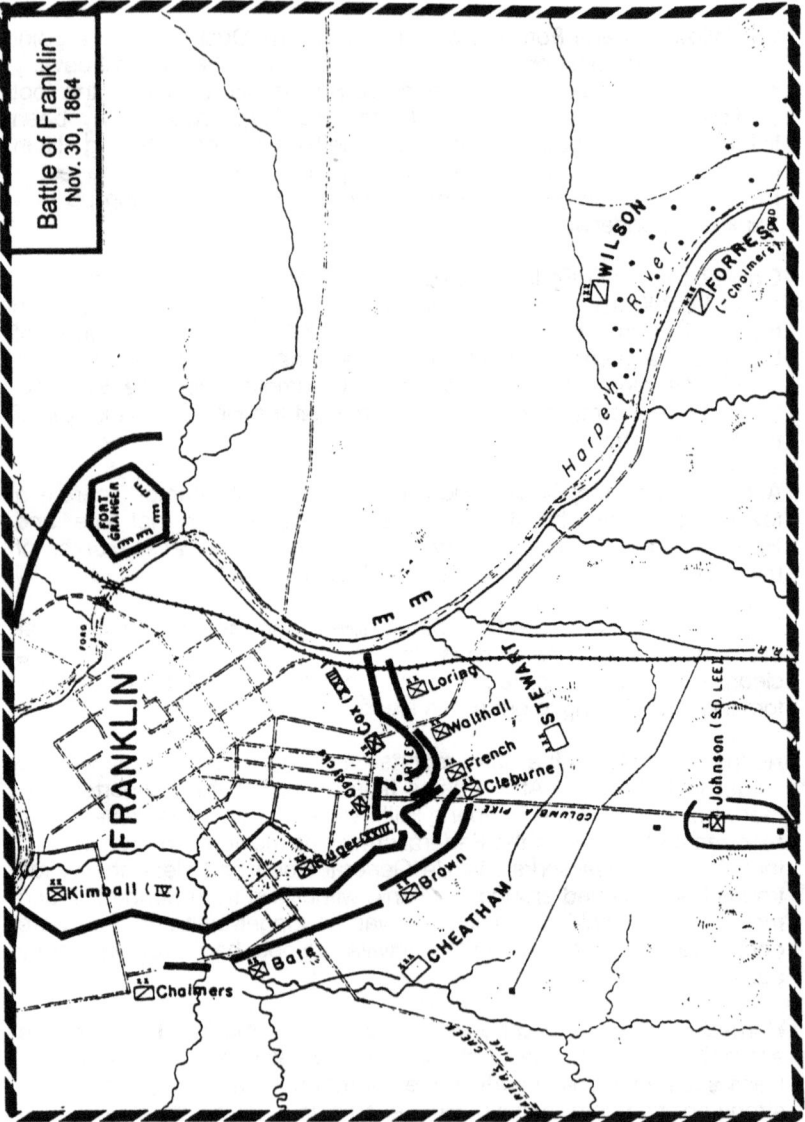

Battle of Franklin
Nov. 30, 1864

FORT GRANGER

FRANKLIN

WILSON

FORREST
(-Chalmers)

Harpeth River

Loring

Cox

Walthall

French

Carter

Cleburne

STEWART

COLUMBIA PIKE

Johnson (S.D. LEE)

Ruggles

Brown

Kimball (IV)

Bate

CHEATHAM

Chalmers

We were now about a mile southeast of Franklin, near the house of Mr. John McGavock, between the Columbia and Lewisburg pikes, when we were ordered to halt for a bit. The various elements of Loring's division formed into line of battle with our brigade, Scott's, on the extreme right. We were to come up the Lewisburg pike and keep contact with either Forrest's cavalry or the Harpeth River.

About 3:00 P.M. the order to move forward was given. Our part of the line was nearest to the crescent shaped trenches around Franklin. For this reason we were instructed to move forward slowly, so that the left of our line could have enough time to reach the enemy at the same time we did. The Union breastworks were about 1200 yards across an open field in front of us.

A signal volley was fired and the 35th started out marching slowly in full view of the enemy, and had only advanced a few hundred yards, when Federal artillery got the range and started cutting great gaps in our line. With each advancing yard, our men were being blown apart. Each Yankee shell would leave a pile of dead and writhing bodies on the ground. To advance slowly was to die!

Ignoring orders, the 35th and the rest of the troops on our end of the line broke into a wild charge and like a tidal wave closed with the enemy. Some of our boys struck the Federal line at a point where it was protected by an Osage Orange hedge which had been cut down to form an obstacle through which it was impossible to pass. They charged right up to that hedge, firing as fast as they could, and every man that reached that point was killed or wounded.

Wave after wave of southern manhood hit the Federal lines again and again. On our left we could see that the Union defenders had been overwhelmed. The Union troops in the rear could not fire on the rebels because the blue and gray troops were mixed together in hand to hand battle. The Confederate soldiers assaulted the Federal lines time after time with the fierce energy of mad despair. The slaughter was terrible. Our Color bearer was hit. Col. Ives was down. All of our officers were dead or wounded. At some locations in front of the enemy, the dead had no place to fall and remained upright.

About 9:00 P.M. Hood called a halt to the carnage. The Union army started north to Nashville two hours later. We let them go because we were busy answering the cry of our wounded. The next morning, those of us still alive were appalled at the sight. For 400 Yards in front of the abandoned trenches, the dead lay like leaves after a storm. The ground could not be seen. The 35th had lost about 150 men in the battle, which was half of our number. Every commanding, field and company officer was lost. Co. B went into battle with 23 men and only

5 were not killed or wounded.

The McGavock home was converted into a field hospital. The wounded overflowed the house and porch. The yard was covered with the dying. I helped carry one of my schoolmates from LaGrange to an operating table under the trees. They had to cut off his leg. It topped a pile of such limbs three foot high.

In five hours yesterday, we had lost over 6,000 men, while only causing about 2.300 Union casualties. More men had been killed in that battle than any in history for a like period of time.

We left Franklin and many of our friends on December 2nd, and headed north toward Nashville.

WEDNESDAY, DECEMBER 14, 1864.

For the last week and a half, we have been camped in front of Nashville. The weather has been very cold, ice is everywhere. Food is in short supply and most of us are dressed in rags. At night we fight to stay warm and during the day we dig trenches, which helps to keep us warm. At this point the army is down to 23,000 effectives, all cold, hungry and dispirited. We neither attack nor retreat, but just wait to see what fate has in store for us at Nashville.

Col. John D. Weeden is in charge of the 27th Consolidated, which includes the remains of the 35th. General Stewart's Corps hold the left end of the CSA army line. Loring's division holds the line between Hillsborough Pike and Granny White Pike. The rest of the corps holds the left flank behind a heavy stone wall along the east side of Hillsborough Pike. The 35th is on top of a hill in the center of our division line, about a mile south of the Union entrenchments.

At 6:00 a.m. on the morning of the 15th, we hear the sounds of battle in the distance, off to our right. The fog is so dense we can not see anything, but we know this is it. The Federals have come out to do battle.

Awhile later the sound of our artillery is heard from our left flank and then the Yankees attacked us. Around 2:00 in the afternoon the sound of fighting on our right and left is getting closer and then word comes in that Hood's army is falling back to the south east.

As we are withdrawing, we pass the home of the widow Bradford. She pleads with us to halt and take up positions on her land. She was a plucky lady, but we have to rejoin the army.

Loring's division crosses the Granny White pike and starts digging in on the east side, just behind a road that runs over to the Franklin pike. We dig and shoot, dig and shoot. As darkness falls, the shooting stops. We can finish our trenches and get a little rest. During the day the 35th retreated about a mile and a half and had stopped about a quarter of a mile south of the Bradford house. I sure hope that lady is all right.

About Mid day on the 16th, the sounds of battle are again heard from our right. Things are starting off just like yesterday. At 4:00 p.m. a massive horde of troops in blue started charging up the hill just to our left. In short order the Yankees storm tactic gained the hill top, at which point they turned their fire on us. Our left was crushed, we were being fired on from the front and our left. At the same time the Union cavalry was moving on our rear! Our line on the right started to crumble. It then started to rain and we started a slow fighting retreat toward the Franklin pike.

The grand army turned over to General Hood by General Johnston was no longer an army, it was just a bunch of old soldiers in a state of confusion. Hood's army had disintegrated. It was a depleted, discouraged, disconsolate mob that started the retreat out of Tennessee.

December 17th, we pass thru Franklin and leave 1800 of our sick and wounded to be captured and cared for by the Union cavalry. On the 18th we pass thru Columbia and have a skirmish with the cavalry. They captured Pvt. Joe Brown of Co. B. We arrive a Bainbridge Ferry on the Tennessee River on the 23rd, a pontoon bridge is built and on Christmas day, the river was crossed. By this time it had been raining for several days and all we had was mud. No clothes, no shoes, no food, no tents, no pay, just mud, more mud and injured Pride. The supply wagons were not empty however, they were jammed with sick and dying.

During the three days it took Hood's beaten army to cross the Tennessee, the 35th became split, with one part making it's way to Montgomery Alabama, while the other trudged south toward Tupelo, Mississippi.

SUNDAY, JANUARY 22, 1885.

For the past three weeks, we have had all we can do just to stay alive. The people around Tupelo have shared what they have with us, but they are all but starving also. The weather has been very cold with some rain and a little snow falling. Most of the men are living in brush huts and dugouts. Half of the Army is sick and, of course, there is no medicine.

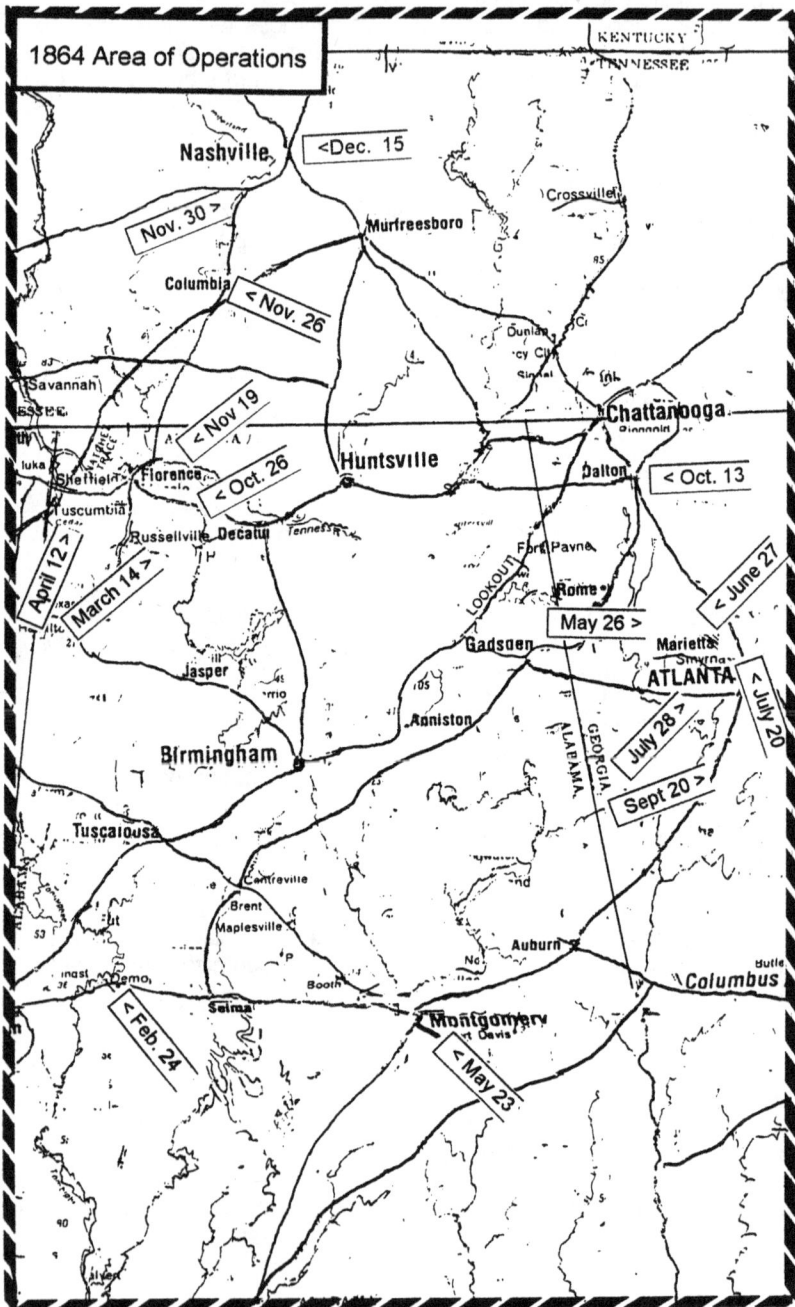

1864 Area of Operations

KENTUCKY
TENNESSEE

Nashville   <Dec. 15
                              Crossville
        Nov. 30 >
                   Murfreesboro
    Columbia   < Nov. 26
                              Dunlap
                              cy City
Savannah   Signal
SSEE   < Nov 19   Chattanooga
                                  Ringgold
iuka   Dalton   < Oct. 13
Sheffield Florence < Oct. 26
Tuscumbia
    Russellville Decatur
April 12 >   Tennessee   Fort Payne
    March 14 >   Rome   < June 27
                    LOOKOUT
                                 May 26 >
              Jasper   Gadsden   Marietta
                                     Smyrna
                           ATLANTA   < July 20
                    Anniston   July 28 >
    Birmingham   GEORGIA
                    ALABAMA
                                Sept 20 >
Tuscaloosa
              Centreville
        Brent
        Maplesville   Auburn
                                      Butle
    nast   emo   Booth   Columbus
        Selma
    < Feb. 24   Montgomery
                           Davis
                    < May 23

68

The dream that was called the Confederated States of America is lying in bits and pieces. The Yankees control the Mississippi River, so everything west of it is lost to us. The Union controls two thirds of Tennessee as well as Northern Alabama and most of Georgia. All of this means that all that is left of the CSA is Virginia, North and South Carolina. Those of us still in the unoccupied part of Mississippi and Alabama are of no use. The Union troops know where we are and can come after us at anytime. Is their any hope?

We had one bit of good news. General Hood was relieved at this own request. We would have a big party to celebrate but no one has the energy. It was just too cold and we have just seen to much. General Beauregard has taken over.

We have just received word that we are to be sent to South Carolina, because it looks like that damn Sherman is getting ready to move out of Georgia and into South Carolina. Our problem is, there is not enough railroad rolling stock to move the men, so we will go a brigade or two at a time.

Finally our time comes and we board the train to Mobile, where we get off and the train returns to Tupelo for another load. We march around Mobile, which Union troops hold, to find another railroad. This is the way it goes, ride and march, ride and march. I guess we should be thankful that it is not march, march, march. By the time we get to South Carolina, Union troops occupy the capitol at Columbia and have burned the city to the ground. We move on to North Carolina, where we find out that our old friend General Joe Johnston has been recalled by Robert E. Lee to be our commander.

After many delays, we arrive at Bentonville North Carolina while a battle is in progress. We are just in time to join up with earlier arrivals from Loring's Division, take part in the last battle and join in the retreat. The division had 150 men killed and wounded. We found out that Loring's division was just about all of Stewart's Corps that is here.

During the march to Raleigh, we are rejoined by the "lost" men of the 35th, those that had gone to Montgomery. At least, those few of us left are together again. It is a time of joy and sadness. We are happy to see old friends and exchange stories, but sad to learn of more stout hearted men lost.

Early April found us near Hillsborough, when word arrived that Federal troops had captured and burned the Confederate capitol at Richmond and that General Lee had surrendered at a place called Appomattox Court House! This leaves General Johnston and his Army, the only Confederate troops still offering resistance.

April 18th saw General Johnston meet with General Sherman near

Raleigh, and sign a broad armistice agreement. The agreement is disapproved by the cabinet in Washington D.C. Johnston and Sherman meet again on April 26th and Johnston surrenders under the same terms Grant gave Lee.

May 2, 1865, General Joe Johnston himself came to us and read his General order No. 22.

"Comrades: In terminating our official relations, I most earnestly exhort you to observe faithfully the terms of pacification agreed upon, and to discharge the obligations of good and peaceful citizens at your homes as well as you have performed the duties of thorough soldiers in the field. By such a course you will best secure the comfort of your families and kindred and restore tranquillity to your country. You will return to your homes with the admiration of your people, won by the courage and noble devotion you have displayed in this long war. I shall always remember with pride the loyal support and generous confidence you have given me. I now part with you with deep regret, and bid you farewell with feelings of cordial friendship and with earnest wishes that you may have hereafter all the prosperity and happiness to be found in the world."

It's over.

Field and Staff Officers
of the
35th Alabama

Colonel:
1. James W. Robertson; resigned
2. Edwin Goodwin; died 2nd half 1863
3. Samuel S. Ives; wounded Nov. 30, 1864
4. A.E. Ashford

Lt. Colonel:
1. Edwin Goodwin; promoted
2. Samuel S. Ives; promoted
3. A.E. Ashford; promoted

Major:
1. William H. Hunt; transferred to 26th Alabama
2. Samuel S. Ives; promoted
3. A.E. Ashford; promoted
4. John S. Dickson; killed Nov. 30, 1864

Adjutant:
1. ? Hanson; resigned 1862
2. Joseph Horn; died June 1864
3. James P. Hennigan; wounded at Atlanta

Surgeon:
1. Dr. W.T. Sanders; resigned Aug. 28, 1862
2. Dr. Isaac F. Deloney; discharged Oct. 1862
3. Benjamin R. King; resigned Feb. 1864

Chaplin:
1. Rev. Robert A. Wilson

Quartermaster:
1. James Latham

Asst. Q/M:
1. Joseph A. Brown

Quartermaster Sgt.
1. James Madden

Commissary Sgt.
1. Isaac L. Pride; promoted

Color Bearers:
1. Lowe A. Dement; killed 1863
2. Marcus D.L. Green; lost let July 1864
3. Robert Wheeler; killed Nov. 30, 1864

Captains and the Counties
From Which Troops Were Raised

Co. A: Lauderdale
1. Samuel S. Ives; promoted
2. John R. Mitchell

Co. B: Franklin
1. W. H. Hunt; promoted
2. Thaddeus W. Felton; killed Oct. 4, 1862
3. John H. Harris; killed late 1863
4. Samuel D. Stewart; killed Nov. 30, 1864

Co. C: Lawrence
1. A.E. Ashford; promoted
2. T.E. Ellett; died Oct. 31, 1863
3. T.A. Tathem

Co. D: Limestone
1. Dr. W.T. Sanders; became Reg. Surgeon
2. John C. Floyd
3. J.N. Martin
4. John Diron; killed Nov. 30, 1864

Co. E: Madison
1. John S. Dickson; promoted 1864
2. Joseph Brown

Co. F: Madison
1. Robert W. Peevey; resigned Nov. 1862
2. A.J. Flanagan

Co. G: Limestone
1. John W. West; resigned

Co. H: Lawrence
1. Richard O. Pickett; promoted to 10th Alabama
2. Ezekiel Johnson

Co. I: Lauderdale
1. J.W. Chisholm; captured sept. 1862
2. W.B. Taylor; resigned Aug. 25, 1863
3. J.B. Patton; wounded Nov. 30, 1864
4. H.B. Irwin

Co. K: Franklin
1. "Red" Jones

ROSTER

35th

ALABAMA INFANTRY REGIMENT

ABERNATHY, CHARLES J.   Co. I   Rank: Pvt.   Source: 7
Born 1845 and enlisted at Florence, Ala on Dec. 1, 1862 by Lt. Patten for a period of three years. Became a nurse at the General Hospital at Lauderdale Springs, Miss. on May 30, 1863. Transferred to the Division Hospital in Marion, Miss. prior to Oct. 31, 1863. He was captured on March 3, 1864 and admitted to McPherson General Hospital, Vicksburg, Miss. with hepatitis on March 5th, 1864. Released June 15, 1864 and exchanged at Vicksburg, Miss. on June 27, 1864.

ABNEY, W.H   Co. C   Rank: Pvt.   Source: 7
Enlisted March 31, 1862.

ADAMS, JOSEPH   Co. G   Rank: Pvt.   Source: 7
Captured at Champion Hill (Big Black River Bridge) on May 16, 1863. Sent to Camp Morton, Ind. Exchanged July 4, 1863 at Ft. Delaware, Del.

ADAY, RUFUS R.   Co. C   Rank: Pvt.   Source: 1,7
Born July 16, 1841 near Hillsborough, Lawrence Co. Ala. Joined the 35th on Jan. 1, 1861 (?) near Moulton, Ala. and continued until captured and paroled. Re-enlisted as a private in Oct. 1862 in Co. F, 5th Ala. Cavalry.

ALDREDGE, WARREN H.   Co. C   Rank: 2nd Lieut.   Source: 7
Joined the 35th on March 31, 1862. Admitted to Miss. C.S.A. Hospital, Jackson, Miss. on July 9, 1863 with acute diarrhea. Had a leave of absence approved by Col. Ives on Nov. 13, 1863 while near Canton, Miss. He had not been home in 13 months and wanted to check on his wife and children. He died Aug. 27, 1864 in a hospital in Ga.

ALLDREDGE, ANDREW P.   Co. C   Rank: Pvt.   Source: 7
Joined the 35th at LaGrange, Ala. in March 1862. Captured Dec. 3, 1862 at Oxford, Miss. Arrived at the Military Prison in Alton, Ill. on Jan. 10, 1863. Died on Feb. 6 or 7 of "Phthisis".

ALLRIDGE, W.H. (or V.)   Co. C   Rank: 2nd Lieut.   Source: 7
Signed a letter, along with other officers dated Aug. 7, 1863.

ALEXANDER, JOHN E.   Co. A   Rank: Pvt.   Source: 7
Joined the 35th in March 1862, at LaGrange, Ala. Captured at Water Valley, Miss. on Dec. 5, 1862. Sent to Holly Springs, Miss. then to Cairo, Ill. in Dec. 1862 Arrived at the Military Prison in Alton, Ill. on Jan. 10, 1863. He was exchanged at City Point, Va. on April 8, 1863 with 855 others.

ALEXANDER, W.W.   Co. C   Rank: ?   Source: 7
Joined the 35th in March 1862, at LaGrange, Ala.

ALLEN, BENJAMIN H.   Co. A   Rank: 2nd Lieut.   Source: 7

His wife, M.J. Allen, filed a claim on Oct. 6, 1864, having to do with the death of her husband. She received $1136,00.

ALLEN, D. McNAIRY   Co. E   Rank: Pvt.   Source: 7

Admitted to 1st Miss. C.S.A. Hospital, Jackson, Miss. on May 31, 1863 with acute diarrhea. Returned to duty June 25, 1863.

ALLEN, JAMES H.   Co. K   Rank: Sgt.   Source: 7

He was captured and paroled by a cavalry division of the 13th U.S. Army Corps during a march to the Mobile & Ohio Railroad in the state of Miss.

ALLEN, ROBERT   Co. A   Rank: Pvt.   Source: 7

Captured at Bridgeport, Ala. on Nov. 29, 1863. He was sent to Louisville, Ky. on Dec. 16th and on to Rock Island, Ill. where he arrived on Dec. 18th. He died Jan. 5, 1864 of measles, and was buried in grave #123, South of the prison barracks.

ANDERSON, JARRET   Co. F   Rank: Pvt.   Source: 7

Living in Jackson Co, Ala. on may 5, 1865. He voluntarily surrendered at Paint Rock, Al. on may 11, 1865 and took the "Oath of Allegiance". He was allowed to return home. He had fair complexion, dark hair, grey eyes and was 6'3" tall.

ANDERSON, ROBERT   Co. D   Rank: Pvt.   Source: 7

Recruited by Capt. J. C. Floyd on March 20, 1862, at LaGrange, Ala. He was born in Bedford Co. Va. in 1817. He was 6' tall, had dark complexion, black hair and eyes and had been a farmer. On Nov. 25, 1862, he was discharged from the 35th, as he had been unfit for duty for 2 months due to age and dysentery.

ARMSTEAD, FOUNTAIN   Co. B   Rank: ?   Source: 2,6

He was from Franklin Co. Ala and was a Cadet at the LaGrange Military Academy in 1861. He joined the 35th when it was formed in March 1862. He died near Tuscumbia, Ala. about 1890.

ARMSTRONG, JAMES G. (or C.)   Co. C or H Rank: Pvt.   Source: 7

Captured at Champion Hill, Miss. (Big Black River Bridge), on May 16, 1863. He was sent to memphis, Tenn. on May 25, 1863 and on to Camp Morton, Ind. By June 9, 1863 he was at Ft. Delaware, Del. and was exchanged on July 4, 1863 with 1697 others. He died July 25, 1863 in the General Hospital at Camp Winder, Richmond, Va. of dysentery.

ARNOT, JAMES   Co. I   Rank: Pvt.   Source: 7

Joined the 35th on Dec. 20, 1862 in Florence, Ala. under Capt. Joiner. He was in French's Division Hospital in Enterprise, Miss. from May 28 to June 30, 1863. He was captured on Nov. 23, 1863 near Corinth, Miss.

ASHFORD, A.E.   Co. C   Rank: Lt. Col.   Source: 1,2,3,4,7

He was from Lawrence Co. Ala. and was elected Capt. of Co. C when the 35th was formed. He was promoted to Major within 90 days. He died prior to 1890.

ASKEW, MARION W.   Co. A   Rank: Pvt.   Source: 7
Captured near Nashville, Tenn. on Dec. 16, 1864. Arrived at the Military
Prison, Louisville, Ky. and was sent on to Camp Chase, Ohio, where he
arrived Jan. 4, 1865. He took the "Oath of Allegiance" on June 12, 1865.
He lived in Lauderdale Co. Ala. He was born about 1832, had dark
complexion and hair, blue eyes and was 5' 7" tall.

ASKEW, QUINTON   Co. A   Rank: Pvt.   Source: 7
Captured near Corinth, Miss. the first week of Oct. 1862. Sent to
Vicksburg, Miss. with 539 others and exchanged on Nov. 8, 1862. Listed
as a deserter on Feb. 29, 1864.

ASTON, WILLIAM M.   Co. C   Rank: Pvt.   Source: 7
Discharged from the 35th on July 22, 1862.

BAGLEY, THOMAS L.   Co. G   Rank: Corporal   Source: 7
Born in Londonderry, Ireland about 1824. He was 5' 4" tall, with light hair,
blue eyes and fair complexion. He was a tailor. Recruited by Capt. J.
West at Athens, Ala. on march 18, 1862. Attached to Loring's Division
Hospital at Lauderdale, Miss on July 1, 1863 as a nurse. The hospital was
moved to Marion, Ala. about Jan. 1864. June 10, 1864 he was sent to the
Wayside Hospital in meridian, Miss. He died in the service on Oct. 30,
1864.

BAILEY, R.H.C.   Co. A   Rank: Sgt.   Source: 7
Captured May 18, 1863 at Big Black Bridge, near Vicksburg, Miss. He
was sent to Memphis, Tenn. on May 25, then on to Camp Morton, Ind.
June 9, 1863 he arrived at Ft. Delaware, Del. and was exchanged on July
4, 1863.

BAILEY, H.J.   Co. G   Rank: ?   Source: 7
Joined the 35th April 1, 1862, at LaGrange, Ala.

BAKER, R.P.   Co. B   Rank: Pvt.   Source: 7
Discharged from the 35th on June 9, 1863.

BAKER, WILLIAM   Co. B   Rank: Sgt. Maj.   Source: 7
He was from Courtland, Ala and was a Cadet at LaGrange Military
Academy from 1860 to March 1862. Joined the 35th on July 12, 1862.
He was shot through the lung at the battle of Corinth, Miss. After the war
he practiced law in Courtland and died in 1875.

BANKS, JAMES   Co. I   Rank: Cpl.   Source: 7
Captured March 26, 1864 at Lauderdale, Ala. Sent to Nashville, Tenn.
and Louisville, Ky.

BARKS, WILLIAM RILEY   Co. I   Rank: Pvt.   Source: 1
Born Dec. 26, 1843 at Dixon, Colbert Co. Ala. Entered the service in April
1862 at Florence, Ala. and served until May 10, 1865 when he
surrendered and was paroled near Greensboro, N.C. with the rest of the

75

35th.

BARKSDALE, ALEXANDER   Co. A   Rank: Pvt.   Source: 7
Captured Dec. 15, 1864 near Nashville, Tenn. Sent to the Military Prison at Louisville, Ky. on Dec. 19 and on to Camp Douglas, Ill. where he arrived on Dec. 22, 1864. In Jan. 1865, he claims he had been loyal to the U.S.A. all along ant=d that he was conscripted into the 35th. April 6, 1865 he takes the "Oath of Allegiance" and is mustered into the 5th U.S. Vol. Infantry.

BARKSDALE, D.A.   Co. G   Rank: Pvt.   Source: 7
Joined the 35th in March 1862, at LaGrange, Ala.

BARKSDALE, DUDLEY R.   Co. ?   Rank: Pvt.   Source: 7
He was living in Limestone Co., Ala. in 1862. He had a fair complexion, light hair, blue eyes and was 5' 10" tall. He was teamster from Jan. 1 thru Oct. 24, 1863 and earned and extra 25 cents per day. He stated he deserted on Dec. 23, 1863. He took the "Oath of Allegiance" on March 19, 1864 and stated that he had no family.

BARNES, F.M.   Co. G   Rank: Pvt.   Source: 7
Listed as "Deserted" from the 35th on Feb. 29, 1864.

BARNETT, L.G.   Co. A   Rank: Pvt.   Source: 7
He was in French's Division Hospital from July 16, 1863 to Aug. 31, 1864.

BARNS, J.   Co. B   Rank: Pvt.   Source: 7
Listed as "Deserted" from the 35th on March 19, 1864.

BARRETT, THOMAS   Co. B   Rank: Pvt.   Source: 7
Listed as "Deserted" from the 35th on March 19, 1864.

BASSETT, JOHN   Co. B   Rank: ?   Source: 2
He was a Cadet at LaGrange Military Academy.

BATES, FRIEND   Co. ?   Rank: ?   Source: 6
He was a Cadet at LaGrange Military Academy prior to 1860 and joined the 35th in 1862. Served throughout the war. After the war, he was a merchant. Died sometime between 1900 and 1907.

BATES, P.   Co. C   Rank: ?   Source: 7
Recruited into the 35th in March, 1862.

BATTLE, JACOB WILLIAM   Co. H   Rank: 2nd Lieut.   Source: 1,6
Born May 2, 1842 in Madison Co. Ala. He was a Cadet at LaGrange Military Academy from Jan. 18, 1859 thru Dec. 1861. Entered the service as a 1st Sgt. on Jan. 1, 1862 (?) at LaGrange, Ala. Promoted to 2nd Lieut. on Oct. 8, 1862 and transferred to Co. C, 50th Ala. Infantry Reg. He was wounded at Murfreesboro and again at Chickamauga, after leaving the 35th. He was living in Huntsville, Ala in 1903. Note: Source 6 indicates he was with the 15th Ala. He attended the LaGrange reunion on May 19, 1905.

76

BATTS, THOMAS   Co. I   Rank: Pvt.   Source: 7
    Discharged from the 35th on July 7, 1862.

BAYLESS, A.M.   Co. A   Rank: Pvt.   Source: 7
    Enlisted March 7, 1862 at Florence, Ala. by Col Ives. He was captured
    Dec. 4, 1862 at Water Valley, Miss. and arrived at the Military Prison in
    Alton, Ill. on Jan. 10, 1863. He was paroled at City Point, Va. on April 8,
    1863 and then admitted to Episcopal Church Hospital in Williamsburg, Va.
    on April 10, release on the 13th, and re-admitted on April 20, 1863. He
    was released again June 5, 1863. He was admitted to the C.S.A. General
    Hospital at Farmsville, Va. and released on May 20, 1863. Feb. 24, 1864
    he was in Loring's Division Hospital and on March 19, 1864, he is listed as
    a deserter from the 35th.

BEARD, HENRY   Co. I   Rank: Pvt.   Source: 7
    Severely wounded at the battle of Baton Rouge, La. Aug. 5, 1862. His
    pay was $11.00 per month. He was still alive on Sept. 16, 1862.

BEASLEY, P.R.   Co. F   Rank: Lieut.   Source: 7
    He signed for an issue of clothing on March 2, 1864. He died July 26,
    1864 at Gilmer Hospital, Ga.

BEAUMONT, RICHARD   Co. ?   Rank: ?   Source: 2
    He was from Tuscumbia, Ala. and was a Cadet at LaGrange Military
    Academy in Aug. 1860. Wounded in the line of duty.

BECKHAM, WILLIAM M.   Co. G   Rank: 2nd Lieut.   Source: 7
    Joined Capt. West's Co. on March 12, 1862 at Athens, Ala. On the 14th
    of Aug. 1862 he was paid $88.00 for service from March 18 to July 31,
    1862. At that time he was a Sgt. and was being promoted to 2nd Lieut.
    He was captured July 4, 1863 when Vicksburg, Miss. fell. He was a
    witness to the parole of several men of the 35th on July 7, 1863 at
    Vicksburg. He was held at Demopolis, Ala. as an unexchanged, paroled
    prisoner on April 30, 1864. Was at the Officers Hospital, Uniontown, Ala.
    on Aug. 16, 1864. At that point he had had chronic diarrhea for 18 months
    and was given 60 days leave. The muster report of Aug. 19, 1864 at East
    Point, Ga. lists him as "sick". He was from Limestone Co. Ala. had fair
    complexion, brown hair, blue eyes and was 6' tall. About Feb. 1, 1865 he
    took the "Oath of Allegiance", at which point he stated he had a family.

BELL, ELISHA   Co. E   Rank: Pvt.   Source: 7
    Enlisted by Capt. John Dickson at Madison Co. Ala. on Oct. 14, 1863. He
    was born in Madison Co. and was 30 years old by Feb. 11, 1864. He was
    5' 6" tall, had florid complexion, hazel eyes, black hair and was a farmer.
    By Feb. 11, 1864 he had been sick for 60 days and was discharged, as
    the Doctor indicated he would never be fit for military service.

BELSHER, COLUMBUS   Co. I   Rank: Sgt.   Source: 7
    Captured at Raymond, Miss. (Big Black River Bridge) on May 16, 1863.
    Sent to Camp Morton, Ind. then on to Ft. Delaware, Del. where he arrived
    on June 9, 1863. He was exchanged with 1697 other POW's on July 4,

1863.

BENTLEY, ALEXANDER J.   Co. B (?) Rank: Pvt.   Source: 1
He was a Cadet at LaGrange Military Academy prior to the war and joined the 35th on March 12, 1862. He was promoted to 2nd Lieut. in June 1862 and transferred to the 33rd Miss.

BENTLEY, N.J.   Co. B Rank: Pvt.   Source: 7
Joined Capt. Hunt's Co. at LaGrange, Ala. on March 31, 1862. He was employed as a teamster from Sept. 1863 to Feb. 1864 and earned and extra 25 cents a day. He was with the 35th in Canton, Miss. on Dec. 31, 1863.

BERKS, WILLIAM R.   Co. I Rank: Cpl.   Source: 7
He was admitted to the 1st Miss. C.S.A. Hospital for rheumatism on Feb. 13, 1864 and returned to duty Feb. 27, 1864.

BERRY, ROBERT HUNTER   Co. H Rank: Pvt.   Source: 7
Captured May 16, 1863 at Champion Hill, Miss. (Big Black River Bridge) and was sent to memphis, Tenn on May 25th where he was placed aboard the steamer "Crescent City" bound for Mound City, Ill. June 1, 1863 he was admitted to the U.S.A. General Hospital in Mound City. He arrived at Camp Morton, Indianapolis, Ind. on July 1, 1863. In Aug. 1863 he joined the U.S. 7th Cav.

BIBB, JAMES   Co. E Rank: Pvt.   Source: 7
He was severely wounded in the mouth at the battle of Baton Rouge, La on Aug. 5, 1862.

BICKHAM, W.M.   See Beckham, William M.

BIGHAM, SAMUEL T.   Co. C Rank: ?   Source: 7
A claim for deceased officers and soldiers was filed on June 8, 1863 by W.W. Bigham.

BINGHAM, ENOCH   Co. F Rank: Pvt.   Source: 7
Born about 1829 in Jackson Co. Ala. Joined the 35th on Dec. 3, 1862 in jackson Co. His pay was $11.00 per month. He was 4' 10" tall, had dark complexion, hazel eyes, dark hair and was a farmer. He was discharged Nov. 30, 1863 as he was having "epileptic attacks".

BINION, JAMES H.   Co. E Rank: Pvt.   Source: 7
He enlisted at Huntsville Ala. on March 20, 1862. He was 33 years old, 6" tall, had fair complexion, gray eyes, dark hair and was a farmer. He died at Camp Preston (?) near Tupelo, Miss. on June 21, 1862. His widow, Martha I. Binion, filed a claim and received $109.10 on Feb. 27, 1864.

BIRD, HUGH L.   Co. G Rank: Pvt.   Source: 7
Enlisted at Athens, Ala. on the 17th day of (?) 1962. He was from Green Co. Ga. and was 50 years old at the time. He was 5' 6" tall, had dark complexion, gray hair and was a farmer. He was discharged due to disability, but no date is given.

BLAKENSHIP, A.   Co. D   Rank: Pvt.   Source: 7
Enlisted by Capt. Sanders at LaGrange, Ala on March 31, 1862. Discharged Oct. 25, 1862.

BLEVINS, WILLIAM S.   Co. F   Rank: Pvt.   Source: 7
Enlisted March 20, 1862 at Marysville, Ala. by Capt. Peavey. At the time he lived in Madison Co, Ala. had fair complexion, light hair, blue eyes and was 6' 1" tall. He had a family. Admitted to the General Hospital in Enterprise, Miss. on April 16, 1863. On Jan. 19, 1865 he deserted. Took the "Oath of Allegiance" on Feb. 4, 1865 and promised to "stay North of the Ohio River until the war was over".

BOATWRIGHT, WILLIAM S.   Co. B   Rank: Pvt.   Source: 7
Enlisted March 12, 1862 in maj. Robertson's Co. at LaGrange, Ala. Admitted to French's Division Hospital at Enterprise, Miss. on May 12, 1863. He died Oct. 15, 1863. he was from Franklin Co. Ala.

BOBBIT, J.J.   Co. A   Rank: Pvt.   Source: 7
Captured at the battle of Corinth, Miss. on Oct. 3 or 4, 1862.

BOLDURAND, H.W.   Co. E   Rank: Pvt.   Source: 7
Discharged Aug. 20, 1862.

BOND, CHARLES J.   Co. C   Rank: Pvt.   Source: 7
The 35th listed him as a deserter on March 19, 1864. he lived in Lawrence Co. Ala. which is where he was captured. He had dark complexion and hair, blue eyes and was 5' 9" tall. He took the "Oath of Allegiance" on July 8, 1864 at Louisville, Ky. and was released North of the Ohio River.

BRACKENS, JONATHAN L.   Co. A   Rank: Pvt.   Source: 7
Died in 1864.

BRADLEY, S.B.   Co. D   Rank: Pvt.   Source: 7
Captured at Greenville, Ala. on April 25, 1865 and was paroled in May.

BRADLEY, WILLIAM L.   Co. B   Rank: Pvt.   Source: 2,7
Sept. 8, 1863 thru Feb. 29, 1864 he worked as a teamster and earned an extra 25 cents a day. He was killed at Franklin, Tenn on Nov. 30, 1864.

BRADSHAW, W.   Co. F   Rank: Pvt.   Source: 7
Listed as a deserter in March 1864.

BRAZELTON, JAMES C.   Co. F or H Rank: Cpl.   Source: 7
Enlisted March 20, 1862 at Marysville, Ala. admitted to the 1st Miss. C.S.A. Hospital, Jackson Miss. on July 9, 1863 with acute diarrhea. Sent to Walker's Division Hospital at Lauderdale, Miss. on July 12, 1863. He died in Aug. 1863 and left $53.00 in cash.

BREWER, A.   Co. A   Rank: Pvt.   Source: 7
He was 5' tall, had light hair, blue eyes and fair complexion. He signed the "Oath" in Montgomery, Ala. on May 27, 1865 and was paroled.

BRICKELL. R.B.   Co. F   Rank: Mst. Sgt.   Source: 7
Captured July 4, 1963 with the fall of Vicksburg, Miss. Paroled about July 10, 1863. Surrendered May 1, 1865 at Greensboro, N.C.

BRIGHAM, J.E.   Co. F   Rank: Pvt.   Source: 7
Enlisted Dec. 3, 1862 in Jackson Co. Ala. in Capt. Fleming's Co. Admitted to Breckinridge's Division Hospital in Marion, Miss. on Oct. 31, 1863.

BRITTON, W.E.   Co. I   Rank: Pvt.   Source: 7
He was from Wayne Co. Miss. Surrendered at Citronville, Ala. on May 4, 1865. Paroled at Meridian, Miss. on May 11, 1865.

BROOKS, HENRY B.   Co. E   Rank: Pvt.   Source: 7
Was a teamster from Jan. 1 to Sept. 1, 1863. Received $66.00 pay for service from April 30, 1863 to Oct. 30, 1863.

BROOKS, JOHN   Co. E   Rank: Pvt.   Source: 7
Recruited March 20, 1863 at Huntsville, Ala. by Col. (Governor ?) A.B. Moore. Was a patient at Loring's Division Hospital at Lauderdale, Miss. from Aug. 8 thru Aug. 31, 1863. By Oct. 31, 1863, he was in Breckinridge"s Division Hospital in Marion, Miss. Admitted to the 1st Miss. C.S.A. Hospital in Jackson, Miss. on Feb. 16, 1864 with "rheumatism". Released Feb. 24. He died March 30, 1864 at Way Hospital in Tuscaloosa, Ala. He left $80.60 in cash.

BROWN, JOSEPH   Co. F   Rank: Capt.   Source: 3,7
He joined the 35th on March 12, 1862, and was promoted to 1st Lieut. on Oct. 30, 1862. He was still listed as a Lieut. on Aug. 7, 1863. Signed approval for payment to feed 22 mules at Canton, Miss. in Dec. 1863. He was acting Quartermaster for the 35th and held that position thru at least Aug. 27, 1864. His pay was $80.00 per month.

BROWN JOSEPH G.   Co. B   Rank: Pvt.   Source: 2,7
He was from Tenn. and had a fair complexion, dark hair, blue eyes as was 5' 6" tall. Captured at Columbia, Tenn. on Dec. 18, 1874. He was in the hospital in Nashville on May 31, 1865. he took the "Oath" on May 19, 1865 and was released.

BROWN, S.H.   Co. B   Rank: Pvt.   Source: 7
Admitted to the Wayside Hospital (general Hospital #9) in Richmond, Va. on June 20, 1864 and was released June 21, 1864.

BROWNE, SAMUEL   Co. E   Rank: Sgt.   Source: 7
On July 31, 1863, he was a Pvt. and received his pay of $11.00 per month plus $50.00 bounty, for the period Dec. 1, 1862 to July 31, 1863. On May 25, 1864 he was at West Point, Ga. as a Sgt. with 6 horses belonging to the field and staff officers of the 35th. A day or two before, they were in Montgomery, Ala. and were to go by rail with the rest of the regiment, but the car with the horses got left behind.

BRUCE, JOHN F.   Co. F   Rank: Pvt.   Source: 7

Captured July 1863 near Jackson, Miss. Arrived at Camp Morton, Indianapolis, Ind. on Aug. 7, 1863. He enlisted in the 12th Michigan Batt. in Aug. 1863.

BURDESHAW, J.T.   Co. K   Rank: Pvt.   Source: 7
No other information.

BURKES, JAMES P.   Co. I   Rank: Sgt.   Source: 7
Joined Capt. Chisholm's Co. at LaGrange, Ala. on March 31, 1862. Listed as a deserter on March 19, 1864. He was captured March 26, 1864 in Lauderdale Co. Ala. and sent to Louisville, Ky. on April 2, 1864. He was sent on to Camp Chase, Ohio on April 13, 1864. He was then sent to City Point, Va. on Feb. 25, 1865 for exchange. He was admitted to Jackson Hospital in Richmond, Va. on March 8, 1865 and released March 12.

BYNUM, BERT   Co. B   Rank: Pvt.   Source: 2,7
He joined Capt. Hunt's Co. at LaGrange, Ala. on March 31, 1862. He was from Lawrence Co. Ala., had fair complexion, light hair, gray eyes and was 5' 6" tall. He took the "Oath" on May 23, 1864.

CAFFEY, H.V.   Co. E   Rank: Pvt.   Source: 7
He may have been in the 33rd Ala.

CAIN, T.J.   Co. D   Rank: Pvt.   Source: 7
Joined Capt. Sander's Co. at LaGrange Ala. in March 1862.

CALDWELL, R.T.   Co. B   Rank: Pvt.   Source: 7
Recruited by Col. Robertson at LaGrange, Ala on March 12, 1862. By Sept. and Oct. 1863 he was in Maj. J. Bingham's Pioneer Corps of General Loring's Division. He was assigned to Camp Smith's ferry on the Pearl River in Miss.

CALL, JOHN   Co. A   Rank: Pvt.   Source: 7
Admitted to the 1st Miss. C.S.A. Hospital at Jackson, Miss. with pneumonia on Feb. 16, 1864. Returned to duty on April 7, 1864.

CALL, THOMAS   Co. A   Rank: Pvt.   Source: 7
He was captured at Water Valley, Miss. on Dec. 4, 1862. Died at the Military Prison, Alton, Ill of "Variola" (small pox).

CAMERON, ROBERT D.   Co. E   Rank: Sgt.   Source: 7
Captured Jan. 31, 1865 in Madison Co. Ala. and sent to Rock Island Barracks, Ill. He was released on May 28, 1865 after signing the "Oath". He was born about 1834, had dark hair, hazel eyes and was 5' 7" tall. He said he was from Huntsville, Ala.

CAMERON, ROBERT NEWTON   Co. B   Rank: Pvt.   Source: 2,7
Joined Capt. Hunt's Co. at LaGrange, Ala. in March 1862 and was wounded at Decatur, Ala. He was involved with a court martial on Feb. 25, 1863.

CAMPBELL, JAMES E.   Co. A   Rank: Pvt.   Source: 7

Captured May 16, 17 or 18, 1863 at Raymond (Edwards Depot), Miss. He was sent to Memphis, Tenn, then Camp Morton, Ind. and on to Ft. Delaware, Del., where he arrived June 9, 1863. He was paroled on July 4, 1863. Entered the Episcopal Church Hospital at Williamsburg, Va. on July 6 with "Febris Ty" (?). He died July 26, 1863 at the South Carolina Hospital in Petersburg, Va., leaving $63.00 in cash.

CAMPER, S.   Co. D   Rank: ?   Source: 7
Joined Capt. Sanders' Co. at LaGrange, Ala. in march 1862.

CAMYSER, BENJAMIN FRANKLIN   Co. D   Rank: Pvt.   Source: 1,7
Recruited by Col. Robertson in Madison Co. Ala on march 14, 1862. He was a patient at Loring's Division Hospital at Lauderdale, Miss. from Aug. 23, 1863 thru Oct. 1863. He stayed with the unit until the end of the war and surrendered at Greensboro, N.C.

CANNADA, W.   See Kennedy, William

CANNAMORE, J.H.   See Kennemer, Joseph H.

CANTERBERRY, WILLIAM JACKSON   Co. D   Rank: Pvt.   Source: 1,7
Entered the service on April 6, 1862 at LaGrange, Ala. Captured at Champion Hill (Big Black River Bridge) on May 16, 1863. He was sent to Camp Morton, Ind. and on to Ft. Delaware, Del. and paroled on July 4, 1863. Returned to the unit and stayed with it until the surrender.

CALDWELL   See Cauldwell

CARLISLES, JNO. H.   Co. K   Rank: Pvt.   Source: 7
Received $44.00 pay for service from Sept. 1, 1863 to Dec. 31, 1863.

CARLOCK, THOMAS V.   Co. H   Rank: Pvt.   Source: 7
Enlisted March 6, 1862. He died Aug. 5, 1862 at the battle of baton Rouge, La. His widow, Fannie Carlock, received $130.36 in back pay and allowances.

CARLOCK, THOMAS W.   Co. H   Rank: 2nd Lieut.   Source: 7
He signed a letter with other officers of the 35th on Aug. 7, 1863. As a part of the 27th Consolidated. He was wounded in the battle of Peachtree Creek, Ga. on July 20, 1864. He tried to resign on Sept. 12, 1864. Dec. 16, 1864, he was captured near Nashville, Tenn. and sent to the Military Prison, Louisville, Ky. From there he was sent to Johnson Island, Ohio. He was released on June 16, 1865. He was from Tuscumbia, Ala. born about 1841, was 5' 10" tall with florid complexion, light hair and gray eyes.

CARTER, THOMAS W.   Co. D   Rank: Pvt.   Source: 7
Enlisted March 20, 1862 at LaGrange, Ala. He was captured in the fall of Vicksburg, Miss on July 4, 1863. and was paroled on July 7, 1863. By April 30, 1864 he was in Co. C, 1st Detachment of Paroled Prisoners at Demopolis, Ala. He was again captured near Nashville, Tenn. on Dec. 16, 1864, sent to Louisville, Ky. and on to Camp Chase, Ohio. He was 39

years old by May 15, 1864 when he signed the "Oath of Allegiance". He was from Madison Co., Ala. had florid complexion, blue eyes and was 5' 9" tall.

CAULDWELL, R.T.   Co. B   Rank: Pvt.   Source: 7,8
Enlisted in 1862 at LaGrange, Ala. On Aug. 2, 1863, he received pay for service from Dec. 1 1862 thru June 30, 1863. He was living in Burleson, Ala. about 1915.

CAYSEY, LEVI   Co. I   Rank: ?   Source: 7
Joined Capt. Chisholm's Co. at LaGrange, Ala in march 1862. A claim was filed on Dec. 15, 1863 in connection with his death.

CHAINEY, HEZEKIAH   Co. C   Rank: Pvt.   Source: 7
Received pay on June 16, 1863. He was listed as a deserter on Feb. 29, 1864.

CHISHOLM, BENJAMIN FRANKLIN   Co. A   Rank: 2nd Sgt.   Source: 1
Born Jan. 23, 1844 at Nashville, Tenn. Joined the 35th on March 18, 1862 at Florence, Ala. He served until June 12, 1865, when he was paroled at Johnson's Island, Ohio.

CHISHOLM, J.W.   Co. I   Rank: Capt   Source: 7
Appointed Capt. on March 12, 1862. He was a prisoner of war sometime prior to Dec. 2, 1863, when he requested and was granted 30 days leave to visit his family and re-equip himself. To gain his release from a POW camp, he signed and oath to the U.S. On July 20, 1864 he was declared unfit for duty due to chronic rheumatism, which had keep him disabled for 6 months.

CHRISTIAN, JAMES   Co. A   Rank: Pvt.   Source: 7
He was captured at Champion Hill (Big Black River bridge) Miss. in May 1863. He received 4 months pay at Richmond Va. on July 18, 1863.

CHUNN, E.L.   Co. E   Rank: Pvt.   Source: 7
From Oct. 1, 1863 thru Feb. 4, 1864 he was the Adjt's. clerk and received and extra 25 cents per day in pay.

CLARK, CHRISTOPHER COLUMBUS   Co. D   Rank: Pvt.   Source: 1,7
Entered service on April 6, 1862 at LaGrange Ala. Captured at Big Black River, Miss. on May 16 or 18, 1863. He was sent to Memphis, tenn., Camp Morton, Ind. and then to Ft. Delaware, Del. He was to be exchanged on July 4, 1863, but was left in a hospital. He was paroled and then exchanged at Point Lookout, Md. on May 3, 1864. He stated he was still with the 35th when it surrendered.

CLARK, JAMES M.   Co. D   Rank: Pvt.   Source: 7
He was admitted to St. mary's Hospital at West Point, Miss. on Jan. 27, 1865, Way Hospital at Meridian, Miss. on March 23, 1865 and Ocmulgee Hospital, Macon, Ga. on April 9, 1865. All three times the problem was chronic diarrhea. He was captured in April 1864, took the "Oath of Allegiance" and was released on May 4, 1865. He was from Madison

Co., Ala, had dark complexion, light hair, grey eyes and was 5' 10" tall.

CLARKSON, JAMES   Co. F   Rank: ?   Source: 7
      He died June 25, 1862 at Newsom Hospital, (Miss?)

CLAUNCH, WILLIAM E.   Co. B   Rank: Pvt.   Source: 8
      Enlisted march 1862 at LaGrange, Ala. Discharged May 17, 1865. He
      was living at Russellville, Ala. about 1915.

CLAY, A.J.   Co. D   Rank: Pvt.   Source: 7
      Joined Capt. Sanders' Co. at LaGrange, Ala. in March, 1862. Discharged
      May 20, 1862. Reason not given.

CLAY, T. S.   Co. D   Rank: Pvt.   Source: 7
      Discharged May 20, 1862. No reason given.

CLEMENT, JAMES FRANK   Co. A   Rank: Pvt.   Source: 1,7,8
      Born Feb. 24, 1852 at Tuscumbia, Ala. He first joined the 2nd Ala. and
      was discharged March 15, 1862. Joined Capt. Chisholm's Co. on April 1,
      1862 at LaGrange, Ala. He was paroled at Pond Springs, Ala. on April 25,
      1865. When he was 56 years old, he applied for a pension.

CLEMENT, W.R.   Co. I   Rank: Pvt.   Source: 8
      Applied for a pension at age 59. He died Jan. 6, 1901.

CLEMENTS, WILLIAM R.   Co. A   Rank: ?   Source: 7
      Nov. 3, 1863, Mrs. C.M. Clements filed a claim in connection with the
      death of her husband, who died at the Clinton Hospital in La. She died in
      Nov. 1908.

CLEMMONS, J.N.   Co. A   Rank: 1st Lieut.   Source: 7
      He was commissioned 1st Lieut. on March 29, 1862. On July 14, 1862 he
      received $274.66 as pay from March 17 thru July 1, 1862. He was
      wounded in the side at the battle of Baton Rouge, la. on Aug. 5, 1862. he
      signed for an issue of clothing for some of his men on Dec. 31, 1863. He
      was listed as AWOL from gen. A.P. Stewart's Corps, Loring's Division,
      Scott's Brigade on Feb. 1, 1864 near Atlanta, Ga.

CLOPTON, JAMES MALVERN   Co. B   Rank: Pvt.   Source: 2,6,7
      Born in Madison, Co. Ala. on Oct. 8, 1844. He was a Cadet at LaGrange
      Military Academy from Feb. 1861 to march 1862. He joined the 35th on
      March 12. He was wounded and captured at the battle of Corinth, Miss in
      Sept. 1862 and sent to a camp at Alton, Ill. He was exchanged due to
      poor health. He enlisted in Russell's 4th Ala. Cavalry. Admitted to St.
      Mary's Hospital, Montgomery, Ala. on May 24th, 1864, and was still there
      Nov. 15.

COBERT, THOMAS W.   Co. H   Rank: 2nd Lieut.   Source: 7
      No information.

COCKEILL, WASHINGTON P.   Co. G   Rank: Pvt.   Source: 2,6,7
      He was from nashville, Tenn. and was a Cadet at LaGrange Military

Academy from Aug. 1860 to July 1861. He had fair complexion, light hair and gray eyes.

COLDMAN, R.D.   Co. D   Rank: ?   Source: 7
He joined Capt. Sanders' Co. in march 1862 at LaGrange, Ala..

COLLIER, JOHN   Co. H   Rank: 2nd Lieut.   Source: 7,9
Wounded in the arm at the battle of Baton Rouge, La. on Aug. 5, 1862. Wounded again at Corinth, Miss. on Oct. 3, 1862. He became Capt. of Co. K, 5th Ala. Calvary.

COLLIER, WILLIAM E.   Co. D   Rank: Pvt.   Source: 7
Joined Capt. Sanders' Co. on march 20, 1862 at LaGrange, Ala. Born in Limestone Co., Ala. about 1832. He was 6' tall with fair complexion, dark eyes and auburn hair. He was a farmer before the war. He was ill 2 months with typhoid fever and was discharged in Oct. or Nov. 1862.

CONNER, GEORGE   Co. B   Rank: ?   Source: 2
He was from Miss. and was a drill instructor at LaGrange Military Academy before the 35th was formed.

CONNER, GEORGE W.   Co. A   Rank: Pvt.   Source: 7
Captured at Tuscumbia, Ala. on Feb. 20, 1865. Sent to Louisville, Ky. and on to Camp Chase, Ohio, where he arrived March 23. He took the"Oath of Allegiance" on June 13, 1865 and was released. He was from Franklin Co. Ala., born about 1841, had florid complexion, dark hair, hazel eyes and was 5' 6" tall.

CONOLEY, JOHN B.   Co. D   Rank: Pvt.   Source: 7
Joined Capt. Sanders' Co. at LaGrange, Ala. on March 20, 1862. He was paid for service from Sept. 30, 1862 to June 30, 1863. Captured at Edwards Depot, Miss. on May 17, 1863 and sent to memphis, Tenn., then Camp Morton, Ind. and on to Ft. Delaware, Del. He was exchanged with 1697 POW's at City Point, VA. on July 6, 1863. He was declared "unfit for field service" on Nov. 19, 1864 and was "detailed as a teamster". He took the "Oath" on May 9, 1865 and stated he was from Limestone Co., Ala. and that he had no family. He had fair complexion, dark hair, blue eyes and was 5' 10" tall.

COONER, JOHN   Co. C   Rank: Pvt.   Source: 7
Received pay for 33 days on Oct. 13, 1863.

COOPER, BERT H.   Co. B   Rank: Pvt.   Source: 2,7
Captured in the fall of Vicksburg, Miss. on July 4, 1863. Paroled July 7, 1863. He was paid on Aug. 1, 1863 for service from Nov. 30, 1862 thru June 30, 1863.

COOPER, JOHN PARKS   Co. B   Rank: Pvt.   Source: 1,2,6,7
Born Tuscumbia, Ala. on Feb. 14, 1844. He was a Cadet at LaGrange Military Academy from 1861 to March 1862, when he joined the 35th. He stayed with the unit until the end of the war and surrendered with Johnson's Army in May 1865 at Greensboro, N.C. He was living in Tuscumbia in

1904 and attended the LaGrange reunion on May 19 of that year. See source 2 for family information.

COOPER, THOMAS J.   Co. C   Rank: Pvt.   Source: 7
Listed as a deserter on Feb. 29, 1864. Captured in Izard Co. Ark in July 1864. He took the "Oath of Allegiance" on July 16, 1864 and was released "North of the Ohio River". He was from Izard Co, Ark. had dark hair, hazel eyes and was 5' 9" tall.

COOPER, U.B.   Co. D   Rank: Pvt.   Source: 7
Captured in the fall of Vicksburg, Miss. on July 4, 1863. He was in the Paroled Prisoners Camp at Demopolis, Ala. on April 1, 1864.

CORNELIUS, F.   Co. C   Rank: ?   Source: 7
Joined Capt. Ashford's Co. at LaGrange, Ala. in March 1862.

CORTER, P.   Co. D   Rank: ?   Source: 7
Joined Capt. Sanders' Co. at LaGrange, Ala. in March 1862.

CORUM, G.   Co. A   Rank: ?   Source: 7
He was born in Alabama and died Aug. 29, 1863 of typhoid fever.

CORUM, JAMES SHELTON   Co. ?   Rank: Pvt.   Source: 1
Born May 28, 1819 near Rogersville, Lauderdale Co. Ala. Joined the 35th in the fall of 1861 (?) at Florence, Ala. Served until the spring of 1865, when his Co. was disbanded at Vicksburg, Miss. (I am not sure he was in the 35th).

COTTINGHAM, D.   Co. C   Rank: ?   Source: 7
He joined Capt. Ashford's Co. in March 1862 at LaGrange, Ala.

COTTINGHAM, J.   Co. C   Rank: ?   Source: 7
He joined Capt. Ashford's Co. in March 1862 at LaGrange, Ala.

COTTINGHAM, W.   Co. C   Rank: ?   Source: 7
He joined Capt. Ashford's Co. in March 1862 at LaGrange, Ala.

CRAIG, J.P.   Co. C   Rank: ?   Source: 7
He joined Capt. Ashford's Co. in March 1862 at LaGrange, Ala.

CRAIG, J.T.   Co. C   Rank: ?   Source: 7
He joined Capt. Ashford's Co. in March 1862 at LaGrange, Ala.

CRAIG, WILLIAM T.   Co. C   Rank: Sgt.   Source: 7
He joined Capt. Ashford's Co. in March 1862 at LaGrange, Ala. Admitted to Ocmulgee Hospital, Macon, Ga. on July 29, 1864. They amputated his left ring finger. Aug. 3, 1864 he received a 30 day furlough to visit his family in Lawrence Co. Ala.

CRITTSENDAM, JOHN C.   Co. K   Rank: Pvt.   Source: 7,8
Enlisted Nov. 1862 at LaGrange, Ala. He was a teamster from Jan. 1, 1863 to Dec. 31, 1863. Discharged May 17, 1865. About 1915 he was

living in Russellville, Ala.

CROSS, C.C.   Co. ?   Rank: ?   Source: 4,6
He was from either the state of Miss. or Cherokee, Ala. and was a Cadet
at LaGrange Military Academy in Aug. 1860. He became a Cadet Drill
Instructor before the 35th was formed. He was living in Carrollton, Miss. in
1903.

CROWELLS, NELSON   Co. B   Rank: ?   Source: 2
No other information.

CRUTCHER, ANDREW BENTON   Co. D   Rank: Lieut.   Source: 1,7
Entered service on April 29, 1861 at Huntsville, Ala. in Co. F of the 4th Ala.
Infty. Discharged Sept. 29, 1861 due to disability, at Richmond, Va. He
then joined the 35th Ala. in March of 1862 at Madison, Ala. as a private.
He was promoted to Lieut. on Nov. 28, 1862. He tried to resign his
commission on Feb. 7, 1863 and again on Sept 12, 1864. Stayed with the
35th until May 18, 1865 when he surrendered with Lt. Gen. R. Taylor.

CRUTCHER, GEORGE W.   Co. D   Rank: Pvt.   Source: 7
He joined Capt. Sanders' Co. at LaGrange, Ala. in March 1862.
Discharged July 15, 1862. No reason given.

CRUTCHER, J.E.   Co. D   Rank: Pvt.   Source: 7
Discharged July 15, 1862. No other information.

DANIEL, J.T.   Co. ?   Rank: ?   Source: 7
Resigned Dec. 2, 1862. No other information.

DARNEL, M.   Co. C   Rank: ?   Source: 7
Joined Capt. Ashford's Co. at LaGrange, Ala. in March 1862.

DAVIS, BEN   Co. G   Rank: ?   Source: 7
Joined Capt. West's Co. at LaGrange Ala in March 1862.

DAVIS, JOHN M.   Co. B   Rank: Pvt.   Source: 7
Joined Capt. Hunt's Co. at LaGrange, Ala. on March 12, 1862. Admitted
to Loring's Division Hospital at Lauderdale, Miss. on June 29, 1863. From
July 1 to Nov. 13, 1863 he is listed as a nurse. On Nov. 21, 1863 he
signed for an issue of clothing. Admitted to Way Hospital, Meridian, Miss.
on Jan. 17, 1865 and listed as wounded. Captured in April 1865. He took
the "Oath" on May 4, 1865 and returned to Athens, Ala. He had dark hair
and complexion, gray eyes and was 5' 8" tall.

DAVIS, WARREN L.   Co. A   Rank: Pvt.   Source: 7
No other information.

DAVIS, WILLIAM J.   Co. A   Rank: Pvt.   Source: 7
Captured May 16, 1863 at Edwards Depot. Exchanged at City Point, Va.
on July 6, 1863 with 1697 POW's.

DAY, LAFAYETTE   Co. E   Rank: Pvt.   Source: 7

His pay from March 20, 1862 to Aug. 31, 1862 was $11.00 per month.

DEAN, JAMES L.   Co. A   Rank: Sgt.   Source: 7
He was from Lauderdale Co. Ala, and a Cadet at LaGrange Military Academy in Aug. 1860. He signed for an issue of clothing on Jan. 11, 1864. Captured near Nashville, Tenn. on Dec. 16, 1864 and was sent to Louisville, Ky. From there he was sent to Camp Chase, Ohio, where he arrived Jan. 4, 1865. Took the "Oath" June 12, 1865 and was released. He was born about 1844, had fair complexion, light hair, dark eyes and was 6' 1" tall.

DeBOW, SOLOMON J.   Co. F   Rank: 2nd Lieut.   Source: 7
Joined the 35th on March 12, 1862. He died May 28, 1862. His widow, Eliza, filed a death claim on May 16, 1863.

DELONEY, ISAAC FOX   Co. D   Rank: Surgeon   Source: 1,7,8,9
Born Dec. 8, 1830 in Madison Co. Ala. Joined the 35th on April 15, 1862 at LaGrange, Ala. He was discharged Oct. 1, 1862 due to bad health, near Grenada, Miss. He was the surgeon for both the 27th and the 35th. He was still living in Oct. 1907.

DELONEY, J.F.   Co. D   Rank: Pvt.   Source: 7
No other information.

DEMENT, LOWE A.   Co. B   Rank: ?   Source: 2,4,6,7
He was from Meridianville, Madison Co. Ala. and was a Cadet at LaGrange Military Academy in Aug. 1860. He became a drill instructor at LaGrange before the 35th was formed. He was the 1st Color Bearer for the 35th. Died at jackson, Miss. in the summer of 1863 wile caring the Colors.

DEMONY, LEWIS   Co. G   Rank: Pvt.   Source: 7
On Sept. 30, 1863 he received pay for the period May 1 thru Aug. 31, 1863.

DENSON, THOMAS J.   Co. I   Rank: 2nd Lieut.   Source: 7
Appointed 2nd Lieut. on march 12, 1862. Resigned Jan. 10, 1863 due to bad lungs.

DERRICK, W. YOUNG   Co. E   Rank: Pvt.   Source: 7
Joined the 35th on March 20, 1862 at Huntsville, Ala. Admitted to Loring's Division Hospital at Lauderdale, Miss. as a patient on July 9, 1863.

DEVAN, E.J.   Co. H   Rank: Sgt.   Source: 7
Captured in the fall of Vicksburg on July 4, 1863. Paroled July 7, 1863.

DICKSON, JOHN S.   Co. E   Rank: Major   Source: 2,3,4,7,9,11
He was from Madison Co. Ala. and was elected Capt. of Co. E when the 35th was formed on March 12, 1862. He signed for an issue of clothing for some of his men on Dec. 31, 1863. Promoted to Major. Killed at the Battle of Franklin, Tenn. on Nov. 30, 1864.

DICKSON, WILLIAM S.   Co. E   Rank: Pvt.   Source: 7

On Oct. 4, 1862 he wrote Gen. Breckinridge, asking how to get back to the 35th. Aug. 31, 1863 he signed for a jacket. July 10 thru Oct. 1863 he is at Breckinridge's Division Hospital at Marion, Miss. He signed the "Oath of Allegiance" in April 1865, stating he lived in Greene, Tenn. and that he had deserted at Bristol, Tenn. on Feb. 15, 1864. He had dark complexion,hair and eyes and was 5' 6" tall.

DINSMORE, JOHN T.   Co. H   Rank: ?   Source: 7

A death claim was filed on Dec. 24, 1864 by D.L. Dinsmore. (His father?)

DIRON, JOHN   Co. D   Rank: Capt.   Source: 2

Joined the 35th as a private. Promoted to Capt. of Co. D in July 1862. He was killed at the Battle of Franklin, Tenn. on Nov. 30, 1864.

DISHON, B.W.   See DUSKIN, DAVID

DISKIN, B.W.   See DUSKIN, DAVID

DOWNS, DANIEL L.   Co. B   Rank: Sgt.   Source: 2,7

He was a Cadet at LaGrange Military Academy. He drew pay for the period Aug. 1, 1863 thru Oct. 31, 1863. He received a gunshot wound in the left let at the Battle of Franklin, Tenn. (Spring Hill) on Nov. 30, 1864. He was captured and his leg was amputated on Dec. 1, 1864 at the U.S.A. General Hospital in Nashville. He was born in 1841 and was from Franklin Co. Tenn. (?), had dark complexion and hair, grey eyes and was 6' tall.

DUNCAN, WILLIAM   Co. B   Rank: Pvt.   Source: 7

Joined the 35th on March 12, 1862. Listed as a deserter on March 19, 1864. March 29, 1865 he took the "Oath of Allegiance" and was paroled to "remain North of the Ohio River during the war." He said he deserted in March 1864 and had no family. He was from Franklin Co. Ala. had fair complexion, brown hair, blue eyes and was 6' tall.

DUSKIN, DAVID W.   Co. F   Rank: Pvt.   Source: 1,7

Joined the 35th in April 1862 at Marysville, Ala. He was captured at Champion Hill (Edwards Depot), Miss. on May 17, 1863. He was sent to Camp Morton, Ind. and on to Ft. Delaware, Del. He was to be exchanged at City Point, Va. on July 4, 1863, but was left in the hospital at Ft. Delaware. He was a POW for 11 months.

DWYER, JAMES A.   Co. A   Rank: Pvt.   Source: 7

Captured at Big Black River or Champion Hill, Miss on May 17, 1863. Exchanged at City Point, Va. on July 6, 1863. At Richmond, Va. on July 18, 1863 he was paid for service from December 1862 to march 31, 1863. He was a teamster from Dec. 1, 1863 thru Feb. 22, 1864. Listed as a deserter on March 19, 1864.

EASON, WILLIAM   Co. ?   Rank: ?   Source: 2,6

He was a Cadet at LaGrange in Aug. 1860 and was from Huntsville, Ala. He joined the 35th and died in the service.

EARSKINE, JAMES A.   Co. E   Rank: Pvt.   Source: 7
        Discharged June 30, 1862.

EDEY,   See ADAY, RUFUS R.

EDEY, NICHOLAS   Co. C   Rank: Pvt.   Source: 7
        Joined Capt. Ashford's Co. in March 1862. He was captured at Iuka or
        Corinth, Miss late in Sept. or early Oct. 1862 and paroled. Listed as a
        deserter March 19, 1864.

EDEY, R.P.   Co. C   Rank: Pvt.   Source: 7
        Joined Capt. Ashford's Co. in March 1862. He was captured a Iuka or
        Corinth, Miss. in Late Sept or early Oct. 1862 and Paroled. Listed as a
        deserter March 19, 1864.

EDWARDS, DAVID   Co. E   Rank: Pvt.   Source: 7
        Captured on March 4, 1865 in Morgan Co. Ala. He was sent to Louisville,
        Ky. and on to Camp Chase, Ohio, where he arrived March 24. He took
        the "Oath of Allegiance" on June 13, 1865 and was released. He was
        from Morgan Co. Ala. had dark complexion, hair and eyes and was 5' 6"
        tall. By June 1865 he was 28 years old.

ELLETT, THEO E.   Co. C   Rank: Capt.   Source: 7,9
        Appointed 1st Lieut. on march 12, 1862. On Sept. 10, 1862 he was sent
        to North Ala. to recruit and arrest deserters. He returned about Oct. 29th
        with 70 men. Theo died in Lawrence Co. Ala. on Oct. 31, 1863.

ELLETT, THOMAS RICHARD   Co. B   Rank: Pvt.   Source: 7
        Joined the 35th in march 1862 at LaGrange, Ala. Wounded in the ankle
        on Aug. 5, 1862 at the Battle of baton Rouge, La. Employed as a
        teamster from Jan. 1, thru Aug. 31, 1863. He earned an extra 25 cents a
        day for this duty. Entered French's Division Hospital at Shelby Springs,
        Ala. on Oct. 3, 1863 with chronic diarrhea. Returned to duty Feb. 17,
        1864.

ELLIDGE, S.L.   Co. E   Rank: Pvt.   Source: 7
        "Wounded severely in both ankles" at the Battle of baton Rouge, La. on
        Aug. 5, 1862.

ELLIOTT, DAVID M.   Co. ?   Rank: Pvt.   Source: 7
        Surrendered and took the "Oath" at Nashville, Tenn. on July 14, 1865 and
        was allowed to return home. He was from Limestone Co. Ala. had fair
        complexion, dark hair, blue eyes and was 6' tall.

ELLIOTT, GEORGE   Co. G   Rank: Pvt.   Source: 7
        Joined Capt. West's Co. at Athens, Ala. Feb. 28, 1863. Admitted to
        Loring's Division Hospital at Lauderdale, Miss. on Aug. 13, 1863 with
        typhoid fever. Died Sept. 19, 1863. He was born in Ala.

ELLIOTT, JOHN K.C.   Co. G   Rank: Pvt.   Source: 2,7
        He was a Cadet at LaGrange in Aug. 1860 from Limestone Co. Ala.

Joined Capt. West's Co. on March 18, 1862. Served as a teamster from Nov. 10, 1863 to Feb. 29, 1864 and was paid an extra 25 cents per day. He took the "Oath" March 30, 1865 and stated that he deserted on Dec. 23, 1864 and had a family. He had dark complexion and hair, hazel eyes and was 5' 11" tall.

ELLIOTT, J.E. Co. C Rank: 1st Lieut. Source: 7
On July 12, 1862, he received pay from Feb. 25, 1862 thru July 30, 1862 at the rate of $90.00 per month. Also see Ellett, T.E.

ELLIOTT, ROBERT Co. G Rank: Pvt. Source: 7
Joined Capt. West's Co. in March 1862. Received pay for the period March 18, 1863 to April 30, 1863, plus a $50.00 enlistment bonus. Surrendered at nashville, Tenn. and took the "Oath of Allegiance" on June 14, 1865. He was from Limestone Co. Ala. and had fair complexion, light hair, gray eyes and was 5'6" tall.

ELLIOTT, W.A. Co. G Rank: Pvt. Source: 7
Joined Capt. West' Co. in March 1862. Discharged June 18, 1862.

ELLIOTT, WILLIAM C. Co. E Rank: Pvt. Source: 7
He was enlisted into the 35th on March 20, 1862 by Gov. A.B. Moore at Huntsville, Ala. and died May 19, 1862 at Lauderdale Springs, Miss. His wife, Emily, filed a death claim for back pay and allowances on March 20, 1863. She received $97.36 on Nov. 30, 1864. He was 36 years old when he died and was 5'10" tall, had fair complexion, light hair, blue eyes and was a painter.

ELLIS, DAVID CABAL Co. A Rank: Pvt. Source: 7
Admitted to the 1st Miss. CSA Hospital at Jackson, Miss. on May 4, 1863 with Chronic Diarrhea. He died June 2, 1863 leaving 50 cents in cash.

ERWIN, WILLIAM Co. E Rank: Sgt. Source: 7
Discharged May 19, 1862. No other information.

ESKEW, MARION W. See ASKEW, MARION

ESTES, W.N.S. Co. A Rank: ? Source: 7
Died May 9, 1863 at Stillman Hospital, Clinton, La. He left $7.00 in cash.

EVANS, AUGUSTUS FRANKLIN Co. G Rank: 1st Lieut. Source: 1,7
He was from Limestone Co., Ala. and entered the service on March 18, 1862 at Athens, Ala. as a 3rd Lieut. with pay of $80.00 per month. Admitted to Ocmulgee Hospital at Macon, Ga. on July 29, 1864 and was "transferred" on Aug. 10. He had "Feb. Peruit." He was a 1st Lieut. when he was paid for service from July 1 to Oct. 30, 1864. On Dec. 7, 1864 he was "on furlough, by order of General Wood, to procure clothing for the command". Captured or surrendered April 20, 1865 at Macon Ga. He signed the "Oath" on May 12, 1865 and allowed to return home. He had dark complexion and hair, hazel eyes and was 5'6" tall.

EVANS, J.M. Co. C Rank: Cpl. Source: 7

Joined Capt. Ashford's Co. in March 1862. Listed as a deserter March 19, 1864.

FAIRCLOTH, JOSEPH   Co. H   Rank: ?   Source: 7
Died July 1, 1862 in a hospital, leaving $21.00 in cash.

FARIS, BLUFORD MARTIN   Co. B   Rank: 2nd Lieut.   Source: 2,6,7
Born Aug. 14, 1840 in Lawrence Co. Ala. Graduated from LaGrange
Military Academy and became assistant Professor of Mathematics.
Joined Capt. hunt's Co. in March, 1862. On Aug. 26, 1863 he drew 47
jackets, 47 drawers, 50 shirts, etc. for his men because "—the men lost the
greater portion of their clothing in the fall of Vicksburg." On Sept. 16, 1863,
he is Acting Quartermaster of the 35th and gets 113 pairs of pants, 227
shirts, etc. On Oct. 1, 1863, he signed for forage for 4 horses and 22
mules belonging to the 35th. Oct. 30 he gets 39 jackets, 125 pairs of
pants, etc. After the war he became a Minister and took over the 1st
Presbyterian Church at Ripley, Miss. in April 1874. He then took a church
in Searcy, Ark. where he died Sept. 9, 1888.

FARLEY, E.A.   Co. H   Rank: Sgt.   Source: 7
Discharged May 25, 1862. No reason given.

FARRISS, B.M.   See FARIS, BLUFORD

FELTON, THADDEUS E. JR.   Co. B   Rank: Capt.   Source: 2,3,4,5,6,7
He was from LaGrange, Ala. and was a Cadet in Aug. 1860. He became
a Cadet Drill Instructor at LaGrange. He was one of only two graduates of
LaGrange Military Academy, completing his studies in 1861. He joined the
35th on March 18, 1862 as a 1st Lieut. Was promoted to Capt. and took
over Co. B about April 20, 1862 when Capt. Hunt was promoted. He was
killed Oct. 4, 1862 while leading a charge at the Battle of Corinth, Miss.
For more family information, see source 2.

FINCH, BERRY ELLIS   Co. B   Rank: Pvt.   Source: 1,7
Born April 11, 1841 in Campbell Co. Ga. Joined the 35th March 12, 1862
at LaGrange, Ala. Served until May 16, 1865. paroled at meridian, Miss.
He was living in Pleasant Site, Ala. in 1907.

FISHER, J.   Co. A   Rank: Pvt.   Source: 7
Captured in the fall of Vicksburg, Miss on July 4, 1863. He signed his
parole July 7, 1863.

FISHER, R.W.   Co. A   Rank: Pvt.   Source: 7
Captured and paroled at Corinth, Miss. Oct. 3 or 4, 1862. Captured in the
fall of Vicksburg, Miss on July 4, 1863. He signed his parole and was
released July 7, 1863.

FLANAGAN, A.S.   Co. G   Rank: Pvt.   Source: 7
Joined the 35th on March 18, 1862 at Athens, Ala. His pay from march 18
thru June 30, 1862 was $11.00 per month. He was a nurse at Walker's
Division Hospital at Brandon, Miss. from Oct. 10 thru Oct. 31, 1863.

FLANAGAN, A.J.   Co. F   Rank: Capt.   Source: 2,3,7
His pay from March 20 thru July 1, 1862 was $90.00 per month. He lead a detail to North Ala. on Nov. 21, 1862 to recruit and arrest deserters. He signed for clothing for his men on Dec. 31, 1863, and was listed as "sick in Hospital" on Aug. 19, 1864. Surrendered at Citronelle with Lieut. General R. Taylor on May 4, 1865. He signed his parole on May 18, 1865 and was released at Grenada, Miss. on May 19, 1865.

FLANNIGAN, J.C.   Co. G   Rank: Pvt.   Source: 7
Listed as a deserter in 1864.

FLEMING, CHARLEY FRANKLIN   Co. B   Rank: Pvt.   Source: 1
Born July 24, 1837 in Monroe Co. Ga. Joined the 35th on march 15, 1862 at LaGrange, Ala. He was captured in March 1865 and paroled at Camp Chase, Ohio in May 1865. He was living in Franklin Co. Ala. in 1907.

FLETCHER, W.E.   Co. D   Rank: Sgt.   Source: 7
He was on detached service as a clerk from Sept. 20 thru Dec. 31, 1862 and April 30 thru Oct. 1, 1863 at a pay rate of 75 cents per day. His pay as a Sgt from Jan. 1 thru Feb. 28, 1863 was $17.00 per month. In Oct. 1863 he was granted 30 days leave to go to his home in Ala. and recover from "dysentery and general disability". He surrendered April 28, 1865 at Greensboro, N.C. with general Joseph E. Johnston.

FLOYD, J.A.   Co. G   Rank: Pvt.   Source: 7
Joined Capt. West's Co. in March 1862. He was part of 197POW's exchanged at Vicksburg, Miss on Dec. 2, 1862.

FLOYD, JOHN C.   Co. D   Rank: Capt.   Source: 7
His pay as 2nd Lieut. from March 20 thru June 30, 1862 was $80.00 per month. By Oct. 30, 1862 he was a Capt.

FOOTE, W.H.   Co. C   Rank: ?   Source: 7
Joined Capt. Ashford's Co. in March 1862 at LaGrange, Ala.

FORD, JOHN H.   Co. C   Rank: Pvt.   Source: 7
Captured at Big Black River, Miss. May 16 or 18, 1863. Sent to memphis, Tenn. and on to Ft. Delaware, Del. where he arrived June 9, 1863. He was to be exchanged on July 3, 1863, but was "left in hospital". He died July 15, 1863.

FORIS, BLUFORD   See FARIS, BLUFORD MARTIN

FOSTER, BENJAMIN   Co. E   Rank: Pvt.   Source: 7
Took the "Oath of Allegiance" at Knoxville, Tenn. on Feb. 11, 1864.

FOWLER, J.W.   Co. A   Rank: Pvt.   Source: 7
He received pay for service from Nov. 1, 1863 thru Feb. 29, 1864.

FRASER, W.W.   Co. G   Rank: ?   Source: 7
Joined Capt. West's Co. in March 1862 at LaGrange, Ala.

FRAZIER, JAMES H.   Co. ?   Rank: ?   Source: 7
    Died at the General Hospital in Okolona, Miss. sometime prior to Aug. 30, 1862. He left 90 cents in cash.

FRIEND, DANIEL B.   Co. B   Rank: Pvt.   Source: 2,6,7
    He was from Madison Co. Ala. and was a Cadet at LaGrange Military Academy in 1861. Joined Capt. Hunt's Co. in March 1862. He took the "Oath" in Feb. 14, 1865 at Louisville, Ky. and stated he deserted on Dec. 21, 1864 and had no family. He had dark complexion, brown hair, hazel eyes and was 5'10' tall. He was released North of the Ohio River.

FUDGE, WILLIAM H.   Co. G   Rank: Pvt.   Source: 7
    Joined Capt. West's Co. in March 1862 at LaGrange, Ala. Captured May 16 or 17, 1863 at Champion Hill (Big Black River), Miss. and was sent to Memphis, Camp Morton, Ohio and on to Ft. Delaware, Del. where he arrived June 9, 1863. He was exchanged with 1697 POW's at City Point, Va. on July 6, 1863.

FULLINGTON, D.H.   Co. F   Rank: Pvt.   Source: 7
    He was discharged from the 35th on May 2, 1862. No reason given.

GAILEY, THOMAS F.   Co. C   Rank: Pvt.   Source: 7
    He was a teamster from Nov. 1862 thru Dec. 31, 1863.

GARNER, JESSE P.M.   Co. F   Rank: ?   Source: 7
    He may have been a member of the 41st Ala Infantry.

GARRETT, C.W.   Co. A   Rank: Pvt.   Source: 7
    Captured in the fall of Vicksburg, Miss. on July 4, 1863. He signed his parole and was released on July 7, 1863.

GARRETT, E.T.   Co. A   Rank: Pvt.   Source: 7
    Died Nov. 3, 1863 at Lauderdale Springs, Miss.

GARRETT, J.   Co. A   Rank: Pvt.   Source: 7
    Listed as a deserter on March 19, 1864.

GARRETT, THOMAS CHINA   Co. A   Rank: Pvt.   Source: 7
    Enlisted March 17, 1862 at Florence, Ala. Entered Loring's Division Hospital at Lauderdale, Miss. on July 9, 1863 as a patient. He was furloughed Sept. 2, 1863.

GASS, GEORGE G.   Co. E   Rank: Pvt.   Source: 7
    He took the "Oath of Allegiance" on Feb. 11, 1864 at Knoxville, Tenn.

GASSAWAY, H.   Co. C   Rank: ?   Source: 7
    Joined Capt. Ashford's Co. in March 1862 at LaGrange. Ala.

GASSAWAY, W.E.   Co. C   Rank: ?   Source: 7
    Joined Capt. Ashford's Co. in March 1862 at LaGrange, Ala.

GAYLEY, D.T.   Co. G   Rank: Pvt.   Source: 7

Admitted to the 1st Miss. CSA Hospital at Jackson, Miss. on Feb. 28, 1864 with Chronic Diarrhea. Released March 7, 1864.

GEORGE, JOHN R.   Co. H   Rank: Pvt.   Source: 7
He received pay from March 6 thru July 31, 1862. His widow, Clea S. George, filed a death claim on Dec. 24, 1862.

GILES, STEVEN COLEMAN   Co. ?   Rank: Pvt.   Source: 1
Entered the service Jan. 1861 and was in Co. G of the 15th Miss. Transferred to the 35th Ala. and served with that unit until the close of the war.

GILES, WILLIAM HOGAN   Co. E   Rank: Pvt.   Source: 1
Joined the 35th in March 1862 at Huntsville, Ala. He stayed with the unit until the end of the war in 1865.

GILLESPIE, STEPHEN   Co. C   Rank: Pvt.   Source: 7
Joined Capt. Ashford's Co. at LaGrange, Ala. in March 1862. Captured at Big Black Rive on May 17, 1863 and was sent to Memphis, Camp Morton, Ind. and arrived at Ft. Delaware, Del. on June 9, 1863. He was exchanged on July 6 at City Point, Va. with 1697 POW's.

GILLUM, MILETUS B.   Co. I   Rank: 2nd Lieut.   Source: 7
Joined Capt. Chisholm's Co. on March 22, 1862 at Florence, Ala. His pay from April 22 thru June 30, 1862 was $80.00 per month. Captured in the fall of Vicksburg, Miss. on July 4, 1863. By April 30, 1864 he was a part of Co. C of the 1st Detachment of Paroled prisoners at Demoplis, Ala. He had fair Complexion, sandy hair, hazel eyes and was 6'1" tall.

GILLUM, WILLIAM W.   Co. I   Rank: Pvt.   Source: 7
Wounded at the Battle of Baton Rouge, La on Aug. 5, 1862. He had a broken leg. Had duty as a "sawyer" from Nov. 11 thru Nov. 30, 1862 at Canton, Miss. Captured March 26, 1864 in Lauderdale Co. Ala. He was sent to Nashville, Louisville, Ky and then on to Camp Chase, Ohio where he arrived April 14, 1864. He died there on May 7, 1864 of pneumonia.

GIPSON, RICHARD   Co. F   Rank: Pvt.   Source: 7
He was a convalescent in a hospital and was released Dec. 22, 1862.

GLAZE, SOC. D.   Co. G   Rank: Pvt.   Source: 7
Enlisted March 2, 1862 at Athens, Ala. He was admitted as to French's Division Hospital in Lauderdale, Miss. on July 1, 1863 with chronic hepatitis and enlargement of the liver. From July 5 thru Sept. 30, 1863 he was listed as a cook at French's Division Hospital. Nov. and Dec. 1863 he is listed as a nurse with pay of $7.50 per month. He was declared unfit for field duty on March 8, 1864 and was detailed to work at Shelby Springs Hospital in Shelby Co. Ala. He was given a furlough on Aug. 8, 1864.

GLOSUP, CLINTON B.   Co. A   Rank: Pvt.   Source: 7
Captured at Water Valley, Miss on Dec. 4, 1862. Sent to the Military Prison at Alton, Ill where he arrived Jan. 10, 1863. Died Feb. 14, 1863 of

"Variola" (smallpox).

CORBAN, W. A.   Co. B   Rank: ?   Source: 7
Enlisted March 2, 1862 into Capt. Hunt's Co.

GODLEY, CHARLES P.   Co. B   Rank: Pvt.   Source: 7
Served as Acting Ordnance Sgt. from June 6 thru Dec. 31, 1863. Died June 23, 1864 at Macon, Ga.

GOOCH, W.H.   Co. I   Rank: Pvt.   Source: 7
Discharged May 27, 1862. No reason given.

GOODLETT, WADDY T.   Co. H   Rank: 2nd Lieut.   Source: 7
Commissioned 2nd Lieut. on March 12, 1862. Died June 10, 1862.

GOODLOE, A.T.   Co. D   Rank: 1st Lieut.   Source: 4,7
He was commissioned Sept. 24, 1862. On Nov. 17, 1863 he asked for 30 days leave to visit his wife and children. Nov. 27, 1863 he signed for 23 pair of shoes, 66 hats, 26 pair of pants, etc. for his men.

GOODWIN, COLUMBUS W.   Co. G   Rank: Pvt.   Source: 7
Captured near Raymond, Miss. (Big Black River) on May 17, 1863 and sent to Memphis, Camp Morton, Ind. and then Ft. Delaware, Del. He was exchanged with 1697 POW's on July 6, 1863 at City Point, Va. He was admitted to the General Hospital at Petersburg, Va. with pneumonia on July 8, 1863. He was given 50 days furlough on Aug. 26, 1863.

GOODWIN, EDWIN   Co. -   Rank: Col.   Source: 2,3,4,5,6,7,8
He was born at Aberdeen, Miss. and graduated from LaGrange in 1851. He lived in Franklin Co. Ala. and became professor of Languages and Literature at LaGrange Military Academy. Elected Lt. Col. when the 35th was formed. Promoted to Col. on Oct. 4, 1862. That same month he went to Northern Ala. to arrest deserters and recruit men. He came back with 60 men. In April 1863 he signed for wood (fuel) for 10 Capt.'s, 30 officers and 450 men. He died in the service in the second half of 1863 at Columbus, Miss. and was buried near the site of LaGrange Military Academy. His widow, A. Goodwin, died in 1902. For more family information, see source 2.

GOODWIN, GEORGE   Co. B   Rank: Pvt.   Source: 7
On July 22, 1864 he was admitted to Ocmulgee Hospital in Macon, Ga. with "Vul. Sclopet".

GOODWIN, J.H.   Co. F   Rank: Pvt.   Source: 7
He was paroled at Talladega, Ala. on May 29, 1865.

GOODWIN, J.W.   Co. G   Rank: Pvt.   Source: 7
Joined Capt. West's Co. in March 1862. He was given 60 days furlough on July 7, 1863.

GOODWIN, V.M.   Co. G   Rank: ?   Source: 7
Joined Capt. West's Co. in March 1862.

GOODWIN, Z.M.   Co. G   Rank: Pvt.   Source: 7
    Captured at Big Black River on May 16, 1863. He was exchanged on July
    4, 1863.

GOSSUP, CLINTON   Co. ?   Rank: ?   Source: 7
    Died at the Military Prison at Alton, Ill. on Feb. 14, 1863.

GRAY, HENRY V.   Co. E   Rank: Cpl.   Source: 7
    He may have belonged to the 35th Miss.

GREEN, JOHN R.   Co. B   Rank: ?   Source: 2,4,7
    Joined Capt. Hunt's Co. in March 1862. Wounded at Decatur, Ala. in Nov.
    1864.

GREEN, MARCUS D.L.   Co. B   Rank: Pvt.   Source: 1,2,4,8
    Born June 28, 1838 at Florence, Ala. He joined Co. E of the 2nd Ala. (The
    Franklin Blues) at Tuscumbia, Ala. on march 2, 1861 and was mustered
    out on March 2, 1862. He then joined the 35th on April 30, 1862 at
    Corinth, Miss. He became Color Bearer sometime in 1863. On July 20,
    1864 he was wounded and lost a leg at Peachtree Creek, Ga. He was
    living in Tuscumbia, Ala. and blind when he applied for a pension.

GREENHAUGH, JAMES   Co. G   Rank: Pvt.   Source: 7
    Joined Capt. West's Co. in March 1862. Died at Columbus Hospital (Miss.
    ?) sometime prior to Aug. 1, 1863.

GREENHILL, SAMUEL E.   Co. B   Rank: Pvt.   Source: 7
    Joined Capt. Hunt's Co. on March 24, 1862 at Frankfort, Ala. Admitted to
    the 1st Miss. CSA Hospital at Jackson, Miss. on Feb. 17, 1864 with
    chronic diarrhea. He was sent to the General Hospital at Shelby Springs,
    Ala. where he had the same problem April 4 to 16 and June 24 to July 28,
    1864. He was furloughed July 28, 1864.

GRENS, G.D.   Co. I   Rank: ?   Source: 7
    May 5, 1863 he was admitted to Hugh Springs Hospital (Miss.?).

GRENS, M.L.   Co. ?   Rank: ?   Source: 7
    May 5, 1863 he was admitted to the Hugh Springs Hospital.

GREY, J. MILTON   Co. C   Rank: Cpl.   Source: 7
    Received pay for the period of Dec. 1, 1862 thru Feb. 28, 1863.

GRIFFIN, J.B.   Co. G   Rank: ?   Source: 7
    Joined Capt. West's Co. in March 1862.

GRISTELL, J.   Co. A   Rank: Pvt.   Source: 7
    Captured at the Battle of Corinth, Miss. on Oct. 3rd or 4th, 1862.

GILLIUM, L.   Co. ?   Rank: 2nd Lieut. Source: 7
    Listed as absent without leave on Aug. 1, 1864 near Atlanta, Ga.

97

GUNTER, MASON J.　　　　Co. C　　Rank: Pvt.　　　Source: 7
　　　Joined Capt. Ashford's Co. at Courtland, Ala. on Feb. 25, 1862. He was
　　　born in Moore Co., N.C. and was 65 years old when he joined. During July
　　　1862 he had duty as a blacksmith. He was discharged on Nov. 25, 1862.
　　　He had dark complexion, gray eyes and hair and was 5'6" tall.

GUTHRIE, J.B.　　　　　Co. F　　Rank: Pvt.　　　Source: 7
　　　Killed at the Battle of Baton Rouge, La. on Aug. 5, 1862.

HADEN, E.B.　　　　　　Co. B　　Rank: ?　　　Source: 7
　　　Died in 1862 in a hospital in Columbus, Miss.

HAINS, B.P.　　　　　　Co. D　　Rank: Cpl.　　　Source: 7
　　　Discharged July 20, 1862.

HALEY, MARK　　　　　See HAYLEY, MARK ROGERS

HALL, WILLIAM C.　　　　Co. F　　Rank: 1st Lieut.　Source: 7
　　　Elected Lieut on march 20, 1862. Captured and paroled near Boonville,
　　　Miss. about June 1, 1862. He was reported as buying cotton for the
　　　Federals in Madison Co. Ala. Dropped from the rolls of the 35th on Nov.
　　　16, 1863.

HANNA, JOHN　　　　　Co. ?　　Rank: Capt.　　Source: 11
　　　Died in the service. No other information.

HANSELL, WILLIAM A.　　Co. B　　Rank: Lieut.　　Source: 2,4,5,6
　　　Born Marietta, Ga. on Aug. 10, 1843. He was a Cadet and Drill Instructor
　　　at LaGrange Military Academy. Elected Adjutant when the 35th was
　　　formed. Resigned in 1862 to take a post in the Engineering Corps.

HAMILTON, EDGAR A.V.　　Co. H　　Rank: Pvt.　　　Source: 7
　　　Received pay from Oct. 1, 1862 thru April 30, 1863. He was from Lincoln,
　　　Co. Tenn. , had fair complexion, light hair, blue eyes, was 5'6" tall and had
　　　a family. He took the "Oath of Allegiance" on Feb. 11, 1865.

HAMILTON, JOSEPH　　　Co. C　　Rank: Pvt.　　　Source: 7
　　　Joined Capt. Ashford's Co. in March 1862. Worked as a teamster from
　　　April 1, 1863 thru Feb. 29, 1864 and earned an extra 25 cents per day.

HAMILTON, R.　　　　　Co. C　　Rank: ?　　　Source: 7
　　　Joined Capt. Ashford's Co. in March 1862.

HAMPTON, CHARLES M.P.　Co. H　　Rank: Pvt.　　　Source: 7
　　　Enlisted March 11, 1862 at Moulton, Ala. He was a patient at the general
　　　Hospital at Enterprise, Miss. in Jan. 1863. Listed as a deserter in March
　　　1864.

HAMPTON, JOHN J.W.　　Co. H　　Rank: Pvt.　　　Source: 7
　　　Admitted to the 1st Miss. CSA Hospital at Jackson on July 9, 1863 with
　　　"Febois Remit." Sent to the General Hospital the next day.

HAMPTON, MANOSH BASLIC   Co. H   Rank: 1st Lieut.   Source: 1,7,8
Born April 16, 1835 at Leighton, Ala. Commissioned a Lieut. in the 35th on March 12, 1862. He signed for forage on Aug. 22, 1862. Resigned from the 35th in Jan. 1864 to take over Co. B of the 11th Ala. Cavalry at Bainbridge, Ala. He stayed with that unit until April 1865 when he was paroled at Pond Springs, Ala.

HANAGAN, A.S.   Co. C   Rank: Pvt.   Source: 7
Received pay from July 1 thru Aug. 30, 1862.

HANSON, JOHN W.   Co. D   Rank: Pvt.   Source: 7
He took the "Oath" on May 25, 1865 at Montgomery, Ala. He was 5'8" tall and had light hair, blue eyes and fair complexion.

HANSON, ?   Co. B   Rank: Lieut.   Source: 4
He was from Ga. and was a Cadet at LaGrange. Joined the 35th in March 1862. Served at Drill Instructor for new recruits. Became Adjutant on March 20, 1862 and resigned in the last half of 1862.

HARDIN, EGBERT B.   Co. B   Rank: ?   Source: 7
His widow, Julia Ann Hardin, filled a death claim on Jan. 6, 1865.

HARDIN, MILTON A.   Co. B   Rank: Pvt.   Source: 7
No other information.

HARDY, CHARLES   Co. B   Rank: ?   Source: 2,7
He was a Cadet at LaGrange before the war. Joined Capt. Hunt's Co. in March 1862. Wounded at the Battle of Peachtree Creek, Ga. Wounded again at Franklin, Tenn. Fell from the top of a rail car near Chapel Hill, N.C. and injured his ankle. Stayed with the unit until the end of the war. For more family information, see source 2.

HARGETT, M.L.   Co. B   Rank: ?   Source: 7
Joined Capt. Hunt's Co. in March 1862.

HARGROVE, WILLIAM S.   Co. G   Rank: Pvt.   Source: 7
Admitted to 1st Miss. CSA Hospital at Jackson on Feb. 28, 1864 with chronic rheumatism. Returned to duty March 29, 1864. Signed the "Oath" on Jan. 20, 1865. He was from Giles Co. Tenn., had dark complexion and hair, hazel eyes and was 6'tall. He said he had a family and deserted July 29, 1864.

HARDING, J.A.   Co. G   Rank: Pvt.   Source: 7
Joined Capt. West's Co. in March 1862. Captured at Big Black River, Miss. on may 16 or 17, 1863. He was sent to Camp Morton, Ind. and on to Ft. Delaware, Del. Exchanged July 6, 1863 with 1697 POW's Listed as a deserter in Feb. 1864.

HARMON, JAMES W.   Co. B   Rank: Cpl.   Source: 6,7
From Lauderdale Co. Ala. Was a Cadet at LaGrange Military Academy in 1861. Captured Dec. 16, 1864 and sent to Camp Chase, Ohio. He

took the "Oath" there on May 15, 1865. He had florid complexion, dark hair, blue eyes and was 5'4" tall.

HARMON, STEVE   Co. B   Rank: ?   Source: 2
Dead. No other information

HARPER, ROBERT L.   Co. D   Rank: Pvt.   Source: 7
Joined Capt. Sanders' Co. on March 18, 1862. He was a teamster in Jan. and Feb. 1864. He said he deserted on Dec. 25, 1864 and had a family. Took the"Oath" on March 19, 1865. He was from Limestone Co. Ala. had fair complexion, brown hair, gray eyes and was 5'10" tall.

HARRINGTON, SCOTT   Co. B   Rank: ?   Source: 2,6,7
He was from Ridge Post Office, Texas and was a Cadet at LaGrange Military Academy from July 1861 until the school closed in March 1862. He then joined the 35th. Killed at the Battle of Atlanta in July 1864.

HARRIS, ARCHIBALD   Co. E   Rank: Pvt.   Source: 2,7
No other information.

HARRIS, BEN   Co. D   Rank: ?   Source: 2,7
From Mooresville, Ala. He was a Cadet at LaGrange in Aug. 1860 Joined Capt. Sanders' Co. in March 1862.

HARRIS, BEVERLY E.   Co. E   Rank: Cpl.   Source: 7
Recruited by Capt. Dickson on March 28, 1862 at Huntsville, Ala. He was in Jackson's Division Hospital at Old Marion, Miss. during Sept. or Oct. 1863. Captured May 25, 1864 at Dallas, Ga. Sent to Louisville, Ky. and on to Rock Island Barracks, Ill. where he arrived June 9, 1864. On March 6, 1865 he was transferred to City point, Va. and was exchanged with 3499 POW's. By May 12, 1865 he was back in Huntsville, Ala. He was from Jackson Co. Ala., had fair complexion, dark hair, hazel eyes and was 5'9" tall.

HARRIS, FRANCIS B.   Co. ?   Rank: Asst. Surgeon Source: 7
Captured at Champion Hill, Miss. on May 28, 1863. Sent to Nashville, Louisville and on to Johnson's Island, Ohio. On Aug. 2, 1864 he was sent to Ft. Delaware, Del. and was exchanged on Aug. 7, with 38 surgeons and chaplains. He surrendered April 20, 1865 at Macon, Ga. He took the "Oath" on May 12, 1865 and was released. He was from Limestone Co. Ala., had fair complexion, brown hair, hazel eyes and was 5'11" tall.

HARRIS, JOHN   Co. A   Rank: Pvt.   Source: 1,2,7
He was a Cadet at LaGrange in Aug. 1860. Joined the 35th in the spring of 1861 (?) at Maysville, Ala. Captured at Nashville, Tenn. on Dec. 17, 1864 and sent to Camp Chase, Ohio. Paroled May 16, 1865. He was from Madison Co. Ala., had dark complexion, black hair, blue eyes and was 5'10" tall.

HARRIS, JOHN H.   Co. B   Rank: Capt.   Source: 2,3,4,6,7
He was from Limestone Co. Ala. and was a Cadet and Drill Instructor at LaGrange Military Academy in 1860 and 1861. He was commissioned a

Lieut. in the 35th on March 12, 1862 and promoted to Capt. on Oct. 4, 1862. Died in the service in Miss. in late 1863.

HARWELL, J.S. Co. H Rank: 2nd Lieut. Source: 7
Surrendered May 12, 1865 at Meridian, Miss.

HAYLEY, MARK ROGER Co. B Rank: Pvt. Source: 1,2,6,7
Born April 15, 1845 at Florence, Ala. He was a Cadet at LaGrange Military Academy July thru Dec. 1861. Joined the 35th in the spring of 1862 at LaGrange, Ala. Wounded at the Battle of Corinth, Miss. and again at Kingston, N.C. Surrendered and signed the "Oath" on Aug. 18, 1865 and was then paroled at Raleigh, N.C. He was farming near Florence, Ala. in 1904.

HAZELWOOD, S. Co. C Rank: ? Source: 7
Joined Capt. Ashford's Co. in March 1862.

HEARN, JOHN A. Co. D Rank: Pvt. Source: 7
Joined the 35th on March 20, 1862 at LaGrand (?). He was a teamster from Dec. 15. 1862 thru April 7, 1863 and earned an extra 25 cents a day. He was a patient at the General Hospital at Point Clear, Baldwin Co. Ala. sometime between July 17 and Aug. 31, 1863.

HEDGEPETH, JESSE T. Co. B Rank: Pvt. Source: 7
He was a teamster from Feb. 16, 1863 thru July 27, 1864 and was paid an extra 25 cents per day. He signed for an issue of clothing on Oct. 29, 1863 and July 11, 1864.

HENNIGAN, ARTHUR P.R. Co. H Rank: 2nd Lieut. Source: 6,7
Born Dec. 27, 1840 at Brickville, Ala and was a Cadet at LaGrange Military Academy from 1858 thru Dec. 1861, During that time he was Sgt. of Cadet Co. A. Joined the 35th when it was formed in March 1862. He died in the service at Lauderdale Springs, Miss. on Aug. 19, 1863 of diarrhea.

HENNIGAN, DALLAS Co. ? Rank: ? Source: 6
Born Oct. 13, 1844 at Brickville, Ala and was a Cadet at LaGrange Military Academy in 1860. He resigned July 5, 1861. Joined the 35th in March 1862 and died at Oxford, Miss. on May 28, 1862.

HENNIGAN, JAMES POLK Co. K Rank: 1st Lieut. Source: 4,5,6,7
Born Nov. 13, 1842. He was a Cadet at LaGrange Military Academy in 1860 and 1861 during which time he was a Lieut. in Cadet Co. B. Upon leaving LaGrange on Dec. 4, 1861, he became Military Instructor in the Confederate service for two months. He joined the 35th on March 12, 1862 and was elected 1st Lieut. Became Adjutant in 1863. He was severely wounded on July 22, 1864 by a shell fragment at the Battle of Atlanta. Admitted to St. Mary's Hospital at LaGrange, Ga. on July 26, 1864. By Aug. 9 he still "could not be moved". He was permanently disabled. He Surrendered on May 17, 1865. Colbert Co. Ala. was his home. In 1903 he was living in Brick, Ala. and was able to attend the LaGrange reunion on May 19, 1904.

HERDY, H.N.   Co. G   Rank: Pvt.   Source: 7
Listed as a deserter in March 1864.

HEVEN, JOHN   Co. D   Rank: Pvt.   Source: ,7
No other information.

HIGHTOWER, W.H.   Co. C   Rank: ?   Source: 7
Joined Capt. Ashford's Co. in March 1862.

HILL, J.S.H.   Co. B   Rank: ?   Source: 2
From Selma, Ala. and was a Cadet at LaGrange in Aug. 1860. No other
information.

HILL, M.S.   Co. A   Rank: Pvt.   Source: 7
Enlisted Dec. 1, 1862 at Center Star, Ala. Admitted to Breckinridge's
Division Hospital at Lauderdale, Miss. as a patient on July 1, 1863.
Furloughed Sept. 2, 1863.

HILL, P.M.   Co. G   Rank: Pvt.   Source: 7
Listed as a deserter in March 1864.

HILL, W.D.   Co. G   Rank: Pvt.   Source: 7
Enlisted March 18, 1861 (?) at Athens, Ala. He was a nurse at the
General Hospital in Lauderdale Springs, Miss. from July 30 thru Sept.
1863. Listed as a deserter in March 1864.

HILL, WILLIAM   Co. I   Rank: Pvt.   Source: 7
Captured and paroled at the Battle of Corinth, Miss. on Oat. 3 or 4, 1862.

HINDS, JOHN B.F.   o. I   Rank: Pvt.   Source: 7
Captured at Big Black River, Miss. on May 17, 1863. Sent to Camp
Morton, Ind. and on to Ft. Delaware, Del. Exchanged July 6, 1863 at City
Point, Va. with 1697 POW's. Captured in Lauderdale Co., Miss. on July
16, 1864 and was sent to the Military Prison in Louisville, Ky. He took the
"Oath of Allegiance" on July 18, 1864 and was released "North of the Ohio
River". He was from Lauderdale Co., Miss., had light complexion, dark
hair, blue eyes and was 5'4" tall.

HINES, H.C.   Co. A   Rank: Pvt.   Source: 7
Listed as a deserter in March 1864.

HOBGOOD, WILLIAM   Co. B   Rank: ?   Source: 2
He was a Cadet at LaGrange. No other information.

HODGE, JAMES D.   Co. G   Rank: Pvt.   Source: 7
Joined the 35th on July 15, 1862. Deserted May 1, 1864. He took the
"Oath" on Jan. 11, 1865. He was from Giles Co., Tenn., had light
complexion and hair, gray eyes and was 5'6" tall. He stated he had no
family.

HODGE, W.B.   Co. A   Rank: Pvt.   Source: 7

Listed as a deserter in March 1864.

HODGE, NEIL B.   Co. A   Rank: Pvt.   Source: 7
      Captured near Nashville, Tenn. on Dec. 16, 1864. Sent to Louisville, Ky.
      and on to Camp Chase, Ohio where he arrived Jan. 4, 1865. Took the
      "Oath of Allegiance" on May 13, 1865 and was released. He was from
      Lauderdale Co. Ala., had florid complexion, dark hair, blue eyes and was
      5'6" tall.

HOLF, J.M.   Co. G   Rank: Pvt.   Source: 7
      Joined Capt. West's Co. in March 1862.

HOLLAND, JACOB   Co. G   Rank: Pvt.   Source: 7
      Captured May 16, 1863 at Champion Hill, Miss. and sent to Memphis,
      Tenn. on May 25, 1863.

HOLLEY, JACOB O.   Co. H   Rank: Pvt.   Source: 7
      Captured near Nashville, Tenn. on Dec. 16, 1864, Sent to Louisville, Ky.
      and on to Camp Chase, Ohio where he arrived Jan. 4, 1864. He died
      Feb. 10, 1865 of pneumonia. Buried 1/8 mile South of Camp Chase.

HOLLIMAN, ROBERT T.   Co. B   Rank: Pvt.   Source: 2,7
      Joined Capt. Hunt's Co. in may 1862. Received pay for service from Oct.
      1, 1862 thru Feb. 1, 1863. Listed as a deserter in March 1864.

HOLT, G.K.   Co. ?   Rank: ?   Source: 7
      He was one of 48 POW's exchanged near Vicksburg, Miss. on board the
      steamer "Metropolitan" on Dec. 2, 1862.

HOLT, J.N.   Co. G   Rank: ?   Source: 7
      Joined the 35th at Athens, Ala. on March 18, 1862. He was born in
      Limestone. Co., Ala. By Oct. 1862 he was 19 years old, 5' tall with florid
      complexion, blue eyes and red hair. He had been a farmer. Discharged
      Oct. 22, 1862 due to a deformity of his left leg caused by a childhood
      fracture.

HOLT, SILAS W.   Co. A   Rank: Pvt.   Source: 7
      Received pay for "rations" from jan. 1 thru April 5, 1863, He signed for
      clothing on Dec. 14, 1863 and again in the 2ns 1/4 or 1864. Captured in
      Sumpter Co. Ala. on July 14, 1864. He took the "oath" on July 16 and was
      released to stay North of the Ohio River for the rest of the war. He was
      from Giles Co. Tenn. and had ruddy Complexion, brown hair, blue eyes
      and was 5'9" tall.

HOOPER, JAMES W.   Co. B   Rank: Pvt.   Source: 2,7,8
      Enlisted in 1862 at LaGrange, Ala. He was in the hospital at Tunnel Hill,
      Ga. with asthma on May 25, 1863 and released on June 8, 1863.
      Discharged in 1864. He was living in Belgreen, Ala. about 1915.

HORN, JOSEPH   Co. B   Rank: Lieut.   Source: 2,4,6,7
      He was from LaGrange, Ala. and was a Cadet and drill instructor at
      LaGrange Military Academy from Feb. 1860 to March 1862. He became

Adjutant of the 35th in late 1862. Died in the service in June, 1864.

HORTON, F.M.   Co. G   Rank: ?   Source: 7
    Joined Capt. West's Co. in March 1862.

HORTON, SAMUEL M.   Co. G   Rank: Pvt.   Source: 7
    Discharged July 24, 1862. No reason given.

HOWARD, CHARLES   Co. G   Rank: Pvt.   Source: 7
    Captured July 20, 1864 at the Battle of Peachtree Creek, Ga. Arrived at
    Chattanooga, Tenn. on Aug. 12, 1864 and took the "Oath".

HOWELL, W.C.   Co. I   Rank: ?   Source: 7
    Born in Ala. Died Aug. 14, 1863 at Lauderdale, Miss. of "paralysia".

HUBBARD, GEORGE C.   Co. F   Rank: Lieut.   Source: 7,8,11
    He was the Adjutant when the 35th was formed. On May 16, 1863 at
    Bakers Creek, Miss. he was visiting Co. F. and the Captain asked him to
    act as his 1st Lieut. during the action. Lieut. Hubbard was killed in that
    action. His widow, M.F. Hubbard was living in Leighton, Ala. when she
    applied for a pension.

HUDLESTON, H.   Co. D   Rank: ?   Source: 7
    Joined Capt. Sanders' Co. in March 1862.

HUDLESTON, J.   Co. D   Rank: Pvt.   Source: 7
    Captured in the fall of Vicksburg, Miss. on July 4, 1863. He signed his
    parole and was released on July 7, 1863.

HUDSON, JOHN DARBY   Co. E   Rank: Cpl.   Source: 1,7
    Born April 15, 1842 at Florence, Ala. and Joined the 35th in the spring of
    1862 at Huntsville, Ala. Served until the end of the war. Paroled at
    Meridian, Miss. on May 14, 1865.

HUNT, JAMES JACKSON   Co. A   Rank: Pvt.   Source: 7
    Joined the 35th on March 7, 1862 at LaGrange, Ala. He was in
    Breckinridge's Division Hospital at Marion, Miss with chronic diarrhea from
    July 9, thru Aug. 31, 1863. Listed as a deserter in March 1864.

HUNT, WILLIAM HENRY   Co. B   Rank: Major   Source: 2,3,4,5,6,7,11
    He was from Ga. This West Point graduate was Commandant of Cadets
    and Instructor of Military Science at LaGrange Military Academy from 1858
    to 1862. He was elected Capt. of Co. B when the 35th was formed. On
    March 20, 1862 he was promoted to Major. Late in 1862 he resigned to
    take command of another regiment. At this point there is some confusion,
    he was Col. of (A) the 26th Ala., (B) a Reg. of Va. infantry, (C) a Ga. Reg.
    serving in Va., or (D) still with the 35th. I think option (A) or (C) is correct.
    In any event, he was killed on Nov. 30, 1864 at the Battle of Franklin, Tenn.
    For more family information, see source 2.

HUNTER, A.D.   Co. K   Rank: 2nd Lieut.   Source: 7,9
    Wounded at the Battle of Corinth, Miss. in Oct. 1862. Resigned his

commission on Feb. 4, 1863 because he did not want to be an officer. He became a private in the 35th.

HUNTER, JAMES   Co. K   Rank: Cpl.   Source: 7
Died at Gilmer Hospital, Atlanta, Ga. on June 27, 1864 leaving $1.00 in cash.

HUNTER, JOHN M.   Co. E   Rank: 1st Lieut.   Source: 7
He was elected 1st Lieut. on March 12, 1862 and died Oct. 30, 1862.

HURN, JOHN A.   Co. D   Rank: Pvt.   Source: 7
Joined Capt. Sanders' Co. on March 20, 1862 at LaGrange, Ala. He was detailed as a nurse at the General Hospital at Point Clear, Ala. from Aug. 28 thru Oct. 31, 1863. He either deserted or was captured Dec. 22, 1864. He took the "Oath" at Nashville, Tenn. on Jan. 21, 1865. He was from Giles Co. Tenn. had dark complexion and hair, hazel eyes and was 5'9" tall. He stated he had no family.

HUTTON, JOHN J.   Co. I   Rank: Pvt.   Source: 7
Enlisted March 22, 1862 at Florence, Ala. He was a patient sometime in July and Aug. 1863 at the Convalescent Hospital at Springhill, Ala.

HUTTON, R.W.   Co. I   Rank: ?   Source: 7
Joined Capt. Chisholm's Co. in March 1862.

IRION, J.P.   Co. I   Rank: ?   Source: 7
Joined Capt. Chisholm's Co. in March 1862.

IRWIN, H.B..   Co. I   Rank: Capt.   Source: 7
He was from Moulton, Ala. Admitted to Pettigrew General Hospital # 13 at Raleigh, N.C. on march 11, 1865 with a fracture of the right leg and left heel.

IRWIN, J.   Co. I   Rank: Sgt.   Source: 7
Listed as a deserter in March 1864.

ISAM, ISAAC   Co. D   Rank: Pvt.   Source: 7
Listed as a deserter in March 1864.

IVES, SAMUEL   Co. A   Rank: Col.   Source: 1,2,3,4,7
Born in Aug. 1836 at Center Star, Lauderdale Co, Ala. He entered the service as a private in May 1861 at Center Star, in Co. I of the 9th Ala. He served with the 9th until wounded in Virginia in early 1862 and discharged. He joined the 35th on March 12, 1862 at Florence, Ala and was elected Capt. of Co. A. Promoted to Major on May 8, 1862. He was wounded in the shoulder at the Battle of Baton Rouge, La. on Aug. 5, 1862 Promoted to Lt. Col. on Nov. 12, 1862. By Feb. 20, 1864 he was a full Col. and was commander of the 35th. By Aug. 19, 1864 he was commanding officer of the 27th, 35th and 49th Consolidated Reg. He was wounded again at the Battle of Franklin, Tenn. on Nov. 30, 1864. Ives served with the 35th until the end. He was paroled at Pond Springs, Ala. in May 1865.

IVES, S.J.W.   Co. A   Rank: 2nd Lieut.   Source: 7
    Joined the 35th on March 12, 1862.

JACKSON, JAMES A.   Co. B   Rank: Pvt.   Source: 2,6,7
    From LaGrange, Ala. and was a Cadet at LaGrange Military Academy in
    Aug. 1860. He died Aug. 14, 1863 at Walker's Division Hospital in
    Lauderdale, Miss. He left $6.00 in cash.

JAMES, N.   Co. C   Rank: ?   Source: 7
    Joined Capt. Ashford's Co. in March 1862.

JAMES, S.H.   Co. C   Rank: ?   Source: 7
    Died Nov. 1, 1863. No other information.

JARMON, JAMES T.   Co. ?   Rank: Capt.   Source: 7
    He was Commissary Officer. Resigned on June 9, 1862 due to poor
    health.

JARRETT, J.J.   Co. G   Rank: ?   Source: 7
    Joined Capt. West's Co. in March 1862.

JOHNSON, CLAUDE   Co. C   Rank: Pvt.   Source: 7
    No other information.

JOHNSON, EZEKIEL T.   Co. H   Rank: Capt.   Source: 3,7
    Joined the 35th as a Sgt. and was then promoted to 2nd Lieut. Became
    Capt. of Co. H. He transferred to Col. Patterson's 5th Ala. Cavalry on
    Sept. 16, 1863.

JOHNSON, FREDRICK V.   Co. E   Rank: Sgt.   Source: 7
    Wounded in the chest at the Battle of Baton Rouge, La. on Aug. 5, 1862.
    Captured in Madison Co. Ala. on jan 31, 1865. Sent to Louisville, Ky and
    on to Rock Island, Ill. where he arrived Feb. 18, 1865. He took the "Oath"
    on May 12, 1865 and was released. He was from Huntsville, Ala. had fair
    complexion, dark hair, hazel eyes and was 5'9" tall. He was 21 years old
    when he was released.

JOHNSON, JAMES L.   Co. G   Rank: Sgt.   Source: 7
    Received pay for service from March 18 thru Aug. 31, 1862. Promoted to
    Sgt on April 29, 1862 at a pay rate of $17.00 per month.

JOINER, BENJAMIN   Co. A   Rank: Pvt.   Source: 7
    Joined the 35th on Oct. 7, 1862 at Florence, Ala. He was a patient at
    Loring's Division Hospital at Lauderdale, Miss. on Aug. 8, 1863..

JOINER, CHARLES   Co. A   Rank: Pvt.   Source: 7
    Captured May 16, 1863 at Champion Hill, Miss. and was sent to Memphis,
    Camp Morton, Ind. and then Ft. Delaware, Del. He was exchanged on
    July 6, 1863 at City Point, Va. with 1697 POW's.

JOINER, JAMES E.   Co. A   Rank: ?   Source: 7
    Died May 21, 1863 at Stillman Hospital in Clinton, La. leaving $47.00 in

cash.

JONES, D.W.   Co. ?   Rank: ?   Source: 7
Exchanged on Dec. 2, 1862 with 48 POW's on board the steamer "Metropolitan" near Vicksburg, Miss.

JONES, JAMES P.   Co. H   Rank: ?   Source: 7
Died June 25, 1862 at Newsom Hospital. A death claim was filed on Nov. 4, 1862 by his widow, Harriet M. Jones.

JONES, JESSE   Co. A   Rank: Cpl.   Source: 7
Admitted to 1st Miss. CSA Hospital at Jackson on July 9, 1863. Transferred on July 12 to the General Hospital at Lauderdale, Miss. with acute diarrhea, where he died Sept. 20, 1863. He was born in Ala.

JONES, J.F.   Co. D   Rank: ?   Source: 7
Joined Capt. Sanders' Co. in March 1862.

JONES, JOHN J.   Co. ?   Rank: Pvt.   Source: 7
Joined the 35th on March 20, 1862. He was from Madison Co. Ala., had fair complexion, light hair, blue eyes and was 5'5" tall. He said he deserted on Dec. 18, 1864 and had no family.

JONES, R.F. "RED"   Co. K   Rank: Capt.   Source: 3,4,5,7
He was from Franklin Co. Ala and joined the 35th as a 2nd Lieut. Elected Capt. on Oct. 9, 1862. On Aug. 21, 1863 he was paid $130.00 per month for service from May 1 thru July 31, 1863. This pay voucher has a note "Officer under sick orders returning from Hospital to his command." Nov. 19, 1863 he requested and received 44 days leave to "visit my aged parents in San Antonio, Tx." On July 27, 1864 in Ga., he is listed as absent with approval. He stayed with the unit until the end.

JONES, S.W.   Co. ?   Rank: ?   Source: 7
His name is on a list of POW's to be exchanged aboard the steamer "Metropolitan" near Vicksburg, Miss. on Dec. 2, 1862. A note states "in U.S. Hospital".

JONES, T.S.   Co. D   Rank: Pvt.   Source: 7
Joined Capt. Sanders' Co. in March 1862. Discharged May 20, 1862.

KEENUM, W.C.   Co. B   Rank: Pvt.   Source: 7
He was a teamster from Dec. 8, 1863 thru Feb. 1, 1864.

KELLOGG, A.T.   Co. D   Rank: ?   Source: 7
Joined Capt. Sanders' Co. in March 1862.

KELLOGG, H.E.   Co. D   Rank: Cpl.   Source: 7
Captured in the fall of Vicksburg, Miss. on July 4, 1863. He signed his parole and was released on July 6, 1863. He was the Adjt's clerk from Jan. 1 to May 17, 1863. On March 2, 1864 he signed for an issue of clothing.

KENNARD, JOHN W.   Co. E   Rank: Pvt.   Source: 7
Discharged May 19, 1862. No reason given.

KENNEDY, A.   Co. A   Rank: Pvt.   Source: 7
Listed as a deserter in March 1864.

KENNEDY, EZEKIEL   Co. F   Rank: Pvt.   Source: 7
Joined the 35th on Dec. 20, 1862. Captured "at home" in Jackson Co. Ala. on Nov. 13, 1863. Sent to Louisville, Ky and then Camp Morton (near Indianapolis), where he arrived Nov. 30, 1863. He was sent by rail to Point Lookout, Md. in March of 1865, and was exchanged with 1011 POW's on the James River in Va. on March 23, 1865. He entered the General Hospital #9 in Richmond, Va. the same day.

KENNEDY, SAMUEL   Co. B   Rank: ?   Source: 2
No other information.

KENNEDY, WILLIAM   Co. A   Rank: Pvt.   Source: 7
Captured at Edwards Depot or Champion Hill, Miss. on May 16 or 17, 1863. Sent to Memphis, Camp Morton, Ind. and arrived at Ft. Delaware, Del. on June 9, 1863. He was exchanged on July 4, 1863, but was "left in the hospital at Ft. Delaware". His widow, Sabre Kennedy, filed a death Claim on Nov. 3, 1863.

KENNEMER, JOSEPH H.   Co. G   Rank: Sgt.   Source: 7
Joined Capt. West's Co. in March 1862. Attached to French's Division Hospital at Lauderdale, Miss. as a nurse. Captured Dec. 16, 1864 near Nashville, Tenn. and sent to Louisville, Ky then Camp Chase, Ohio. Released on May 15, 1865. He was from Limestone Co. Ala., had florid complexion, dark hair, blue eyes and was 5'10" tall. He was 22 when released.

KENNEMUR, FRANKLIN   Co. A   Rank: Pvt.   Source: 7
Captured on May 16 or 17, 1863 at Big Black River, Miss. Sent to Camp Morton, Ohio and then to Ft. Delaware, Del. to be exchanged on July 4, 1863, but was "left in the hospital". He died July 6, 1863.

KIDD, W.R.   Co. H   Rank: Pvt.   Source: 7
Captured and paroled near Kingston, Ala. on May 12, 1865.

KING, BENJAMIN RUSH   Co. D   Rank: Surg.   Source: 1,7,8
Born Oct. 20, 1833 at Leighton, Ala. Joined the 35th on Oct. 1, 1862 at Grenada, Miss. Served with the 35th until Feb. 1864 when he resigned and joined Major William Warren's Battalion as surgeon. he was living in Colbert Co. Ala. in 1907.

KING, C.D. Jr.   Co. E   Rank: Pvt.   Source: 7
Captured July 4, 1863 in the fall of Vicksburg, Miss. He signed his parole and was released on July 7, 1863.

KING, GEORGE W.   Co. A   Rank: Pvt.   Source: 2,7
He was a Cadet at LaGrange in Aug. 1860. Listed as a deserter in March,

1864.

KING, J.C.   Co. H   Rank: Pvt.   Source: 7
Entered the General Hospital #9 in Richmond, Va. on May 31, 1864 and was released June 1, 1864.

KING, J.S.   Co. K   Rank: Pvt.   Source: 7
Paroled June 20, 1865 at Telladega, Ala.

KINNEY, HUGH J.   Co. E   Rank: Pvt.   Source: 7
Enlisted March 31, 1862 at Huntsville, Ala. Admitted to Loring's Division Hospital at Lauderdale, Miss. as a patient on Aug. 13, 1863. He was still there on Sept. 1.

KINNEY, JOHN   Co. H   Rank: Pvt.   Source: 7
Died Oct. 3, 1862. A death claim was filled on Jan. 23, 1863 by his widow, Ellen Kinney. She received $82.63 on Feb. 16, 1864.

KINNEY, WILLIAM M.   Co. E   Rank: Pvt.   Source: 7
Enlisted March 31, 1862 at Huntsville, Ala. Admitted as a patient to Loring's Division Hospital on Aug. 13, 1863. He was still there on Oct. 31, 1863. Entered 1st Miss. CSA Hospital at Jackson on Feb. 16, 1864 with chronic diarrhea. Returned to duty April 21, 1864.

KINSEY, M.R.   Co. H   Rank: Pvt.   Source: 7
He was part of a detail sent to North Ala. on Nov. 21, 1862 to recruit.

KOONCE, JOHN E.   Co. I   Rank: ?   Source: 7
A death claim was filed April 3, 1863 by a lawyer.

LAMBERT, M.H.   Co. G   Rank: Pvt.   Source: 7
Joined the 35th on March 18, 1862.

LANCASTER, SAMUEL P.   Co. A   Rank: Pvt.   Source: 7
Captured and paroled about Oct. 3, 1862 at Corinth, Miss.

LANDERS, L. CLARK   Co. F   Rank: Pvt.   Source: 7
Captured May 16 or 18, 1863 at Big Black River, Miss. Sent to Memphis, Camp Morton, Ind. and then Ft. Delaware, Del. He was exchanged on July 6, 1863 at City Point, Va. with 1697 POW's.

LATHAM, JAMES W.   Co. ?   Rank: Capt.   Source: 2,7
Elected Quartermaster when the 35th was formed. He was from Leighton, Ala.

LATHAM, T.A.   Co. C   Rank: 1st Lieut.   Source: 7
Commissioned a 2nd Lieut on Sept. 24, 1862. By Aug. 7, 1863 he was a 1st Lieut.

LAWLER, JAMES H.   Co. F   Rank: Pvt.   Source: 7
Discharged May 2, 1862. No reason given.

LAWLER, JOHN   Co. F   Rank: Pvt.   Source: 7
    Discharged May 2, 1862. No reason given.

LAWLER, WILLIAM   Co. F   Rank: 2nd Lieut.   Source: 7,9
    He was shot in the left leg at the Battle of Corinth, Miss. on Oct. 3, 1862.
    Received pay from July 24 thru Oct. 24, 1863. Resigned Jan. 11, 1864.

LEAVELL, THOMAS S.   Co. A   Rank: Pvt.   Source: 7
    Joined the 35th on March 17, 1862 in Lauderdale Co. Ala. Captured Nov.
    10, 1863 in Giles Co. Tenn. by U.S. Scouts. Sent to Louisville, Ky and
    Camp Morton, Ind. where he arrived on Nov. 25, 1863. He signed the
    "Oath" and was released on May 22, 1965, saying he was going to Pulaski
    Co. Tenn. He had florid complexion, dark hair, blue eyes and was 6' tall.

LEMAY, C.W.   Co. ?   Rank: Pvt.   Source: 1
    Born March 11, 1842 at Mountain Springs, Lawrence Co. Ala. Entered the
    service on Oct. 16, 1861 at Knoxville, Tenn as a member of Co. I of the
    16th Ala. as a replacement for his brother. Served until the Battle of
    Fishing Creek, Ky. in 1862. Enlisted for himself in the 35th on March 1,
    1862. at LaGrange, Ala. Served with the 35th until they reached Augusta,
    Ga. There he was detailed with the 2nd Reg. Engineering Troops.

LEMAY, N.E.   Co. A   Rank: Pvt.   Source: 7
    Served as a teamster from jan. 1 thru Feb. 29, 1864 and earned an extra
    25 cents per day.

LEMAY, WEST   Co. H   Rank: Pvt.   Source: 7
    Wounded slightly at the Battle of Baton Rouge, La. on Aug. 5, 1862.

LEWIS, JOHN   Co. C   Rank: ?   Source: 7
    Joined Capt. Ashford's Co. in March 1862.

LEWIS, LEVI   Co. F   Rank: Pvt.   Source: 1
    Joined the 35th in April 1863 at Marysville, Ala. Captured near Florence,
    Ala. in Jan. 1865. Sent to Camp Chase, Ohio. Paroled in June 1865.

LEWIS, SAMUEL RAGLAND   Co. D   Rank: Pvt.   Source: 1,7
    Joined the 35th on Jan. 3, 1862 (?) at Mooresville, Ala. "Served on the
    staff of Gen. John Breckinridge as express messenger from Jan. until Oct.
    when the Gen. was transferred from Miss. to Tenn." Stayed with the 35th
    until June 10, 1865.

LEWIS, W.M.   Co. G   Rank: 2nd Lieut.   Source: 7
    Commissioned Nov. 28, 1862.

LILE, THOMAS J.   Co. K   Rank: 2nd Lieut   Source: 7
    He signed a letter, with other officers of the 35th on Aug. 7, 1863. Entered
    Way Hospital at Meridian, Miss. on Feb. 15, 1864, and was furloughed.
    Surrendered May 11, 1865 at Meridian, Miss.

LISLE, JOHN S.   Co. I   Rank: ?   Source: 7
    Joined Capt. Chisholm's Co. at Florence, Ala. on March 22, 1862.

Discharged Sept. 25, 1862 because of disability due to typhoid fever. He was from Lauderdale Co. Ala. and was 17 years old in 1862. Had fair complexion, light hair, hazel eyes and was 5'10" tall. He had been a farmer.

LOCKLEY, I.E.   Co. C   Rank: Pvt.   Source: 7
No other information.

LONG, ANDREW J.   Co. C   Rank: Pvt.   Source: 7
He said he joined the 35th on Dec. 5, 1861 (?) and deserted on March 29, 1864. and had no family. He took the "Oath of Allegiance" on April 4, 1865. He was from Lawrence Co. Ala. Had fair complexion, dark hair, hazel eyes and was 5"7" tall.

LONG, H.A.   Co. C   Rank: ?   Source: 7
Joined Capt. Ashford's Co. in March 1862.

LOONEY, G.C.   Co. A   Rank: Pvt.   Source: 7
Joined the 35th on March 17, 1862 at Florence, Ala. He was detailed to Maj. J. Bingham's Pioneer Corps at Smith's Ferry on the Pearl River in Miss. in Sept. and Oct. 1863. Listed as a deserter in March 1864.

LOONEY, GEORGE W.   Co. A   Rank: Pvt.   Source: 7
He was a teamster July 1, thru Aug. 31, 1863 and earned an extra 25 cents per day.

LOVELL, THOMAS S.   See LEAVELL, THOMAS S.

LOWE, J.D.   Co. I   Rank: ?   Source: 7
Died in the General Hospital at Okolonan (?), Miss. leaving $31.15 in cash.

LYLES, J.S.   See LISLE, JOHN S.

MADDIN, JOHN W.   Co. ?   Rank: Surgeon   Source: 2
Born Aug. 28, 1834 in Columbia, Tenn. In March of 1862 he arrived in LaGrange, Ala. from Waco, Tx and joined the 35th. He was transferred to the 30th Texas Cav. in 1863. For more family information, see source 2.

MADDING, JAMES A. (or M.)   Co. E   Rank: Capt.   Source: 2,4,5,7
Appointed Quartermaster on Dec. 12, 1862. Captured in the fall of Vicksburg, Miss. on July 4, 1863. Signed his parole on July 6, 1863. Received 10 days leave on Feb. 24. 1864. Captured March 2, 1864 at Summerville, Ala. Sent to Nashville, Louisville and on to Jackson Island, Ohio (near Sandusky) where he arrived April 25, 1864. He was sent to City Point, Va. on Feb. 24, 1865 and exchanged.

MALONE, W.E.   Co. G   Rank: ?   Source: 7
Joined Capt. West's Co. in March 1862.

MANDLEY, WILLIAM E.   Co. B   Rank: Pvt.   Source: 7
Captured at the Battle of Corinth, Miss. on Oct. 3 or 4, 1862. He was probably wounded. He was placed on board the steamer "Dacotah" with

539 POW's. Exchanged near Vicksburg, Miss. on Nov. 8, 1862. He died at Selma, Ala. on Oct. 2, 1863.

MAPLES, EDWARD N.   Co. F   Rank: Pvt.   Source: 7
Received pay for service from Nov. 30, 1862 thru June 30, 1863. Captured at the Battle of Champion Hill, Miss. on May 17, 1863. He was sent to Memphis, Camp Morton, Ind. and them Ft. Delaware, Del. and exchanged at City Point, Va, on July 6, 1863 with 1697 POW's.

MARCHEY, ALEX   Co. A   Rank: Pvt.   Source: 7
Captured and paroled at the Battle of Corinth, Miss. on Oct. 4, 1862.

MARTIN, JAMES L.   Co. D   Rank: Pvt.   Source: 7
Joined Capt. Sanders' Co. in March 1862. Captured at the Battle of Nashville, Tenn. on Dec. 16, 1864. He was sent to Louisville, Ky. and then Camp Chase, Ohio. He signed the "Oath" and was released on May 13, 1865. He had dark complexion and hair, gray eyes and was 5'9" tall.

MARTIN, JOHN N.   Co. D   Rank: Capt.   Source: 3,7
Joined the 35th on March 12, 1862 as a 2nd Lieut. By Dec. 31, 1863 he was a Capt. in charge of Co. D.

MARTIN, WILLIAM L.   Co. E   Rank: Cpl.   Source: 7
His pay from march 20 thru Aug. 31, 1862 was $13.00 per month. Wounded in the leg at the Battle of Baton Rouge, La on Aug. 5, 1862. Captured in the fall of Vicksburg, Miss. on July 4, 1863. Paroled on July 6, 1863.

MASTERSON, JOHN H.   Co. C   Rank: Pvt.   Source: 7
Joined Capt. Ashford's Co. in March 1862. Discharged May 28, 1862.

MATHEWS, JOHN N.   Co. B   Rank: Pvt.   Source: 7
Discharged July 26, 1862. No other information.

MATTHEWS, ELLIE   Co. B   Rank: Pvt.   Source: 6
He was from Huntsville, Ala. and was a Cadet at LaGrange Military Academy from July 1861 to March 1862. He was living in Huntsville in 1903.

McBRIDE, JAMES   Co. ?   Rank: Pvt.   Source: 7
Exchanged on board the steamer "Metropolitan" near Vicksburg, Miss. on Dec. 4, 1862.

McCARTEY, M.K.   Co. D   Rank: Pvt.   Source: 7
Joined Capt. Sanders' Co. in March 1862. He was a teamster from Jan. 1 thru June 30, 1863.

McCLESKEY, J.E.   Co. I   Rank: ?   Source: 7
Joined Capt. Chisholm's Co. in March 1862.

McCLESKY, SAMUEL M.   Co. C   Rank: ?   Source: 7
Joined Capt. Ashford's Co. in March 1862. Died at Lauderdale Springs,

Miss. A death claim was filed by Caroline McClesky. Date not listed.

McCLUSKEY, WILLIAM M.   Co. A   Rank: ?   Source: 7
Died at Clinton, La. A death claim was filed by a lawyer on July 14, 1863.

McDADE, W. J.   Co. B   Rank: Sgt.   Source: 7
Joined

McDAIRD, JOHN J.   Co. E   Rank: 2nd Lieut.   Source: 7
Joined the 35th as a Lieut. on March 12, 1862. He resigned on Nov. 26, 1862 due to physical disability. He had chronic diarrhea and other ailments.

McELYEA, J.A.   Co. A   Rank: Pvt.   Source: 7
Joined the 35th on March 14, 1862 at Florence, Ala. Captured at the Battle of Corinth, Miss. on Oct. 3 or 4, 1862. Placed on board the steamer "Dacotah" with 539 POW's and exchanged near Vicksburg, Miss. on Oct. 18, 1862. Discharged on Jan. 18, 1864 due to a double hernia. He was born in Lauderdale Co. Ala. and was 35 years old when discharged. he was 5'9" tall, had dark complexion, hair and eyes. He had been a farmer.

McELYEA, W.H.   Co. A   Rank: Pvt.   Source: 7
Enlisted Sept. 1, 1862 at Florence, Ala. On Nov. 1, 1863 he was at Jackson's Division Hospital at Old Marion, Miss. Admitted to Breckinridge's Division Hospital #2 at lauderdale Springs, Miss. as a patient on Dec. 13, 1863. He was still there on Dec. 31, 1863.

McGATA, J.C.   Co. F   Rank: Pvt.   Source: 7
Captured in the fall of Vicksburg, Miss. on July 4, 1863. Paroled on July 6 and released.

McGAUGHY, C.S.   Co. C   Rank: ?   Source: 7
Joined Capt. Ashford's Co. in March 1862.

McILWIN, J.W.   Co. A   Rank: Pvt.   Source: 7
Captured May 1, 1865 at New Orleans, la. Exchanged May 23, 1865.

McKIMON, W.   Co. G   Rank: Pvt.   Source: 7
Wounded in the left side by a "ball" at the Battle of Franklin, Tenn. on Nov. 30, 1864 and captured. Admitted to the USA General Hospital in Nashville, Tenn. on Dec. 26, 1864. He was 22 years old at the time.

McLOUGHLIN, HENRY B.   Co. A   Rank: 2nd Lieut.   Source: 7
He was part of a detail sent to North Ala. on Nov. 21, 1862 to recruit. Captured May 17, 1863 at the Battle of Champion Hill, Miss. Listed as AWOL on May 16, 1863. He took the "Oath" at Johnson's Island, Ohio on Jan. 24, 1865. He was from Florence, Ala. had light complexion, dark hair, gray eyes and was 5'7" tall. There is a note in the file which reads; "Was born in Indianapolis, Ind. Joined the 35th as a private July 1, 1861 in which capacity he served until the following Oct. 1862, when he was promoted 2nd Lieut. of his Company, and served as such until he was captured May 17, 1863. Say's he was always for the Union for which reason he was obliged to join the Conf. Army, as they were suspicious of him and would not allow him to sell his property and return North as he wished to do. That

he was elected Lieut. by the influence of a relative and also by becoming popular with the men. He wishes to take the "Oath" as he was never a rebel and always opposed to secession. Says he tried to desert several time but was watched by a vigilance committee so that no opportunity presented it's self."

McMAHAN, L.H. Co. A Rank: Pvt. Source: 7
Captured in the fall of Vicksburg, Miss. on July 4, 1863 while in Gen. Smith's Division CSA Hospital. Died July 24, 1863. He was born in Ala.

McMURTRY, CURTIS Co. A Rank: Pvt. Source: 7
Enlisted by Capt. Mitchell on Dec. 1, 1862 in Lauderdale, Ala. He was a patient in the General Hospital at Point Clear, Baldwin Co. Ala. on Aug. 31, 1863.

McWILLIAMS, S.A. See WILLIAMS, SAMUEL

MEADOWS, A.M. Co. G Rank: ? Source: 7
No other information.

MEADOWS, RILEY B. Co. ? Rank: Pvt. Source: 7
Joined the 35th on March 18, 1862. He was from Marshall Co. Tenn. He said he deserted on Dec. 28, 1864 and had no family. He took the "Oath of Allegiance" at Nashville, Tenn. on Jan. 27, 1865. He had fair complexion, sandy hair, hazel eyes and was 5'5" tall.

MEADOWS, TERRY H. Co. G Rank: Pvt. Source: 7
Joined Capt. West's Co. on March 18, 1862. He was from Marshall Co. Tenn. He said he deserted on Dec. 28, 1864 and had no family. He signed the "Oath" at Nashville, Tenn. on Jan. 27, 1865. He had fair complexion, sandy hair, gray eyes and was 5'4" tall.

MELER, J.M. Co. A Rank: Pvt. Source: 7
Received pay from March 15 thru Aug. 31, 1862. He was a teamster from Jan. 1 thru June 1, 1863, and was paid an extra 25 cents per day.

MEYERS, JAMES S. Co. H Rank: Pvt. Source: 7
From Lawrence Co. Ala. Admitted to the 1st Miss. CSA Hospital at Jackson on June 9, 186(?) with chronic diarrhea. Sent to the General Hospital on July 7. Admitted to Ocmulgee Hospital at Macon, Ga. on July 5, 1864 with diarrhea. Furloughed on July 16, 1864.

MIERS, WILLIAM Co. A Rank: Pvt. Source: 7
Captured near Columbia, Tenn. on Dec. 22, 1864 by a Cavalry Troop. Sent to Louisville and Camp Chase, Ohio. Died (?) 28, 1865. Buried in grave 983.

MILLER, BURGESS M. Co. F Rank: Pvt. Source: 1,7
Joined the 35th on April 1, 1862 at Marysville, Ala. Captured in the fall of Vicksburg, Miss. on July 4, 1863. He signed his parole and was released July 7, 1863, but was no longer fit for duty.

MILLER, J.A.   Co. F   Rank: Pvt.   Source: 7
Signed for an issue of clothing on Aug. 3, 1863. Listed as a deserter on March 1864.

MILLER, W.   Co. D   Rank: ?   Source: 7
Joined Capt. Sanders' Co. in March 1862.

MINCHEW, J.J.   Co. D   Rank: Cpl.   Source: 7
Given 30 days furlough on Jan. 9, 1863.

MINER, JOSEPH R.   Co. G   Rank: Pvt.   Source: 7
Joined Capt. West's Co. in March 1862. Signed for an issue of clothing on April 24, 1863. On that same day he entered St. Mary's Hospital in Dalton, Ga. with "debilitas" or extreme weakness of the body. Returned to duty May 6, 1863. Captured at Murfreesboro, Tenn. on Aug. 16, 1863 and was sent to Louisville, Ky. and Camp Chase, Ohio where he arrived Sept. 5, 1863. On Jan. 14, 1864 he was sent to Rock Island Barracks, Ill. On Oct. 17, 1864 he enlisted in the U.S. Army for "frontier service".

MITCHELL, JOHN D.   Co. G   Rank: Pvt.   Source: 7
Joined Capt. West's Co. on March 18, 1862. He signed the "Oath" at Nashville, Tenn. on March 19, 1865 and stated that he deserted on Dec. 23, 1864 and had no family. He was from Limestone, Co. Ala, had fair complexion, light hair, gray eyes and wad 5'11" tall.

MITCHELL, JOHN ROBERT   Co. A   Rank: Capt.   Source: 1,2,3,7,9
Born May 31, 1835 at Lexington, Lauderdale Co. Ala. Entered the service as a 3rd Sgt. in Co. I, 9th Ala. Infty. Reg. on June 10, 1861 at Florence, Ala. He was paid as a 1st Lieut. in the 35th from March 17 thru July 1, 1862. Wounded at the battle of Corinth, Miss. on Oct. 2, 1862. In Aug. 1863 he was being paid as a Capt. There is a note in the file that states, (1) He was on detached service per Gen. Johnston, (2) Promoted to Capt. March 8, 1862. He served until the spring of 1865 when he surrendered at Decatur, Ala.

MITCHELL, RANDOLPH   Co. G   Rank: Pvt.   Source: 1,7
Born Nov. 16, 1834 in Limestone Co. Ala. Joined the 35th on March 20, 1862 at Athens, Ala. Captured near Nashville, Tenn. on Dec. 16, 1864 and was sent to Louisville, Ky. and on to Camp Chase, Ohio. He took the "Oath" on May 15, 1865 and was released. He had light complexion and hair, blue eyes and was 5'6" tall.

MITCHELL, W.H.   Co. E   Rank: Pvt.   Source: 7
Joined the 35th on Oct. 25, 1862 at Huntsville, Ala. Served at Breckinridge's Division Hospital #1 at Lauderdale Springs, Miss. as a nurse from June 22 thru Sept. 30, 1863. Attached to Hospital #2 as a carpenter Oct. 13, 1863. He signed for an issue of clothing on Oct. 26, 1863.

MONROE, T.M.   Co. I   Rank: ?   Source: 7
Joined Capt. Chisholm's Co. in March 1862.

MOODY, JAMES HENRY   Co. C   Rank: Pvt.   Source: 7

Joined Capt. Ashford's Co. in March 1862. Entered 1st Miss. CSA Hospital at Jackson on July 9, 1863 with chronic diarrhea, and was sent to the General Hospital the next day. Died Aug. 27, 1863 at Enterprise, Miss. He was from Ala.

MORAND, J.W.   Co. C   Rank: Cpl.   Source: 7
Joined Capt. Ashford's Co. in March 1862. Entered the 1st Miss. CSA Hospital at Jackson with Chronic diarrhea on Feb. 28, 1864. Returned to duty March 14, 1864.

MORGAN, J.   Co. E   Rank: Pvt.   Source: 7
He was a POW that was paroled at Talladega, Ala. on May 29, 1865.

MORRIS, WILLIAM H.   Co. C   Rank: Sgt.   Source: 7
Discharged Aug. 12, 1862. No other information given.

MORRISON, J.W.   Co. B   Rank: Pvt.   Source: 7
Joined the 35th on March 29, 1862 at LaGrange, Ala. Discharged Aug. 29, 1862. Born in Ala. about 1843, had fair Complexion, blue eyes, light hair and was 5'8" tall. He had been a farmer.

MORSELY, J.P.   Co. D   Rank: ?   Source: 7
Joined Capt. Sanders' Co. in March 1862.

MOSELEY, ANTHONY WADDY   Co. B   Rank: Pvt.   Source: 1,2,7
Joined Capt. Hunt's Co. March 12, 1862 at LaGrange, Ala. Had extra duty as acting Commissary Sgt. from Aug. 1 thru Nov. 30, 1863 for which he received an extra 25 cents per day. He was wounded at the battle of Franklin, Tenn. in Oct. 1864. He surrendered in 1865 at Danville, Morgan Co. Ala.

MOSS, JOSEPH   Co. A   Rank: Pvt.   Source: 7
Captured on Dec. 10, 1862 at Oxford, Miss. and was sent to the Military Prison in Alton, Ill. Died Jan. 16, 1863 of pneumonia. A death claim was filed by his father, Samuel Moss.

MURPHY, C.B.   Co. I   Rank: Pvt.   Source: 7
Joined the 35th on March 22, 1862. Captured and paroled on Oct. 3 or 4, 1862 at the battle of Corinth, Miss.

MURPHY, JAMES O.   Co. B   Rank: ?   Source: 2
Wounded at the battle of Franklin, Tenn. on Nov. 30, 1864.

MURPHY, R.J.   Co. ?   Rank: ?   Source: 7
No other information.

MYERS, WILLIAM   See MIERS, WILLIAM

NAIL, THOMAS J.   Co. D   Rank: Pvt.   Source: 7
Enlisted March 23, 1862 at Huntsville, Ala. On Oct. 31, 1863 he was at Breckinridge's Division Hospital at Marion, Miss. Captured Aug. 20, 1864 near Atlanta, Ga. Sent to Nashville, Louisville and on to Camp Chase,

Ohio, where he arrived Sept. 3, 1864. Signed the "Oath" and was released June 11, 1865. He was from Madison Co. Ala. had fair complexion, dark hair, gray eyes and wad 5'7" tall. He was 22 years old when released.

NEAL, FRANK   Co. B   Rank: ?   Source: 2,7
He was a Cadet at LaGrange and joined Capt. Hunt's Co. in March 1862.

NEAL, FRANKLIN   Co. E   Rank: ?   Source: 7
Captured at the battle of Champion Hill, Miss. on May 16, 1863. He was in the Mound City, Ill. Hospital in July and was then sent to Camp Morton, Ind. where he arrived July 22, 1863. Sent to Point Lookout, Md. for exchange on Feb. 19, 1865. Also see NOEL, FRANK.

NEAL, R.R.   Co. G   Rank: Sgt.   Source: 7
Joined Capt. West's Co. in March 1862. Discharged Oct. 25, 1862. No reason given.

NEELEY, J.G.   Co. A   Rank: ?   Source: 7
Born in Ala. Died Aug. 10, 1863 at Lauderdale, Miss.

NELMS, W.B.   Co. H   Rank: Pvt.   Source: 7,8
Joined the 35th on March 15, 1862 at LaGrange, Ala. Discharged July 15, 1862 due to disability. Rejoined the 35th in Aug. 1862, as a member of Co. I. He was born in Lawrence Co. Ala. and was 35 years old when discharged. He had dark complexion, blue eyes, light hair and was 6' tall. He was 72 years old and living in Leighton, Ala. when he applied for a pension.

NELSON, FREDERICK MOSLEY   Co. B   Rank: ?   Source: 2,6
Born May 22, 1845 in Athens, Ala. He was a Cadet at LaGrange Military Academy and joined the 35th in March 1862. He was discharged due to poor health in late 1862. He then joined Co. A of the 7th Tenn. Cav. He surrendered a Greensboro, N.C. in 1865. He was living in Memphis, Tenn. when he attended the LaGrange reunion on May 19, 1904. For more family information, see source 2.

NEWBY, HENRY J.   Co. G   Rank: Pvt.   Source: 7
Joined Capt. West's Co. on March 18, 1862. Captured June 29, 1864 near Athens, Ala. Sent to Louisville, Ky, then to Camp Morton, Ind. where he arrived July 7, 1864. Sent by B&O railroad to Point Lookout, Md. to be exchanged with 1011 POW's on March 23, 1865. Entered the General Hospital at Edwards Grove, Richmond, Va. the next day. He was released on March 27, 1865 and furloughed home. He was from Limestone Co. Ala. had fair complexion, dark hair, gray eyes and was 5'11" tall. He said he had a family in 1865.

NEWMAN, YANCY P.   Co. B   Rank: ?   Source: 2,6,7
He was from Huntsville, Ala. and was a Cadet at LaGrange Military Academy in Aug. 1860. Joined Capt. Hunt's Co. in March 1862. From Sept. 22 thru Nov. 20, 1863 he served as "acting hospital steward" Admitted to 1st Miss. CSA Hospital at Jackson on Feb. 28, 1864 with

117

acute rheumatism. After the war he lived in Huntsville and then moved to Birmingham, Ala. where he was a merchant. He died about 1904.

NEWNAN, H.M.   Co. I   Rank: ?   Source: 7
    Joined Capt. Chisholm's Co. in March 1862.

NICHOLSON, HENRY   Co. C   Rank: Pvt.   Source: 7
    Discharged Aug. 12, 1862. No other information given.

NICKELS, J.J.   Co. G   Rank: ?   Source: 7
    Joined Capt. West's Co. in March 1862.

NOEL, FRANK   Co. E   Rank: ?   Source: 7
    He was a POW that arrived at Mound City, Ill aboard the steamer "Crescent City" and was admitted to the USA General Hospital on June 1, 1863. NOTE: This may be the same person as NEAL, FRANKLIN.

NUNN, J.E.   Co. D   Rank: Coms'y Sgt. Source: 7
    Joined Capt. Sanders' Co. on March 20, 1862 at LaGrange, Ala. Captured in the fall of Vicksburg, Miss. on July 4, 1863. He signed his parole on July 7, 1863. By April 30, 1864 he was part of Co. C. of the 1st Detachment of Paroled Prisoners at Demopolis, Ala.

O'BRYAN, WILSON JOSEPH   Co. I   Rank: Pvt.   Source: 1,7
    Born April 4, 1844 at Cloverdale, Lauderdale Co. Ala. Joined the 35th on March 22, 1862 at Florence, Ala. He states that he "Served in another place the first 12 months." (Could be the Franklin Blues of the 9th Ala.) From Jan. thru March 1863 he was a teamster. From May thru June 1863 he was attached to Co. A of the 24th S.C. Vol. He was then with the 35th again until the end. Discharged at Tuscumbia, Ala.

ODELL, THOMAS   Co. I   Rank: Pvt.   Source: 7
    Joined Capt. Chisholm's Co. in March 1862. Discharged July 15, 1862.

ODEM, ELIJAH M.   Co. D   Rank: Pvt.   Source: 7
    Joined the 35th on March 20, 1862 at LaGrange, Ala. On Dec. 5, 1862 he is attached to City Hall Hospital at Jackson, Miss. as a nurse. Captured in the fall of Vicksburg, Miss. on July 4, 1863. By April 30, 1864 he is part of Co. C of the 1st Detachment of Paroled Prisoners. Captured near nashville on Dec. 16, 1864. Died Jan. 2, 1865 enroute to Louisville Military Prison. He is buried in grave 107, Range 1, in Cave Hill Cemetery in Louisville, Ky.

ODEM, D.S.   Co. D   Rank: Pvt.   Source: 7
    Joined Capt. Sanders' Co. in March 1862.

OLD, HENRY D. (or N.)   Co. B   Rank: ?   Source: 2,7
    He was a Cadet at LaGrange and joined Capt. Hunt's Co. in March 1862.

OLIVER, JOHN C.   Co. D   Rank: Pvt.   Source: 1,7
    Born Sept. 30, 1841 in Virginia. Joined Capt. Sanders' Co. in March 1862 at Athens, Ala. Admitted to CSA General Hospital # 1 at Charlotte, N.C.

on April 10, 1865 with typhoid fever. Paroled at Talladega, Ala. May 17, 1865.

O'NEAL, A.J.   Co. F   Rank: Pvt.   Source: 7
Captured May 16 or 17, 1863 at Big Black River (Champion Hill), Miss. and was sent to Memphis, Camp Morton, Ind. and then on to Ft. Delaware, Del. He was to be paroled on July 6, 1863, but was "left in hospital at Ft. Delaware".

ORRILL, J.W.   Co. I   Rank: Pvt.   Source: 7
Received pay from March 1 thru June 30, 1863.

PAINE, GEORGE W.   Co. C   Rank: Pvt.   Source: 7
Joined Capt. Ashford's Co. in March 1862. Captured May 16 or 18, 1863 near Big Black River, Miss. Sent to Ft. Delaware, Del. and exchanged at City Point, Va. on July 6, 1863 with 1697 POW's.

PARHAM, GEORGE W.   Co. D   Rank: Pvt.   Source: 7
Joined Capt. Sanders' Co. on March 21, 1862. Discharged Oct. 29, 1862 because he had "phthisis palmonalis" He was born in Limestone Co. Ala. and was 33 years old when discharged. He had fair complexion, gray eyes, light hair and was 5'10" tall. He had been a farmer.

PARKE, M.   Co. A   Rank: Sgt.   Source: 7
He passed thru General Hospital # 9 in Richmond, Va. on Feb. 27, 1865.

PARKER, W.   Co. C   Rank: Pvt.   Source: 7
Joined Capt. Ashford's Co. in March 1862. Killed at the battle of Baton Rouge, La. on Aug. 5, 1862.

PATTERSON, BENJAMIN   Co. E   Rank: 2nd Lieut.   Source: 1,7
Joined the 35th in March 1862 as a private at Huntsville, Ala. He was appointed Sgt. and then elected 2nd Lieut of Co. B. at Grenada, Miss. on Jan. 7, 1863. Sept. 1, 1863 thru April 1, 1864 he received 40 cents per day "for use and risk of horse". His pay from March 1 thru Aug. 31, 1864 was $80.00 per month. He stayed with the unit thru the period of Consolidation and was with Johnson's Army when it surrendered at Greensboro, N.C. He surrender at Huntsville, Ala. in 1865.

PATTERSON, JACKSON   Co. I   Rank: ?   Source: 7
Died prior to March 1864, leaving $4.00 in cash.

PATTERSON, JAMES ANDREW   Co. K   Rank: Pvt.   Source: 7
No other information.

PATTON, J.B.   Co. I   Rank: Capt.   Source: 3,7,11
Wounded at the Battle of Franklin, Tenn. He was a 1st Lieut. on July 31, 1864, with pay of $90.00 per month. Paroled at Meridian, Miss. on May 13, 1865.

PATTON, SAMUEL   Co. I   Rank: Pvt.   Source: 7

119

Joined Capt. Chisholm's Co. in March 1862. Discharged May 10, 1962.

PAYNE, D.W.   See PAINE, GEORGE W.

PEACE, JAMES P.   Co. G   Rank: Pvt.   Source: 7
Joined Capt. West's Co. on March 18, 1862 at Athens, Ala. Discharged
Oct. 21, 1862 due to "phthisis retmonalis" He was born in Limestone Co.
Ala. and was 19 years old when discharged. He had fair complexion, blue
eyes, light hair and was 5'7" tall. He had been a farmer.

PEACE, M.N.   Co. G   Rank: Pvt.   Source: 7
Joined Capt. West's Co. on March 18, 1862 at Athens, Ala. Discharged
Oct. 30, 1862 at 21 years of age. He was from Limestone Co. Ala. and
was 5'5" tall, had fair complexion, gray eyes, dark hair and had been a
farmer.

PEDEN, W.W.   Co. B   Rank: Pvt.   Source: 7
Joined Capt. Hunt's Co. in March 1862. Discharged May 14, 1862.

PEEBLES, THOMAS W   Co. B   Rank: Sgt.   Source: 2,6,7
He was a Cadet at LaGrange Military Academy until March 1862 when he
joined Capt. Hunt's Co. On Feb. 1, 1864 he requested a commission and
assignment to a cavalry division. he received no reply. Killed at the battle
of Franklin, Tenn. in Oct. 1864.

PEETE, SAMUEL   Co. D   Rank: Pvt.   Source: 7
Joined Capt. Sander's Co. on March 20, 1862 at Mooresville, Ala. Born in
Limestone Co. Ala. Admitted to French's Division Hospital at Lauderdale
Springs, Miss. as a patient on July 1, 1863. He had chronic rheumatism
and was detailed for hospital duty on Aug. 20, 1863. In Sept. he was a
cook. Oct. thru Dec. 1863 he was a nurse at the hospital in lauderdale
Springs and was paid $7.50 per month. By Aug. 1863 he was 29 years
old, 6'3" tall, had fair complexion, blue eyes and light hair. He had been a
lawyer.

PEEVEY, ROBERT W.   Co. F   Rank: Capt.   Source: 3,4,7
From Jackson Co. Ala. He was elected Capt. of Co. F when the 35th was
formed. His pay from March 20 thru June 30, 1862 was $130.00 per
month. He resigned Nov. 6, 1862 due to chronic inflammation of the liver
and kidney.

PENCE, ALLEN   Co. F   Rank: Pvt.   Source: 7
Received pay for service from July 21, 1862 thru Feb. 28, 1863 at $11.00
per month. A note on his pay voucher states "soldier furloughed home
from General Hospital Braudon(?), Miss."

PETTIFORD, J.W.   Co. I   Rank: ?   Source: 7
Joined Capt. Chisholm's Co. in March 1862.

PETTITT, BENJAMIN   Co. A   Rank: Pvt.   Source: 7
Joined the 35th on April 2, 1862 at Scoton (?), Ala. Discharged at age 18
on Sept. 6, 1862, due to chronic diarrhea. He was born in lauderdale Co.

Ala. and was 5'9" tall, had fair complexion, blue eyes, light hair and had been a farmer. His name appears on a list of clothing left by deceased soldiers at Gate City Hospital in Atlanta, Ga. The list is dated June 6, 1863.

PETTUS, S.J.   Co. D   Rank: ?   Source: 7
Joined Capt. Sander's Co. in March 1862. He was born in Ala. and died Sept. 27, 1863 from Typhoid fever at Morton, Miss.

PETTUS, W.D.   Co. D   Rank: ?   Source: 7
Joined Capt. Sander's Co. in March 1862.

PHELPS, J.M.   Co. E   Rank: Pvt.   Source: 7
Listed as a deserter in March 1864.

PHILLIPS, J.M.   Co. I   Rank: Pvt.   Source: 7
Joined Capt. Chisholm's Co. in March 1862.

PICKETT, RICHARD 0.   Co. H   Rank: Capt.   Source: 2,3,4,7
He was from Lawrence Co. Ala. Elected Capt. of Co. H when the 35th was formed. He was captured at Corinth, Miss. Exchanged Oct. 9, 1862 on board the steamer "Louis D'Or" near Baton Rouge, La. He was a lawyer, politician and orator. On Aug. 7, 1863 all the officers of the 35th as well as the 27th, signed a letter recommending Pickett as Judge Advocate. No reply was received. Resigned to become Col of the 10th Ala. Cav.

PIKE, JEFF   Co. G   Rank: Pvt.   Source: 7
Captured at Talahoma, Miss.(?) on July 4, 1863 and sent to Camp Douglas, Ill.

PITTS, J.M.   Co. F   Rank: Pvt.   Source: 7
Wounded in the hand at the battle of Baton Rouge, La. on Aug. 5, 1862.

PITTS, JOHN B.   Co. I   Rank: Pvt.   Source: 7
Born in Ala. Died Aug. 15, 1863 at Lauderdale, Miss. of chronic diarrhea.

PONDER, W.J.   Co. C   Rank: ?   Source: 7
Joined Capt. Ashford's Co. in March 1862.

POPE, JAMES   Co. B   Rank: ?   Source: 2
On other information.

POPE, ROBERT   Co. B   Rank: ?   Source: 2,6
He was from LaGrange, Ala. and was a Cadet at LaGrange Military Academy in Aug. 1860. He died in the service.

POPE, W.H.   Co. B   Rank: ?   Source: 2,7
He was from Tenn. and was a Cadet at LaGrange Military Academy in Aug. 1860. Joined Capt. Hunt's Co. in March 1862.

POTER, R.B.   Co. C   Rank: Sgt.   Source: 7

He was a wagonmaster during the month of Oct. 1863. On Nov, 13, 1863 he was transferred to Capt. May's Co. of Col. Patterson's Ala. Cav. and was commissioned a 2nd Lieut.

POUNDER, PRESTON   Co. A   Rank: Pvt.   Source: 7
Captured in the fall of Vicksburg, Miss. on July 4, 1863. Paroled on July 13, 1863.

PREWITT, MARSHALL P.   Co. I   Rank: Pvt.   Source: 7
Joined the 35th on March 22, 1862 at Florence, Ala. He was 19 years old when discharged on Sept. 23, 1862 due to "Phthisis Pulmonalia" (bad lungs". He was born in Lauderdale Co. Ala. had fair complexion, hazel eyes, brown hair and was 5'11" tall. He had been a farmer.The records also indicate he signed the "Oath" on March 8, 1865 and was released.

PRICE, JAMES R.   Co. A   Rank: Pvt.   Source: 7
Wounded severely in the chest at the battle of Baton Rouge, La. on Aug. 5, 1862. From Jan. 1 thru Sept. 30, 1863 he served as Adj't Clerk and earned an extra 25 cents per day.

PRICE, JOHN H.   Co. ?   Rank: Sgt.   Source: 7
He was from Tenn. He took the "Oath" on Feb. 1, 1864 saying he deserted on Oct. 15, 1864 and had a family. He had fair Complexion, light hair, blue eyes and was 5'9" tall.

PRIDE, ISAAC L.   Co. ?   Rank: Capt.   Source: 4,5,7
He was elected Commissary Sgt. on March 20, 1862, when the 35th was forming. He was promoted to Capt. on May 15, 1862, and was made Brigade Commissary Officer. He was captured in the fall of Vicksburg, Miss. on July 4, 1863. By April 1864 he was at the "Parole Camp" at Demopolis, Ala.

PRIEST, R.   Co. C   Rank: ?   Source: 7
Joined Capt. Ashford's Co. in March 1862.

PRIEST, SAMUEL   Co. H   Rank: Pvt.   Source: 7
Died in 1864 leaving $13.00 in cash.

PRIEST, WILLIAM   Co. C   Rank: Pvt.   Source: 7
Captured near Columbia, Tenn. on Dec. 22, 1864 and was sent to Louisville, Ky. and then Camp Chase, Ohio, where he signed the "Oath" on June 12, 1865. He was 32 years old at the time. He was from Lawrence Co. Ala. had dark complexion and hair with brown eyes.

PROTECT, SAMUEL   Co. A   Rank: Pvt.   Source: 7
No other information.

PROVENCE, RUBEN   Co. A   Rank: Pvt.   Source: 7
Captured near Nashville, Tenn. on Dec. 16, 1864 and sent to Louisville, Ky. and on to Camp Chase, Ohio. He died in the hospital at Camp Chase on Feb. 23, 1865 of pneumonia. Buried in grave #1393, 1/3 mile South of the camp.

PRUITT, ROBERT W.   Co. B   Rank: Pvt.   Source: 2,6,7

He was from Meridianville, Ala. and was a Cadet at LaGrange Military Academy in Aug. 1860. Joined Capt. Hunt's Co. on March 12, 1862 at LaGrange. Ala. On Feb. 28, 1864 he entered the 1st Miss. CSA Hospital at Jackson with chronic diarrhea. Surrendered at Citronelle, Ala. on May 4, 1865 and was paroled at Meridian, Miss. on May 13.

PUTMAN, S.   Co. A   Rank: Pvt.   Source: 7

He was a teamster from March 17 thru May 20, 1863. Listed as a deserter in March 1864.

PYLES, J. L.   Co. C   Rank: Pvt.   Source: 7

No other information.

RAMBERT, M.H.   Co. G   Rank: Pvt.   Source: 7

Joined Capt. West's Co. in March 1862 at LaGrange, Ala.

RAMBO, J.M.   Co. B   Rank: Pvt.   Source: 7

Joined Capt. Hunt's Co. in March 1862.

RAPER, JESSE   Co. C   Rank: Pvt.   Source: 7

Joined Capt. Ashford's Co. in March 1862 at LaGrange, Ala. He was captured around Corinth, Miss sometime between Sept. 19 & Oct. 6, 1862.

RATHER, JOHN WILLIAM   Co. B   Rank: 2nd Lieut.   Source: 1,27,8

He was born Dec. 14, 1828 at Elkton, Giles Co. Tenn. By May 8, 1862 he was with the 35th. In Dec. 1862 his pay was $80.00 per month. he continued with the unit until May 1865 and was paroled at Pond Springs, Ala. He was alive and living in Spring Valley in 1907.

RAY, GEORGE H.   Co. B   Rank: Pvt.   Source: 7

Employed as a teamster at Canton, Miss in Nov. and Dec. 1863.

REDDIN, ALLEN   Co. B   Rank: Pvt.   Source: 2,7

Listed as a deserter on March 19, 1864.

REDUS, WILLIAM M.   Co. G   Rank: 1st Lieut.   Source: 7

Joined the 35th on March 18, 1862. His pay was $90.00 per month. Died Aug. 8, 1862.

RENICK, J.A.   Co. H   Rank: Pvt.   Source: 7

Admitted to the 1st Miss. C.S.A. Hospital at Jackson, Miss. on Feb. 28, 1864 with diarrhea. Returned to duty March 14, 1864.

RICE, GEORGE N.   Co. A   Rank: Pvt.   Source: 2,7

Killed at the battle of Baton Rouge, La. on Aug. 5, 1862.

RICHARDSON, GEORGE E.   Co. B   Rank: Pvt.   Source: 2,8

He was born about 1840 and joined the 35th in Oct. 1862. He was living in Tuscumbia, Ala. in 1901.

RICHARDSON, J. HENRY P.   Co. B   Rank: Pvt.   Source: 2,7
          Joined Capt. Hunt's Co. on March 25, 1862 at LaGrange, Ala. Entered
          Walker's Div. Hospital at Lauderdale, Miss. on July 16, 1863, and was
          there thru Aug. 31. Sept. and Oct. of 1863, he is shown at Jackson's Cav.
          Div. Hospital at Old Marion, Miss. He is listed as "sick". Pay was $11.00
          per month.

RIDDLE, HENRY O.   Co. C   Rank: Pvt.   Source: 7
          He may have been with the 35th Miss., not the 35th Ala.

RIGGANS, W.   Co. E   Rank: Pvt.   Source: 7
          He was from Bibb Co. Ala. He surrendered in May 1865 and was paroled
          at Selma, Ala. on May 28, 1865.

RITCHESON, H.S.   Co. B   Rank: Pvt.   Source: 7
          He was wounded and captured at the battle of Champion Hill (Big Black
          River), Miss. on May 16, 1863.

ROBARTS, N.   Co. D   Rank: ?   Source: 7
          Joined Capt. Sanders' Co. in March 1862 at LaGrange, Ala.

ROBERTS, MATHEW Z.   Co. C   Rank: 4th Sgt.   Source: 1,7
          Born Feb. 27, 1835 near Mooresville, Limestone Co. Ala. Joined the 35th
          at LaGrange, Ala. in 1862. Captured May 11, 1864 at Morrisville, Ala. He
          was sent to Louisville, Ky. and on to a POW camp at Rock Island, Ill.
          where he arrived June 1, 1864. On May 3, 1865 he was sent to New
          Orleans, La and exchanged "at the mouth of the Red River" on May 23,
          1865.

ROBERTSON, G.C.   Co. G   Rank: ?   Source: 7
          Joined Capt. West's Co. at LaGrange, Ala. in March 1862.

ROBERTSON, JAMES W.   Reg. 35th Rank: Col.   Source: 2,3,4,5,6,7
          He was from Marietta, Ga. and was Superintendent of LaGrange Military
          Academy as well as Professor of Engineering, before the 35th was
          formed. He was elected Col. of the 35th when it was organized.
          Resigned on Nov. 12, 1862 due to illness. Jan. 5, 1863 he was assigned
          to duties in the Engineering Det. of the Confederate Army and sent to
          Mobil, Ala. to take charge of the defense of the lower bay. Later he was
          sent to Charleston, S.C. in 1864 he was sent to Florida and placed in
          charge of fortifications. After taking up his new duties, he always signed
          himself as "Col., 35th Ala." His pay was $195.00 per month. After the
          war, he was placed in charge of rebuilding some of the railroads in Fla.,
          Ga., and Ala. He was appointed Railway Commissioner of the state of
          Ga. in 1880. He was living in Marietta, Ga. on Jan. 25th 1905.

ROBERTSON, JOHN TIRY   Co. A   Rank: Pvt.   Source: 1,7
          Born Nov. 7, 1838 at Greenhill, Ala. Joined Capt. Ives's Co. on March 17,
          1862 at Florence, Ala. and served until March 1864. During July and Aug.
          1863 he was at Breckinridge's Div. Hospital at Marion, Miss. He was listed
          as a deserter in March 1864. He stated he "resigned at Franklin, Tenn."

(Oct. 1864.)

ROBERTSON, N.F.   Co. D   Rank: Pvt.   Source: 7
Recruited March 20, 1862 by Col. J.W. Robertson. During Sept. and Oct. 1863, he was in Jackson's Cavalry Div. Hospital at Old Marion, Miss.

ROBINSON, GALE C.   Co. C   Rank: Sgt.   Source: 7
He was wounded nov. 30, 1864 by a "gun shot fracture of the right ankle joint" at the battle of Franklin, Tenn. Captured on Dec. 18, 1864 at Columbia, Tenn. He was sent to Louisville, Ky on Feb. 25, 1865 and on to Camp Chase, Ohio where he arrived on March 5th. March 25, 1865, he was sent to Point Lookout, Md. He died June 14, 1865 of chronic diarrhea and buried in POW grave #2129 at Point Lookout.

ROBINSON, IRA   Co. G   Rank: Sgt.   Source: 7
Captured on Dec. 15, 1864 near Nashville, Tenn. He was sent to the Military Prison in Louisville, Ky. and on to Camp Douglas on Dec. 20, 1864

ROBINSON, RICHMOND L.   Co. G   Rank: Pvt.   Source: 7
He may have been in the 35th Miss.

ROBINSON, SILAS   Co. ?   Rank: Pvt.   Source: 7
Lived in Giles Co. Tenn. He had fair complexion, dark hair, blue eyes and was 5'61/2" tall. He joined the 35th on Jan. 20, 1863. He stated he deserted on March 4, 1865. Took the "Oath of Allegiance" on May 9, 1865 and indicated he had a family.

ROBINSON, S.T.   Co. A   Rank: Pvt.   Source: 7
He was wounded on Aug. 5, 1862 at the battle of Baton Rouge, Al.

ROBINSON, THOMAS H.   Co. A   Rank: Pvt.   Source: 7
Captured near Big Black River Bridge, Miss. on May 16 or 17, 1863. Arrived at Ft. Delaware, Del. on June 9, 1863 and was exchanged July 6, 1863.

ROBINSON, W.N.   Co. G   Rank: Pvt.   Source: 7
Joined Capt. West's Co. at LaGrange, Ala. on March 31, 1862. Listed as a deserter in March 1863.

ROCHEL, E.S.   Co. G   Rank: Pvt.   Source: 7
Joined Capt. West's Co. at LaGrange, Ala. on March 31, 1862. From Aug. 1 to Aug. 31, 1862 he was a nurse at the Blind Asylum Hospital in Jackson, Miss.

ROGERS, WILLIAM   Co. D   Rank: Pvt.   Source: 7
From Nov. 1, 1863 to June 30, 1864 his pay was $18.00 per month.

ROMINE, W.M.   Co. B   Rank: Pvt.   Source: 7
Joined Capt. Hunt's Co. at LaGrange, Ala. on March 31, 1862. Died July 1, 1862.

ROSCO, JOHN W.   Co. I   Rank: Pvt.   Source: 7

Joined the 35th at Florence, Ala. on Feb. 16, 1864. Admitted as a patient to the 1st Miss. CSA Hospital at Jackson and was transferred to a hospital in Shelby Springs, Ala. He was there thru Aug. 31, 1864 with "Hemephlegia".

ROSS, RUBEN M.   Co. I   Rank: Pvt.   Source: 7
Joined Capt. Chisholm's Co. at LaGrange, Ala. in March 1862. He was captured near Corinth, Miss. between Sept. 19 and Oct. 6, 1862. Sent to Columbus, Ky on Oct. 9, 1862 On Oct. 18th he was with 539 POW's on the steamer "Dacotah" to be exchanged at Vicksburg, Miss. on Nov. 8, 1862.

RUSSELL, G.D.   Co. B   Rank: ?   Source: 2,6,7
He was from Pickens Co. Ala. and was a Cadet at LaGrange Military in Aug. 1860. Joined Capt. Hunt's Co. in March 1862. For more information, see source 6.

RUSSELL, J.E.   Co. D   Rank: Pvt.   Source: 7
Joined Capt. Sanders' Co. at LaGrange, Ala. in March 1862. Discharged June 15, 1862. No reason given.

RUSSELL, W.A.   Co. D   Rank: Pvt.   Source: 4,7
He was from Madison Co. Ala. and was a Cadet Drill Instructor at LaGrange Military Academy before the 35th was formed. He joined Capt. Sanders' Co. on March 20, 1862. His pay was $11.00 per month.

SANDEFUR, T.B.   Co. D   Rank: Pvt.   Source: 7
Discharged July 10, 1862. No other information.

SANDLIN, JAMES W.   Co. C   Rank: Pvt.   Source: 7
His pay from April 2, 1862 thru June 30, 1862 was $11.00 per month.

SAUNDERS, W.T.   Co. D   Rank: Capt.   Source: 2,4,5,7
He was from Limestone Co. Ala. Joined the 35th on March 12, 1862 and was elected Capt. of Co. D. when the 35th was formed. He was made Regimental Surgeon on March 20, 1862, as he was a medical doctor. Resigned Aug. 28, 1862.

SCHRIMSHER, THOMAS M.   Co. F   Rank: 2nd Lieut.   Source: 7
He was from Madison Co. Ala. and was born in 1843. He was 5'11" tall, had dark complexion, hazel eyes, dark hair and was a farmer. Enlisted at Maysville, Ala. on March 10, 1862. Elected 2nd Lieut. on Nov. 25, 1862. He received 30 days furlough on March 20, 1863. As of Oct. 1863 no one had heard from him. He was dropped from the roster on Nov. 23, 1863.

SCRIMPSHER, WILLIAM A.   Co. F   Rank: Pvt.   Source: 7
Enlisted in the 35th at Maysville, Ala. on March 20, 1862. by Col. Lowe. Employed as a teamster from jan. 1, 1863 to June 1, 1863 and earned an extra 25 cents per day. Sept. 1, 1863 he is listed as a nurse at Loring's Div. Hospital in Lauderdale, Miss. He hospital moved to meridian, Miss. where he remained a nurse thru Jan. 1864.

SCRIMSCHER, ANDERSON Co. F   Rank: Cpl.   Source: 1
Joined the 35th in March 1862 at Marysville, Ala. and was with the unit until the surrender in 1865.

SCRIMSCHER, RUSSELL JAMES Co. F   Rank: ?   Source: 1
Joined Co. E. of the 37th Tenn. Infantry in July 1861 at New Hope, Ala. He was with that unit until Sept. 1864. At that point, at Jonesboro, Ga. he was transferred to Co. F. of the 35th Ala., but was "not able to do any more service on account of wounds".

SCRIMSHEW, S. Co. F   Rank: Pvt.   Source: 7
Listed as a deserter in March 1864.

SEAMENS, J.C. Co. C   Rank: Pvt.   Source: 7
Captured near Corinth, Miss. sometime between Sept. 19 and Oct. 6, 1862.

SHARP, ANDREW JACKSON Co. F   Rank: Pvt.   Source: 1
Born Nov. 19, 1838 in Madison Co. Ala. Joined the 35th in March 1862 at Maysville, Ala. and stayed with the unit until Oct. 1864. Died Feb. 24, 1919 in Cleveland Co. Okla. Buried at Ft. Townsen, Okla.

SHARP, WILLIAM H. Co. F   Rank: Pvt.   Source: 7
He was from Madison Co. Ala. and had fair complexion, dark hair, hazel eyes and was 5'9" tall. Surrendered on May 10, 1865 at Huntsville, Ala. He took the "Oath" and returned home on May 11.

SHARPLESS, JAMES Co. A   Rank: Pvt.   Source: 7
Captured May 16, 1863 at Champion Hill (Big Black River), Miss. Arrived at Ft. Delaware, Del. on June 9, 1863 and was exchanged at City Point, Md. on July 6, 1863 with 1697 CSA POW's.

SHEPHARD, C.D. Co. D   Rank: Pvt.   Source: 7
His name appears on a list of people enrolled into Capt. Sanders' Co. dated March 31, 1862 at LaGrange, Ala. He was discharged Aug. 13, 1862.

SHERRED, HENRY J. Co. I   Rank: Pvt.   Source: 7
Captured at Champion Hill (Big Black River), Miss. on May 16, 1863. Sent to Camp Morton, Ind. and on to Ft. Delaware, Del. where he arrived on June 9, 1863. He was exchanged July 6, 1863 with 1697 CSA POW's at City Point, Va.

SHERROLD, J. Co. C   Rank: Pvt.   Source: 7
Listed as a deserter on Feb. 29, 1864.

SHILTON, SAMSON Co. A   Rank: Pvt.   Source: 7
Captured between Sept. 19 and Oct. 6, 1862. He was sent to Columbus, Ky. on Oct. 9 and exchanged on Nov. 8, 1862.

SILES, J.M. Co. I   Rank: Pvt.   Source: 7
Joined the 35th on March 26, 1862.

SIMMONS, C.J.   Co. A   Rank: ?   Source: 7
Died July 11, 1863 as a CSA POW at Memphis, Tenn.

SIMMONS, CALVIN J.   Co. I   Rank: Pvt.   Source: 7
Captured at Big Black River Bridge (Champion Hill), Miss. on May 16, 1863 and was sent to Memphis, Tenn. to Camp Morton, Ind. and then to Ft. Delaware, Del. where he arrived June 9th. He was exchanged July 6, 1863.

SIMMONS, JAMES CALLOWAY   Co. C   Rank: Pvt.   Source: 7
His name appears on a roster of men enrolled in Capt. Ashford's Co. dated March 31, 1862 at LaGrange, Ala. He was captured on Oct. 3 or 4, 1862 at the battle of Corinth, Miss. He was either wounded or acting as a nurse at the time. He was captured again on May 17 at Big Black River (Champion Hill), Miss. and sent to Memphis, Tenn. where he arrived May 25, 1863. He was then sent to Camp Morton, Ind. and on to Ft. Delaware, Del. where he arrived June 9, 1863. He signed his parole there on July 3rd and was exchanged at City Point, Va. on July 6, 1863.

SIMMONS, W.S.   Co. C   Rank: ?   Source: 7
His name appears on a list of men enrolled in Capt. Ashford's Co. dated March 31, 1862 at LaGrange, Ala.

SIMMS, A.M.   Co. H   Rank: Pvt.   Source: 7
Joined Capt. Pickett's Co. March 6, 1862. He was born in Lawrence Co. Ala. about 1834, had dark complexion, black eyes and hair and was 5'10" tall. He was a blacksmith before joining the 35th. He was wounded in the battle of Corinth, Miss. and had a limb amputated. Discharged Oct. 30, 1862.

SIMPSON, JAMES E.   Co. G   Rank: Pvt.   Source: 7
Joined the 35th on March 18, 1862 at Athens, Ala. Discharged Sept. 28, 1863 as he had been ill for 2 months. He was born in Limestone Co. Ala. about 1842. He had dark complexion, gray eyes, dark hair, was 6'2" tall and a carpenter before signing up. He was "physically disabled" on Sept. 22, 1862.

SIMPSON, J.W.   Co. ?   Rank: Ord. Sgt.   Source: 7
Captured July 4, 1863 in the fall of Vicksburg, Miss. Paroled July 7, 1863.

SKIPWORTH, J. F. Jr.   Co. A   Rank: Pvt.   Source: 7
Died sometime in 1863. Left $4.70 in cash.

SLAUS, HYRAM   Co. F   Rank: Pvt.   Source: 7
Discharged June 15, 1862. No reason given.

SLEDGE, WILLIAM   Co. H   Rank: Pvt.   Source: 7
Wounded in the arm at the battle of Baton Rouge, La. on Aug. 5, 1862. He was a part of a detail sent to north Ala. on Nov. 21, 1862 to recruit.

SLOAN, A.   Co. D   Rank: Pvt.   Source: 7

Recruited by Col. Robinson in Limestone Co. Ala. on March 20, 1862. He was born in Tuscaloosa Co. Ala. about 1812. He was 5'5" tall, had dark complexion and eyes with gray hair. By Nov. 8, 1863 he had been unfit for duty due to chronic rheumatism in his left hip and knee and had been in the hospital a Marion, Miss. for 5 months. Discharged on the 30th of Nov. 1863. There is indication that his real year of birth was 1801.

SMITH, ALER.   Co. B   Rank: ?   Source: 2,7
His name is on a list of men that were recruited into Capt. Hunt's Co. dated at LaGrange, Ala. March 31, 1862.

SMITH, BARNET G.   Co. G   Rank: Pvt.   Source: 7
Enlisted by Capt. West at Athens, Ala. on March 18, 1862. He was born in Beckingham Co. Va. in 1810. He was 5'6" tall, had fair complexion, blue eyes, gray hair and was a farmer before signing up. Discharged Nov. 18, 1862 as unfit for duty due to old age.

SMITH, F.M.   Co. B   Rank: ?   Source: 7
His name appears on a list of men recruited into Capt. Hunt's Co. dated March 31, 1862 at LaGrange, Ala. He transferred to the 10th Ala. Infty. on Nov. 15, 1863.

SMITH, G.W.   Co. F   Rank: Pvt.   Source: 7
He was in a hospital and captured in the fall of Vicksburg, Miss. on July 4, 1863. He signed his parole on July 14 and was put on board the steamer "S.S. Crescent" with 611 POW'sa and exchanged in Mobile Harbor, Ala. on Aug. 4, 1863.

SMITH, GEORGE WASHINGTON   Co. G   Rank: Pvt.   Source: 7
Admitted to the 1st Miss. CSA Hospital at Jackson, Miss. with diarrhea on July 9, 1863 and released July 10, 1863. Listed as a deserter in March, 1864.

SMITH, JOHN C.   Co. A   Rank: Pvt.   Source: 7
He was in the 35th by Sept. 5, 1862 and was paid on May 12, 1863. He was captured at Champion Hill (Big Black River), Miss. and sent to Memphis where he was placed on the steamer "Crescent City". Upon arrival at Mound City, Ill. on June 1, 1863, he was admitted to USA General Hospital. He was to go to Ft. Delaware, Del. but was left at Cairo, Ill.

SMITH, JOHN EVANS   Co. A   Rank: Pvt.   Source: 1
Born April 28, 1834 in Lauderdale Co. Ala. Joined the 35th in Dec. 1861 (?) at Florence, Ala. and served until the spring of 1865. Discharged at Tuscumbia, Ala.

SMITH, LEMUEL D.   Co. B   Rank: Pvt.   Source: 7
Captured Dec. 16, 1864 at Nashville, Tenn. He was sent to Louisville, Ky. and on to Camp Douglas.

SMITH, M.A.   Co. B   Rank: Sgt.   Source: 7
He may have been a member of the 32nd Ala. rather than the 35th.

SMITH, WILLIAM M.   Co. A or B   Rank: Pvt.   Source: 7

Joined the 35th on March 12, 1862. He lived in Franklin Co. Ala. and had fair complexion, brown hair, blue eyes and was 5'10" tall. He said he had no family and that he deserted on Oct. 29, 1864. He took the "Oath" on March 30, 1865 and agreed to stay "North of the Ohio River" until the war was over.

SOWELL, W.O.   Co. D   Rank: ?   Source: 7

His name appears on a list of men enlisted into Capt. Sanders' Co. dated at LaGrange, Ala. on March 31, 1862.

SPEARS, D.G.   Co. A   Rank: Pvt.   Source: 7

He was a POW on Jan. 23, 1863.

SPIVEY, RUBEN M.   Co. B   Rank: Pvt.   Source: 2,4,6,7

He was from Madison Co. Ala. and was a Cadet at LaGrange Military Academy in Aug. 1860. He was enlisted by Col. Robinson at LaGrange, Ala. on March 12, 1862. He was accidentally shot in the arm on April 14, 1862 and became the first casualty in the 35th. They had to amputate his right arm. Discharged Nov. 2, 1862. He was born about 1844, had light complexion, black eyes and hair and was 5'11" tall. After the war he lived in Huntsville, Ala. then moved to Topeka, Ks. where he was alive in 1903.

SPOTSWOOD, IRBY E.   Co. E   Rank: Sgt.   Source: 7

He signed for an issue of clothing on Sept. 14, 1864.

STANBURY, J.F.   Co. C   Rank: ?   Source: 7

His name appears on a list of men recruited by Capt. Ashford dated at LaGrange, Ala. March 31, 1862.

STANLEY, E.J.   Co. ?   Rank: ?   Source: 8

He died about 1915. His wife's name was Mary E.

STANLEY, JOSEPH H.   Co. H   Rank: 1st Lieut.   Source: 7

Joined the 35th as a 2nd. Lieut on March 12, 1862. Admitted to 1st Miss. CSA Hospital at Jackson with acute diarrhea on July 9, 1863. Admitted to St. Mary's Hospital in Lagrange, Ga. with acute diarrhea and said to be "ready for railroad transportation" on Aug. 9, 1864. Returned to duty Aug. 10. His pay that year was $90.00 per month.

STARKEY, JOHNATHAN S.   Co. G   Rank: Pvt.   Source: 7

He was listed as a deserter in March of 1864. He was captured near Athens, Ala. on Jan. 1, 1865 and sent to Nashville ant then Louisville, Ky. where he arrived Jan. 11, 1865. He was then sent to Camp Chase, Ohio and arrived there Jan. 25, 1865. He was from Limestone Co. Ala., born about 1844, had dark complexion, light hair and was 5'7" tall.

STEPHENSON, WILLIAM W.   Co. B   Rank: Pvt.   Source: 2,7

He joined Capt. Hunt's Co. in March 1862. Captured July 4, 1863 in the fall of Vicksburg, Miss. He signed his parole on July 9, 1863 and was sent to Memphis, Tenn. on July 20.

STERLING, J.M.   Co. C   Rank: ?   Source: 7
        His name appears on a list of men recruited into Capt. Ashford's Co. dated
        at LaGrange, Ala. March 31, 1862.

STEVENS, WILLIAM S.   Co. C   Rank: Pvt.   Source: 7
        Recruited by Capt. Ashford at LaGrange, Ala. Feb. 25, 1862. He was
        from Lawrence Co. Ala. and had fair complexion, brown hair, gray eyes
        and was 5'9" tall. He said he deserted on Nov. 12, 1864. He took the
        "Oath" April 28, 1865 at Nashville.

STEWART, JOHN A.   Co. C   Rank: 2nd Lieut.   Source: 7
        Joined Capt. Ashford's Co. at LaGrange, Ala. in Feb. 1862. In 1864 his
        pay was $80.00 per month. He was a patient in a hospital and was
        recovering from a wound on July 20, 1864. He resigned Sept. 12, 1864.
        John was from Limestone Co. Ala had dark complexion and hair, hazel
        eyes and was 5'10" tall. He said he deserted on Dec. 20, 1864, and had a
        family. He took the "Oath" on April 28, 1865.

STEWART, SAMUEL D.   Co. B   Rank: Capt.   Source:
2,3,4,6,7,9,11
        He was from Dallas Co. Ala. and was a Cadet Drill Instructor at LaGrange
        Military Academy before the 35th was formed. He joined Capt. Hunts Co.
        at LaGrange on March 12, 1862 as a 2nd Lieut. Wounded in the foot at
        the battle of Baton Rouge, La. on Aug. 5, 1862. Received his first
        promotion on Oct. 4, 1862. On Nov. 11, 1863 he was granted 15 days
        leave to visit an "aged parent and his brothers and sisters". On Dec. 3,
        1863 he signs for clothing for his men. He was killed at the battle of
        Franklin, Tenn. on Nov. 30, 1864.

STEWART, THOMAS C.   Co. I   Rank: Cpl.   Source: 7
        Feb. 28, 1864 he entered the 1st Miss. CSA Hospital with "neuralgia".
        Released March 7, 1864. Listed as a deserter in March 1864. Captured
        at Florence, Ala. on March 26th and sent to Louisville, Ky. April 4, 1864.
        He was then sent to Camp Chase, Ohio where he arrived April 13, 1864.
        Died of pneumonia Feb. 14, 1865 and was buried 3 miles South of Camp
        Chase.

STEWART, WILLIAM   Co. C   Rank: ?   Source: 7
        His name appears on a list of men recruited by Capt. Ashford, dated
        March 31, 1862 at LaGrange, Ala.

STEWART, WILLIAM P.   Co. I   Rank: Cpl.   Source: 7
        He enlisted at Florence, Ala. on March 22, 1862. Died Nov. 2, 1862 at
        Holly Springs, Miss. His wife, Elizabeth Stewart, received $88.86 in back
        pay. He was from Lauderdale Co. Ala.

STOCKTON, WILLIAM A.   Co. C   Rank: Pvt.   Source: 7
        He was recruited by Capt. Ashford at Courtland, Ala. on Feb. 25, 1862.
        He was born in Lawrence, Co. Ala. about 1839 and was 5'8" tall, had fair
        complexion, blue eyes, dark hair and was a farmer. Discharged Nov. 20,
        1862.

STOUT, WILLIAM E.   Co. A   Rank: Pvt.   Source: 7

Wounded at the battle of Franklin, Tenn. on Nov. 30, 1864. Captured Dec. 22, 1864 at Columbia, Tenn. and sent to Nashville. Admitted to USA General Hospital at Nashville. Sent to Louisville, Ky. on March 8, 1865 and on to Camp Chase, Ohio and then Lookout Point, Md. where he arrived March 31, 1865. He took the "Oath" on June 5th and was released June 21, 1865.

STRONG, D.C..   Co. E   Rank: Pvt.   Source: 7

He was enlisted by Gov. Moore at Huntsville, Ala. on March 20, 1862. He was part of a detail sent to north Ala. on Nov. 21, 1862 to recruit men and arrest deserters. Admitted to Jackson's Cavalry Div. Hospital at Old Marion, Miss. in Oct. 1863.

STROTHER, W.H.   Co. B   Rank: Pvt.   Source: 2,6,7

He was from Madison Co. Ala. and a Cadet at LaGrange in Aug. 1860. His name appears on a list of men recruited by Capt. Hunt, dated March 31, 1862 at LaGrange, Ala. Died in 1862 or '63. He left $13.25 in cash. for more information, see source 6.

STURDIVANT, J.J.   Co. D   Rank: Pvt.   Source: 7

Discharged May 2, 1863. No other information.

SULLIVAN, JAMES S.   Co. A   Rank: Cpl.   Source: 7

He was wounded in the ankle at the battle of Baton Rouge, La. on Aug. 5, 1862. Listed as a deserter in March 1864. Captured near Florence, Ala. March 29, 1864 and sent to Nashville, Louisville, Ky. and on to Camp Morton, Ind. where he arrived April 23, 1864. He signed the "Oath" and was released March 6, 1865.

SWANSAN, W.   Co. B   Rank: Pvt.   Source: 7

Listed as a deserter in March 1864.

TANNER, P.R.   Co. G   Rank: 2nd Lieut.   Source: 7

Joined the 35th on March 12, 1862. Died July 15, 1862.

TARKEY, J.H.   Co. G   Rank: Pvt.   Source: 7

His name appears on a list of men recruited by Capt. West, dated March 31, 1862 at LaGrange, Ala.

TATHUM, T.A.   Co. C   Rank: Capt.   Source: 3,7

Joined Capt. Ashford's Co. in March 1862 at LaGrange, Ala. as a 2nd Lieut. Promoted to Capt. in Jan. or Feb. 1864. His pay in March 1864 was $130.00 per month. He is listed as sick on June 18, 1864.

TAYLOR, WILLIAM B.   Co. I   Rank: Capt.   Source: 2,3,4,7

Joined the 35th on March 12, 1862 as a 1st Lieut. Promoted to Capt. on Sept. 25, 1862. On May 24, 1863, near Jackson Miss. he requested a 30 day leave of absence due to "lateral curvature of the spine". Leave was granted June 5, 1863. He had back trouble for 10 years and camp life made it worse. He resigned on Aug. 25, 1863.

TAYLOR, W.R.   Co. F   Rank: Pvt.   Source: 7
Captured at the battle of Champion Hill (Big Black River), Miss. on May 17, 1863. He was sent to Memphis, Camp Morton, Ind. and then to Ft. Delaware, Del. where he arrived June 9, 1863. He was paroled and exchanged with 1697 POW's on July 6, 1863 at City Point, Va.

TEAGUE, JAMES ANDERSON   Co. F   Rank: Pvt.   Source: 7
Admitted to the 1st Miss. CSA Hospital at Jackson with acute diarrhea on July 9, 1863. Sent to "General Hospital" on July 10th.

TEAT, SAMUEL   Co. A   Rank: Pvt.   Source: 7
Captured at the battle of Nashville, Tenn. on Dec. 15, 1864. He was sent to Louisville, Ky. on Jan. 3 and then to Camp Chase, Ohio, where he arrived Jan. 11, 1865. He died Feb. 13th of Pneumonia and was buried in grave #1225 south of the camp.

TERRY, J.F.   Co. G   Rank: ?   Source: 7
His name appears on a list of men enlisted by Capt. West, dated March 31, 1862 at LaGrange, Ala.

THACH, W.T.   Co. D   Rank: 1st Lieut.   Source: 7
Joined the 35th on March 12, 1862. He resigned Aug. 11, 1862 due to illness.

THOMAL, LEMIUL D.   Co. B   Rank: Pvt.   Source: 7
Captured at the battle of Nashville, Tenn. on Dec. 16, 1864. He arrived at the Military Prison at Louisville, Ky. on Dec. 20 and was sent to Camp Douglas, near Chicago, Ill. where he arrived Dec. 24, 1864. Discharged June 20, 1865 and returned to Franklin, Ala.

THOMAS, DILLARD   Co. B   Rank: ?   Source: 2
No other information.

THOMAS, L.E.   Co. B   Rank: ?   Source: 7
His name appears on a list of men enlisted by Capt. Hunt dated March 31, 1862 at LaGrange, Ala.

THOMASSON, WILLIAM J.   Co. E   Rank: Pvt.   Source: 7
He was from Madison Co. Ala. and had fair complexion, light hair, hazel eyes and was 5'11" tall. He surrendered at Atlanta, Ga. on May 6, 1865. He signed the "Oath" on May 12 and returned home.

THOMPSON, BUCK   Co. B   Rank: ?   Source: 2
This person may be the same as one of the Thompson's listed below.

THOMPSON, GEORGE W.   Co. A   Rank: Pvt.   Source: 7
He was from Lauderdale Co. Ala. had light hair, gray eyes and was 5'9" tall. From Jan. 1st to April 1st, 1863 he was a teamster and received an extra 25 cents per day pay. He was listed as a deserter in March 1864. He was captured at Florence, Ala. on March 26, 1864 and sent to Nashville, Louisville, Ky. and then to Camp Chase, Ohio, where he arrived

April 14, 1864. He signed the "Oath" on May 13, 1865 and was released.

THOMPSON, H.H.   Co. E   Rank: Pvt.   Source: 7
    Admitted to the 1st Miss. CSA Hospital at Jackson, on March 3, 1865 (?)
    and returned to duty March 20, 1865 (?).

THOMPSON, JAMES N.   Co. B   Rank: Pvt.   Source: 7
    No other information.

THOMPSON, JOSEPH NICHOLAS   Co. B   Rank: Cpl.   Source: 2,4,5,6,7
    He was from Franklin or Colbert Co. Ala. and was the Military Instructor at
    LaGrange Military Academy, after he graduated from LaGrange. He
    joined the 35th and was wounded at the battle of Peachtree Creek, Ga. in
    1864. Just prior to being wounded, he and two others went over the
    breastworks to "capture or kill a Yankee each". His comrades made their
    charge and killed their man, but Thompson's rifle had a bad cap and failed
    to fire. He recapped his gun and pursued his man, but as he fired, his
    enemy fell to his knees and begged for mercy. The man was taken
    prisoner and turned over to the guard. Thompson was again wounded by
    a shell at the battle of Franklin, Tenn. and had the lower third of his leg
    amputated in the field. He was captured in this condition on Dec. 17, 1864
    and sent to Nashville, where he was admitted to the 1st USA General
    Hospital on Jan. 27, 1865 and released on Feb. 24. He was sent to the
    Military prison at Lousiville, Ky., Camp Chase, Ohio and on to Lookout,
    Md., where he arrived March 26, 1865. He was released as a "sick
    prisoner" on July 4, 1865. He was living in Tuscumbia, Ala. in 1903.

THOMPSON, ROBERT H.   Co. G   Rank: Pvt.   Source: 7
    Listed as a deserter in March 1864. He was from Giles Co. Tenn., had
    dark hair and complexion, gray eyes and was 6'1" tall. He signed the
    "Oath of Amnesty" on June 11, 1865 at Pulaski, Tenn. At that time he
    stated he had on family and had joined the 35th on March 18, 1862, and
    had deserted on May 1, 1864.

THOMPSON, W.J.   Co. K   Rank: Pvt.   Source: 7
    Enlisted Oct. 9, 1862 at LaGrange, Ala. by Col. Goodwin. He was
    admitted to Walker's Div. Hospital at Lauderdale, Miss. on Aug. 16, 1863
    and to French's Div. Hospital at Lauderdale on Sept. 4, 1863 as a patient.
    By Sept. 18th he is listed as a nurse, for which he received an extra 25
    cents per day in pay.

THOMPSON, WILLIAM   Co. B   Rank: Pvt.   Source: 2,7
    Listed as a deserter in march 1864.

THORN, JOHN WILLAFORD   Co. B   Rank: Pvt.   Source: 1
    Born June 30, 1839. Joined the 35th in April 1862 at LaGrange, Ala. He
    signed his parole at Pond Springs, Ala. in May 1865. He was living in
    Franklin Co. Ala. in 1907.

TIPTON, H.   Co. F   Rank: Pvt.   Source: 7
    Listed as a deserter in March 1864.

134

TIPTON, JONATHAN HENRY   Co. F   Rank: Pvt.   Source: 1
Born Nov. 19, 1842. Joined the 35th in Dec. 1862 at Grenada, Miss. and
stayed with the unit until May 1864.

TIPTON, T.T.   Co. F   Rank: ?   Source: 7
Died July 21, 1862 and left $16.00 in cash.

TIPTON, W.   Co. F   Rank: Sgt.   Source: 7
Listed as a deserter in March 1864.

TOONE, G.S.   Co. G   Rank: Cpl.   Source: 7
His name appears on a list of men enlisted by Capt. West, dated March
31, 1862 at LaGrange, Ala. He received $43.83 as pay from Nov. 18,
1862 to Feb. 28, 1863.

TORIAN, SAMUEL THOMAS   Co. B   Rank: ?   Source: 2,6
He was from Mountain Home, Ala. and was a Cadet at LaGrange Military
Academy in Aug. 1860. He joined the 35th when it was formed and then
transferred to Roddy's Cavalry Div. as a Lieut. By 1903 he was living at
Courtland, Ala. and had outlived two wives. He attended the LaGrange
reunion on May 19, 1904.

TRIBLE, D.   Co. D   Rank: ?   Source: 7
His name appears on a list of men recruited by Capt. Sanders' dated
March 31, 1862 at LaGrange, Ala.

TROLMAN, H.T.   Co. E   Rank: ?   Source: 7
Died in Miss. on Oct. 7, 1863.

TROTMAN, Y.P.   Co. E   Rank: 2nd Lieut.   Source: 7
Joined the 35th as a pvt. and was wounded slightly at the battle of Baton
Rouge, La. on Aug. 5, 1862. Promoted to 2nd Lieut. on Oct. 30, 1862.
He is listed as in the hospital at Lauderdale, Miss. part or all of the time
from Feb. 1 to Aug. 31, 1863. His pay at that time was $80.00 per month.
On Nov. 30, 1863, he asked for and was granted 30 days leave of
absence stated he had not been away from his command, other than
while ill and in the hospital since joining the 35th.

TROUSDALE, BENJAMIN FRANKLIN Co. A   Rank: Pvt.   Source: 1,7,8
Born March 2, 1835 at Center Star, Lauderdale Co. Ala. Joined the 35th
on March 15, 1862 at LaGrange, Ala. Captured after the battle of
Champion Hill, near Big Black River, Miss. on May 16, 1863. He was sent
to Memphis, Camp Morton, Ind. and then to Ft. Delaware, Del. where he
arrived June 9, 1863. He was paroled and exchanged with 1697 POW's
at City Point, Va. on July 6, 1863. He took the "Oath" at Pond Springs,
Ala. on April 25, 1865. He was living in Florence, Ala. in 1907.

TYLER, HICKMAN   Co. ?   Rank: Pvt.   Source: 7
He was from Giles Co., Tenn. and had dark complexion and hair, hazel
eyes, was 5'6" tall and had no family in 1865. He stated he volunteered for
the 35th in Sept. 1861 (?) and deserted in Nov. 1864. He took the "Oath
of Allegiance" on March 19, 1865.

VANDERVER, ED   Co. B   Rank: Pvt.   Source: 2,7
Recruited by Maj. Robinson on March 12, 1862 at LaGrange, Ala. He was in the General Hospital at Marion, Miss. on July 30, 1863.

VAUGHN, ROBERT A.   Co. D   Rank: Pvt.   Source: 7
His name appears on a list of men recruited by Capt. Sanders dated March 31, 1862 at LaGrange, Ala. On Dec. 31, 1863 he was listed as the "Brig. Butcher" and was paid for 425 days of service. He lived in Limestone Co., Ala had dark complexion, brown hair, hazel eyes and was 5'9" tall. He said he had a family and deserted on Dec. 10, 1864. He took the "Oath" on Jan. 27,1865 and was paroled Jan. 31, 1865, but he had to stay "North of the Ohio River".

VENABLE, WILLIAM G.   Co. G   Rank: Pvt.   Source: 7
Joined the Capt. West's Co. at Athens, Ala. on March 18, 1862. He was born in Marshall Co. Tenn. about 1826. He had fair Complexion, blue eyes and was 6 feet tall. Discharged May 2, 1863 due to Physical disabilities at Meridian, Miss.

VINSON, J.L.   Co. B   Rank: ?   Source: 2,7
He was a Cadet at LaGrange in Aug. 1860, and his name appears on a list of men recruited by Capt. Hunt, dated March 31, 1862 at LaGrange, Ala.

VOLDRICK, A.   Co. C   Rank: ?   Source: 7
He was a POW sent from Holly Springs, Miss. to Cairo, Ill. in Dec. 1862.

WALKER, JOHN   Co. C   Rank: Pvt.   Source: 7
His name is on a list of recruits received into Capt. Ashford's Co. dated March 31, 1962 at LaGrange, Ala. He died in 1863 and left $5.00 in cash.

WALKER, JOHN B.   Co. A   Rank: Pvt.   Source: 7
Joined the 35th at Florence, Ala. on Feb. 19, 1862. He was born in Tenn. about 1803 and had dark complexion, black eyes, gray hair and was a farmer prior to joining. He was discharged Nov. 14, 1862 due to "dropsy, disability and impaired vision".

WALKER, R.R.   Co. C   Rank: ?   Source: 7
His name appears on a list of men received into Capt. Ashford's Co. dated March 31, 1862 at LaGrange, Ala.

WALLACE, SAMUEL MARION   Co. A   Rank: Pvt.   Source: 1
Born Oct. 29, 1833 at Fayetteville, Lincoln Co. Ala. He joined the 35th in Dec. 1863 (1862?) at Florence, Ala. In May, he was transferred to the 27th Ala. at Port Hudson, La. He served until Nov. 1864, the "deserted and never re-enlisted".

WARD, FLEMING. D.   Co. E   Rank: Pvt.   Source: 7
Joined the 35th on March 20, 1862. Discharged Sept. 1, 1862.

WARREN, A.J.   Co. C   Rank: 2nd Lieut   Source: 7

Joined the 35th as a 2nd Lieut. on March 12, 1862. Died July 16, 1862.

WATKINS, JOHN C.   Co. C   Rank: 2nd Lieut.   Source: 7
Joined the 35th on Feb. 25, 1862. Promoted to 2nd Lieut. on March 12, 1862. His pay on June 30, 1862 was $80.00 per month. He either died or was promoted on Nov. 19, 1862.

WATKINS, R.J.   Co. E   Rank: 1st Sgt.   Source: 7
He was born about 1841 in Madison Co. Ala. He had black eyes and hair, fair complexion and was 5'8" tall. He joined the 35th in Corinth, Miss. on May 12, 1862 and was received into Capt. Dickson's Co. His pay for Nov. to Dec. 1862 was $20.00 per month. He was captured during the fall of Vicksburg, Miss. on July 4, 1863 and paroled on July 7th. By April 30, 1864, he was in Co. C., 1st Detachment, Paroled Prisoners, at Demopolis, Ala.

WATSON, W.M.   Co. I   Rank: Pvt.   Source: 7
He was discharged from the 35th on July 25, 1863. No reason given.

WATTS, P.F.   Co. H   Rank: Pvt.   Source: 7
He received $22.00 for pay from March 1 to April 30, 1864.

WEATHERFORD, THOMAS L.   Co. G   Rank: Sgt.   Source: 7
Enlisted by Capt. West at Athens, Ala. on March 18, 1862. He was born in Limestone Co. Ala. in 1838, was 6'1" tall, had fair complexion, blue eyes, brown hair and was a farmer before joining the 35th. He was discharged due to poor health, "phthisis pulmonalia", on Oct. 19, 1863 at Point Clear Hospital, Baldwin Co. Ala. His pay was $20.00 per month.

WEBB, JOHN R.   Co. D   Rank: Pvt.   Source: 7
His name appears on a list of men received into Capt. Sanders' Co. dated March 31, 1862 at LaGrange, Ala. He was in the General Hospital at Marion, Miss. at least from June 30 thru Oct. 31, 1863 as either a patient or nurse.

WESSON, LEE L.   Co. ?   Rank: Ensign (?)   Source: 7
Captured near Nashville on Dec. 16, 1864. He arrived at the Military Prison, Louisville, Ky. on Jan. 2, 1865 and was then sent to Camp Chase, Ohio. He died Feb. 14, 1865 and was buried 1/3 mile south of Camp Chase.

WEST, JOHN W.   Co. G   Rank: Capt.   Source: 2,3,4,7
He was from Limestone Co. Ala. and was elected Capt. on March 12, 1862 when the 35th was formed. His 1st pay period was from March 18 to June 30, 1862 at $130.00 per month. He was ill on July 28, 1864 in Ga. He surrendered with Lt. Gen. R. Taylor at Meridian, Miss. on May 11, 1865.

WEST, LEVI   Co. A   Rank: Pvt.   Source: 7
Captured at the fall of Vicksburg, Miss. on July 4, 1863. He signed his parole on July 7. The witness was W.M. Bickham, a 2nd Lieut. in the 35th. West was captured again a Florence, Ala. on March 26, 1864 and sent to

Louisville, Ky. and on to Camp Chase, Ohio where he arrived April 14, 1864. He was released May 15, 1865. He had fair complexion, light hair, blue eyes and was 6'1" tall, and was from lauderdale Co. Ala.

WESTON, JOHN RANDOLPH   Co. D   Rank: Pvt.   Source: 7
He was captured at Edwards Depot, near Champion Hill, Miss. on May 16, 1863. He was sent to Memphis, Camp morton, Ind. and then Ft. Delaware, Del. where he arrived June 9, 1863. He was paroled and exchanged at City Point, Va. on July 6, 1863 with 1697 POW's.

WEATHERFORD, T.L.   Co. G   Rank: Ord. Sgt.   Source: 7
Joined Capt. West's Co. on March 18, 1862 at Athens, Ala. He was a patient in the General Hospital at Point Clear, Baldwin Co. Ala. some time from July 7 to Aug. 31, 1863.

WHEELER, JOHN   Co. C   Rank: Pvt.   Source: 7
Recruited by Col. Robinson at LaGrange, Ala. in March 1862. He was in French's Div. Hospital at Lockhart, Miss. sometime in Aug. 1863. Captured at Jonesboro, Ga. on Sept. 4, 1864 and sent to Nashville, then on to Louisville, Ky. where he arrived Oct. 28, 1864. The next day he was sent to Camp Douglas, Ill. On March 24, 1865 he enlisted into Co. D. of the 6th U.S. Vol.

WHEELER, ROBERT   Co. B   Rank: ?   Source: 2,4,7
His name is on a list of men recruited by Capt. Hunt at LaGrange, Ala. dated March 31, 1862. He became Color Bearer after the battle of Peachtree Creek, Ga. and was killed at the battle of Franklin, Tenn. in Nov. 1864.

WHITE, HENRY M.   Co. B   Rank: Pvt.   Source: 2,7
On Aug. 5, 1864 he was admitted to Floyd House Hospital in Russellville, Ala. with diarrhea and general disability.

WHITE, IRA A.   Co. G   Rank: Pvt.   Source: 7
Joined the 35th on March 18, 1862. He had extra duty as a teamster from Sept. 1863 thru Feb. 1864 at Canton, Miss. for which he was paid an extra 25 cents per day. In Jan. 1865, he stated that he had no family and deserted on Dec. 1, 1864. He was from Giles Co. Tenn. had fair complexion, light hair, blue eyes and was 5'11" tall. He then took the "Oath of Allegiance"

WHITE, M.   Co. A   Rank: Pvt.   Source: 7
Discharged on Dec. 19, 1862. No other information.

WHITE, WILLIAM   Co. B   Rank: ?   Source: 2
No other information.

WHITFIELD, WILLIAM G.   Co. D   Rank: Sgt.   Source: 7
Admitted to Ocmulgee Hospital, Macon, Ga. on July 22, 1864. I think he was from Person, N.C.

WHITTEN, WILLIAM S.   Co. C   Rank: Pvt.   Source: 7

His name is on a list of men recruited by Capt. Hunt, dated March 31, 1862 at LaGrange, Ala. He was captured between Sept. 19 and Oct. 6, 1862 near Corinth, Miss. He was placed on board the steamer "Dagotha" with 539 POW's and exchanged Nov. 8, 1863. He was back with the 35th by Jan. 1, 1863 and discharged April 27, 1863 because he was underage.

WHITWORTH, W.J.   Co. D   Rank: ?   Source: 7
His name is on a list of men recruited by Capt. Sanders, dated March 31, 1862 at LaGrange, Ala.

WIGGINS, ROBERT EMMETT   Co. D   Rank: Sgt.   Source: 1,2,4,6,7
He was from Madison Co. Ala. and was a Cadet at LaGrange, Military Academy in Aug. 1860. His name is on a list of men recruited by Capt. Sanders, dated March 31, 1862 at LaGrange, Ala. He was captured in the fall of Vicksburg, Miss. on July 4, 1863. He signed his parole on July 7th and was released. By Aug. 15, 1864 he was back with the 35th as he signed for clothing on that date. He was severely wounded at Franklin, Tenn. in Nov. 1864 and was sent home. In 1903 he was living in Athens, Ala. He attended the LaGrange reunion on May 19, 1904.

WILDER, J.M.   Co. F   Rank: Pvt.   Source: 7
Joined the 35th in Sept. 1862. He was captured Aug. 30, 1863 near Maysville, Tenn. and sent to Nashville. He was then sent to the Military Prison at Louisville, Ky. where he arrived Sept 5, 1863. On Sept 28, 1863, he took the "Oath of Allegiance" and joined the Independent Alabama Cav. of the U.S. Army. He was from Madison Co. Ala. had fair Complexion, light hair, blue eyes and was 5'9" tall.

WILEY, W.H.   Co. I   Rank: Pvt.   Source: 7
His name is on a list of men recruited by Capt. Chisholm dated March 31, 1862 at LaGrange, Ala. He was discharged May 11, 1862 due to poor health.

WILKS, W.J.   Co. I   Rank: Pvt.   Source: 7
His name is on a list of men recruited by Capt, Chisholm dated March 31, 1862 at LaGrange, Ala. On Dec. 19, 1863 he was paid $50.00 bounty for joining. His pay was $11.00 per month.

WILLBANKS, J.   Co. C   Rank: ?   Source: 7
His name is on a list of men trying to enlist in Capt. Ashford's Co. dated March 31, 1862 at LaGrange, Ala. He was rejected due to physical disability.

WILLIAMS, C. A.   Co. E   Rank: Pvt.   Source: 7
No other information.

WILLIAMS, FRANCIS M. A.   Co. A   Rank: Pvt.   Source: 7
Recruited by Capt. Mitchell at Florence, Ala. on March 17, 1862. Admitted to Loring's Div. Hospital at Lauderdale, Miss. on June 27, 1863 as a patient. He was still there Sept. 1, 1863. Captured at Paducah, Ky. on Dec. 7, 1863, and sent to Rock Island Barracks, Ill. on Dec. 15, 1863. He was released May 17, 1865 and returned to Lauderdale Co. Ala. They

furnished transport to Paluski, Tenn. He was born in 1841, had light complexion and hair, blue eyes and was 5'11" tall.

WILLIAMS, GEORGE W.   Co. C   Rank: Pvt.   Source: 7
Captured between Sept. 19 and Oct. 6, 1862 around Corinth, Miss.

WILLIAMS, JAMES   Co. A   Rank: Cpl.   Source: 7
Listed as a deserter in March 1864.

WILLIAMS, JAMES J.   Co. C   Rank: Pvt.   Source: 7
From Sept. to Dec. 1861 he was with the 50th Ala. Infty. His mane is on a list of men enlisted by Capt. Ashford, dated March 31, 1862 at LaGrange, Ala. He was captured near Atlanta, Ga. on Aug. 21, 1864 and sent to Nashville, the Military Prison at Louisville, Ky. and then to Camp Chase, Ohio, where he arrived on Sept. 3, 1864. He was paroled and exchanged at Vicksburg, Miss. on May 12, 1865.

WILLIAMS, JOHN   Co. G   Rank: Pvt.   Source: 7
Deserted on July 20, 1864 after the battle of Peachtree Creek, Ga. Arrived at the Military Prison at Chattanooga, Tenn. on Aug. 12, 1864.

WILLIAMS, MARION   Co. A   Rank: Pvt.   Source: 7
Captured Nov. 23, 1863 by the 7th Ill. Mounted Infty. during an "expedition to Corinth, Miss." He was turned over to the Provost Marshall at Eastport, Miss.

WILLIAMS, SAMUEL   Co. G   Rank: Sgt.   Source: 7
Wounded and captured May 16, 1863 at Champion Hill (Big Black River) Miss. and sent to Memphis, Tenn. He was admitted to Overton Hospital on May 31, 1863 where he "died on June 27, 1863 from the effects of gunshot wounds".

WILLIAMS, W.   Co. C   Rank: ?   Source: 7
His name is on a list of men recruited by Capt. Ashford, dated March 31, 1862 at LaGrange, Ala.

WILLIAMSON, J.A.   Co. G   Rank: Pvt.   Source: 7
Captured at the fall of Vicksburg, Miss. on July 4, 1863. He was in Gen. Smith's Div. Hospital at the time. He signed his parole July 14 and was delivered to Mobile Harbor, Ala. on Aug. 4, 1863 with 611 POW's by ship.

WILLIAMSON, J.K.   Co. G   Rank: ?   Source: 7
His name is on a list of men recruited by Capt. West, dated March 31, 1862 at LaGrange, Ala.

WILLMORE, C.J.   Co. ?   Rank: Pvt.   Source: 7
Captured at Perryville (?). Died at City Hospital, St. Louis, Mo. on Feb. 4, 1863 of "Pneumonia and Typhoid fever". He was born about 1843.

WILLMORE, CHARLES A.   Co. E   Rank: Pvt.   Source: 7
Captured at Big Black River (Champion Hill), Miss. on May 17, 1863 and sent to Memphis, Camp Morton, Ind. and then Ft. Delaware, Del. where

he arrived June 9, 1863. He was paroled and exchanged at City Point, Va. on July 6, 1863 with 1697 POW's. July 8th he was issued clothing and on Aug. 20, he was paid $66.00 for service from Jan. 1 to June 30, 1863. On Nov. 2, 1863 he was issued a pair of shoes at the Medical College Hospital, Atlanta, Ga.

WILSON, DALLAS   Co. I   Rank: Pvt.   Source: 7
Captured at Champion Hill (Big Black River), Miss. on May 16, 1863 and sent to Memphis, Camp Morton, Ind. and then to Ft. Delaware, Del. where he arrived June 7, 1863. He was to have been exchanged on July 4, but was "left in Hospital at Ft. Delaware".

WILSON, ROBERT A. (REV.)   Co. D   Rank: Chaplin   Source: 2,7
His name is on a list of men recruited by Capt. Sanders, dated March 31, 1862 at LaGrange, Ala. He was assigned to duty as Post Chaplin by General Bragg at Kingston, Ga. on July 22, 1863. His pay from July 1862 thru Nov. 1863 was $80.00 per month.

WILSON, R.B.   Co. I   Rank: ?   Source: 7
His name is on a list of men recruited by Capt. Chisholm dated March 31, 1862 at LaGrange, Ala.

WILSON, R.N.   Co. B   Rank: Pvt.   Source: 7
Enlisted by Capt. Felton at LaGrange, Ala. on March 12, 1862. Feb. 1865 he is in a detachment of paroled prisoners at Camp Lee, near Richmond, Va.

WILSON, ROBERT H.   Co. E   Rank: ?   Source: 7
He received a slight wound at the battle of Baton Rouge, La. on Aug. 5, 1862. He was captured at Champion Hill (Big Black River), Miss. on May 16, 1863, and sent to Memphis, Tenn. Camp Morton, Ind. and on to Ft. Delaware, Del. where he arrived June 9, 1863. He was paroled and exchanged at City Point, Va. on July 6, 1863 with 1697 POW's. On Sept. 14, 1864 he signed for a pair of shoes and a coat at Macon, Ga.

WINBURN, JOHN W.   Co. I   Rank: 2nd Lieut.   Source: 7
His name is on a list of men recruited by Capt. Chisholm, dated March 31, 1862 at LaGrange, Ala. Promoted to 2nd Lieut on Sept. 24, 1862. His pay from Feb. 1 thru July 31, 1863 was $80.00 per month. On Aug. 22, 1863 he was in the Officers Hospital at Lauderdale, Miss. He was dropped from the rolls of the 35th on Nov. 23, 1863. He was in Ocmulgee Hospital at Macon, Ga. from July 2 thru July 8, 1864 with "catarrhous". Captured at Gravelly Springs, Ala. on Oct. 8, 1864 and sent to Nashville, Louisville, Ky and then Johnson's Island, Ohio, where he arrived Nov. 19, 1864. He signed the "Oath" on June 16, 1865 and was released. He was born about 1844, and lived in Gravelly, Lauderdale Co. Ala. had fair complexion, light hair, blue eyes and was 5'11" tall.

WINFREY, JOHN M.   Co. E   Rank: Pvt.   Source: 7
Captured at Big Black River (Champion Hill), Miss. on May 17, 1863. Sent to Memphis and on to Mound City Hospital. He arrived at Camp Morton, Ind. on July 22, 1863. He died of chronic diarrhea on Aug. 15, 1864, and

was buried at Green Lawn Cemetery in grave # 1066.

WOOD, BENNETT H.   Co. I   Rank: Pvt.   Source: 7
  Captured at Big Black River (Champion Hill), Miss. on May 16 or 18, 1863.
  He was sent to memphis, Camp Morton, Ind. and then to Ft. Delaware,
  Del. where he arrived on June 9, 1863. He was exchanged with 1697
  POW's on July 6, 1863.

WOOD, D.S.   Co. G   Rank: Pvt.   Source: 7
  Listed as a deserter on March 19, 1864.

WOOD, W.   Co. C   Rank: Cpl.   Source: 7
  His name appears on a list of men recruited into Capt. Ashford's Co. dated
  March 31, 1962 at LaGrange, Ala. Listed as a deserter on March 19,
  1864.

WOODEN, JAMES C.   Co. I   Rank: Pvt.   Source: 7
  Captured at Big Black River (Champion Hill), Miss. on May 16-18, 1863.
  Sent to Memphis, Camp Morton, Ind. and then to Ft. Delaware, Del. where
  he arrived July 9, 1863. He was paroled and exchanged with 1697 POW's
  at City Point, Va. on July 6, 1863.

WOODFORD, JOHN B.   Co. D   Rank: Pvt.   Source: 7
  Employed as a wagonmaster from Jan. 1, 1863 thru Feb. 29, 1864 and
  earned an extra 25 cents per day.

WOODFORD, WILLIAM   Co. B   Rank: ?   Source: 2
  Wounded at the battle of Franklin, Tenn. in Nov. 1864.

WOODRUFF, NATHAN   Co. C   Rank: Pvt.   Source: 7
  Captured at Champion Hill (Big Black River), Miss. on May 16-23, 1863.
  He was sent to Memphis, Camp Morton, Ind. and then to Ft. Delaware,
  Del. where he arrived June 9, 1963. He died there on July 25, 1863.

WOODS, ANDREW   Co. C   Rank: Pvt.   Source: 7
  His name appears on a list of men recruited into Capt. Ashford's Co. dated
  March 31, 1962 at LaGrange, Ala. Listed as a deserter in the 1st quarter
  of 1864.

WOODS, JOHN H.   Co. K   Rank: Pvt.   Source: 7
  On Aug. 17, 1863 he was tried by a military court of Hill's Corps for
  "Attempt to execute a mutiny". The death penalty was suspended.

WOODWARD, J.H.   Co. E   Rank: Pvt.   Source: 7
  Captured at Big Black River (Champion Hill), Miss. on May 16-18, 1863.
  Sent to Memphis, Camp Morton, Ind. and then to Ft. Delaware, Del. where
  he arrived July 9, 1863. He was paroled and exchanged with 1697 POW's
  at City Point, Va. on July 6, 1863.

WORD, B.   Co. D   Rank: ?   Source: 7
  His name appears on a list of Men recruited by Capt Sanders, dated March
  31, 1862 at LaGrange, Ala.

142

WORLY, N.E.   Co. K   Rank: Pvt.   Source: 7
       He died in 1863 and left $11.15 in cash.

WORTHY, JOHN T.   Co. C   Rank: Pvt.   Source: 7
       He was from alabama and died Aug. 25, 1863 at Lauderdale, Miss. from
       diarrhea, leaving $13.00 cash.

WORTHY, J.T.   Co. E   Rank: Pvt.   Source: 7
       Died in 1863 and left $50.75 in cash.

WORTHY, THOMAS   Co. C   Rank: ?   Source: 7
       Died Aug. 29, 1863 at the General Hospital, Lauderdale, Miss. All he had
       were "Sundries".

WRAY, E.   Co. C   Rank: ?   Source: 7
       He was from Alabama and died Aug. 20, 1863 at Macon, Miss.

WRAY, J.   Co. C   Rank: Pvt.   Source: 7
       Listed as a deserter in the 1st 1/4 of 1864.

WRAY, N.V.   Co. A   Rank: Pvt.   Source: 7
       Listed as a deserter in March 1864.

WRIGHT, G.   Co. I   Rank: Sgt.   Source: 7
       Listed as a deserter in March 1864.

WRIGHT, J.   Co. D   Rank: ?   Source: 7
       His name appears on a list of men recruited by Capt. Sanders dated
       March 31, 1862 at LaGrange, Ala.

WRIGHT, JONATHAN R.   Co. F   Rank: Pvt.   Source: 7
       Recruited at Brownsborough, Ala. by Capt. Lowe or Perry on March 20,
       1862. He was a patient at the General Hospital at Point Clear, Baldwin
       Co. Ala. form July 17, to 26, 1863. He then took extra duty as a nurse. He
       was admitted to Ross Hospital at Mobil, Ala. with acute diarrhea on Nov.
       12, 1863 and released on Jan. 14, 1864.

WRIGHT, PHILLIP WASHINGTON   Co. I   Rank: Cpl.   Source: 1,7
       Born Sept. 7, 1836 at Nashville, Tenn. Joined the 35th on April 1, 1862 at
       LaGrange, Ga. (?) Captured near Corinth, Miss. sometime between Sept.
       19 and Oct. 6, 1862. He was a POW at Camp Chase, Ohio at the time of
       surrender.

YORK, J.W.   Co. G   Rank: ?   Source: 7
       His name appears on a list of men recruited by Capt. West, dated March
       31, 1862 at LaGrange, Ala. He died, date unknown, and left $42.85 in
       cash.

YOUNG, JAMES B.   Co. I   Rank: Pvt.   Source: 7
       Captured between Sept. 19 and Oct. 6, 1862. Died at Ripley, Miss. A
       death claim was filled on Fed. 16, 1863.

PRINCIPAL BATTLES AND ENGAGEMENTS

of the

35th ALABAMA

Corinth, Miss. (Union advance April 29, thru May 25, 1862.)

Vicksburg, Miss.	July 1862
Baton Rouge, La.	August 5, 1862
Corinth, Miss.	October 4, 1862
Port Hudson, La.	March 13, 1863
Enterprise, Miss.	April 24, 1863
Jackson, Miss.	May 14, 1863
Champion Hill, Miss.	May 16, 1863
Big Black River, Miss.	May 17, 1863
Vicksburg, Miss.	May 22 thru July 4, 1863

After Consolidation

New Hope Church, Ga.	May 25-28, 1864
Kennesaw Mountain, Ga.	June 27, 1864
Chattahoochee River, Ga.	July 3-9, 1864
Peachtree Creek, Ga.	July 20, 1864
Atlanta, Ga.	July 22, 1864
Ezra Church, Ga.	July 28, 1864
Decatur, Ala.	October 26, 1864
Franklin, Tenn.	November 30, 1864
Nashville, Tenn.	December 15-16, 1864
Bentonville, N.C.	March 19, 1865
Surrendered, Greensboro, N.C.	May, 1865.

CHART A
Number of Men Captured by Co. and Time Period
As Indicated by the Roster

Time Period	Co. A	Co. B	Co. C	Co. D	Co. E	Co. F	Co. G	Co. H	Co. I	Co. K	Co. ?
Up to Nov. 1862	1	2	1	0	2	1	0	0	0	0	4*
Near Corinth	13	2	9	0	0	0	1	1	5	0	1
Black River '63	13	1	5	4	5	4	7	2	7	0	1
Vicksburg, May '63	6	2	0	7	4	5	3	1	2	0	2
4th 1/4, 1863	4	0	0	0	0	2	1	0	2	0	0
1st 1/4, 1864	2	0	0	0	0	0	0	0	5	0	0
Before Atlanta	0	0	1	2	2	0	1	0	0	1	0
July- Oct. '64	1	0	3	1	0	0	2	0	1	0	1
Franklin/ Nashville	9	6	2	4	0	0	3	2	0	0	1
1st 1/4, 1865	2	1	0	1	3	1	1	0	0	0	0
2nd 1/4, 1865	2	1	0	0	0	0	1	1	0	0	0
Total Captured	54	15	21	19	16	13	20	7	22	1	9

* These 4 men were exchanged in Dec. 1862.

Note: The above chart reflects only the men that were listed as captured in official records. Record keeping was poor and after Atlanta, almost non existant. Also Many records were lost or destroyed.

CHART B

Number of Men Wounded by Co. and Battle
As Indicated by the Roster

Battle & Date	Co. A	Co. B	Co. C	Co. D	Co. E	Co. F	Co. G	Co. H	Co. I	Co. K	Co. ?
Baton Rouge, 1862	5	2	0	0	6	1	0	3	2	0	0
2nd Corinth, 1862	0	3	0	0	0	1	0	1	0	1	0
Black River, 1863	0	1	0	0	0	0	1	0	0	0	1
Peachtree Creek, 1864	0	3	0	0	0	0	0	1	0	0	0
Decatur, 1864	0	3	0	0	0	0	0	0	0	0	0
Franklin, 1864	1	5	1	1	0	0	1	0	1	0	1
Total Captured	54	15	21	19	16	13	20	7	22	1	9

Note: The above chart reflects only the men that were listed as wounded in official records. Record keeping was poor and to non existent. Also Many records were lost or destroyed.

CHART C

Number of Men Died by Co. and Cause
As Indicated by Official Records

Cause of Death	Co. A	Co. B	Co. C	Co. D	Co. E	Co. F	Co. G	Co. H	Co. I	Co. K	Co. ?
Cause unknown	10	12	10	0	7	2	5	7	5	2	4
While POW	11	0	4	1	1	0	0	1	2	0	3
From diarrhea	1	0	2	0	1	0	0	3	1	0	0
Typhoid fever	2	1	0	1	0	0	0	1	0	0	0
Other illness	2	0	0	0	0	0	1	0	1	0	0
From wounds	0	0	0	0	0	0	1	0	0	0	0
In Battle	1	8	1	1	1	2	0	1	0	0	0
Total Captured	27	21	17	3	10	4	7	13	9	2	7

Note: The above chart reflects only the men who's death were listed in official records. Record keeping was poor to non existent. Also many records were lost or destroyed.

CHART D

Number of Men on Roster and Recap by Co.
As Indicated by the Official Records and Print Sources

Number of men	Co. A	Co. B	Co. C	Co. D	Co. E	Co. F	Co. G	Co. H	Co. I	Co. K	Co. ?
On roster	101	108	94	79	55	50	86	38	62	14	39
Deserters	17	7	12	3	2	8	18	1	3	0	8
Captured	54	15	21	19	16	13	20	7	22	1	0
Wounded	6	17	1	1	7	2	2	5	3	1	1
Died	27	21	17	3	10	4	7	13	9	2	7

In addition, there were 3 Regimental Officers, none deserted, 1 captured, 1 wounded and 1 died.

The grand totals are: On roster, 726; deserted, 71; captured, 188; wounded, 46; dead, 120. Please keep in mind that these totals are not complete.

SOURCES

1. United States Census Bureau. "1907 Census of Confederate Soldiers in Colbert, Franklin, Jefferson, Lauderdale, Limestone, Madison, Morgan and Chilton County, Alabama" Washington, D.C.

2. McGregor, A.A. "History of LaGrange College", Publisher and date not shown. Circa 1910.

3. Alabama Civil War Centennial Commission, "Brief Historical Sketches of Military Organizations Raised in Alabama During the Civil War", 1962.

4. Thompson, Joseph N. "War Record of the 35th Alabama Infantry Regiment, Confederate States of America", Unpublished, 1924. (Alabama State Archives)

5. Leftwich, Nina. "200 years at Muscle Shoals", Birmingham, Ala. Multigraphic Advertising Co. 1935.

6. Wyeth, John Allan. "History of LaGrange Military Academy and the Cadet Corps", New York, Brewer Press, 1907.

7. National Archives, "Compiled Service Records of Confederate Soldiers Who Served in Organizations From the State of Alabama, 35th Infantry Reg.", Washington, D.C., General Services Adm., 1960.

8. Alabama Archives. "List of Confederate Soldiers or their Widows Who Received Pensions While Residing in Colbert or Franklin Co. Alabama. Montgomery, Alabama.

9. U.S. War Department, "Official Records of the Union and Confederate Armies in the War of the Rebellion", 128 Volumes, Washington, D.C., U.S. Government Printing Office, 1901.

10. Catton, Bruce, "American Heritage Picture History of the Civil War", New York, America Heritage Publishing Co., 1960

11. Evans, Clement A., "Confederate Military History; A Library of Confederate States History", Volume 12, Atlanta, Ga., Confederate Publishing Co., 1899.

12. Lamb, Osie Kyle, "A Study of the Social Development and Social Structure of the Community of Leighton, Alabama", Tuscaloosa, Alabama, University of Alabama, 1931.

OTHER SOURCES

Davis, Major George B., "The Official Military Atlas of the Civil War", New York, Fairfax Press, 1983.

Everhart, William C., "Vicksburg National Military Park, Mississippi", Washington D.C., U.S. Government Printing Office, 1954.

151

Foote, Shelby, "The Civil War, A Narrative", New York, Random House, 1958.

Key, William C., "The Battle of Atlanta", Atlanta, Ga., Peachtree Publishing Co., 1981.

Livermore, Thomas Leonard, "Numbers and Losses in the Civil War in America: 1861-65", Bloomington, Ind. University Press, 1957.

Parish, Peter J., "The American Civil War", New York, Holmes & Meier Publishers, 1976.

Loosing, Benson J., "Matthew Brady's Illustrated History of the Civil War", New York, Fairfax Press, 1912.

www.ingramcontent.com/pod-product-compliance
Lightning Source LLC
Chambersburg PA
CBHW060351090426
42734CB00011B/2104